THE ARCTIC

a cameraman's story in words and pictures of five journeys into the far north

by RICHARD HARRINGTON

The face of the Arctic is seen here at close range. For this book is the record in words and photographs, by a distinguished cameraman, of the people and things he saw on five journeys to the Canadian Far North. Harrington travelled more than 3000 miles by dogteam, sharing the life of the Eskimo and living in caribou skin tents and igloos.

In 1947 he lived with the Chipewyans of northern Manitoba; in 1948 he travelled along the greater portion of the eastern shores of Hudson Bay; in 1949 he accompanied a Royal Canadian Mounted Police constable on a patrol of the sparsely inhabited lands of the Coppermine Eskimo; in 1950 he visited the Padleimiuts in the land of the Little Sticks; in 1951 he made his journey farthest north, to Boothia Peninsula.

The last three journeys are treated in greatest detail in this book, providing a picture of the Arctic in the season of winter darkness, and the miraculously beautiful season of eternal sunlight.

The story is sometimes grave, sometimes gay. On one of his journeys, to the eastern Arctic, he saw the starvation among the Padleimiuts, and he gives us a harrowing picture of famine. On another journey, to Boothia Peninsula, he witnessed the enchantments of the Arctic spring and mingled with the people in their sports and games.

The obstacles to good photography in the Arctic are many. At sub-zero temperatures cameras freeze and lenses blur. In the winter season of darkness, the dim light of a snowy landscape blots out contours. In the summer season

a comprehensive map appears on the rear endpapers

CONTINUED ON NEXT PAGE

CONTINUED FROM PRECEDING PAGE

of continual level sunlight, the glare on the the snow and ice presents another difficulty. Harrington has somehow overcome these obstacles, and his photographs speak for themselves.

Travelling for months on end with Eskimos and sharing all the pleasures and hardships of their life — he photographed these people in their natural attitudes. We are therefore able to visualize what life is like there, and to share Harrington's admiration for an indomitable people.

In addition to Eskimo life, the reader sees what Arctic life is like for white people. We sleep on the hard benches of isolated Roman Catholic missions, never before visited by a white man. We meet an Anglican missionary visiting his widely scattered parishioners, and talk with white trappers who have lived in solitude for twenty years.

This is a warm and human book about the cold North, not a scientific book, nor one of special pleading. It is the record of a sensitive cameraman, in love with the Arctic, whose pictures of a unique people, still living in a stone-age culture, will find a special place in the reader's memory.

RICHARD HARRINGTON

is Canada's outstanding documentary photographer. His work has taken him to the far corners of the world, to tropical lands and to frozen lands. The main object of all of his journeys is to become acquainted with and to record the life of primitive peoples. No land and no people exercised a greater attraction for Harrington than did the frozen lands and their people — so much so that he felt impelled to return to those regions five times.

HENRY SCHUMAN, INC.
20 East 70th Street, New York 21

THE FACE OF THE ARCTIC

THE FACE OF
THE **ARCTIC**

a cameraman's story in words
and pictures of five journeys
into the far north

by   RICHARD HARRINGTON

maps by bunji tagawa

henry schuman · new york

copyright 1952 by henry schuman, inc.
lithographed in the united states of america by
general offset co. inc. bound by h. wolff
designed by robert goldston

contents

author's preface

IT WAS NOT PHOTOGRAPHY ALONE THAT DREW ME BACK again and again to the Far North. There I felt a peace I could not feel Outside. It was a way of life—the calm, the force, the relentless ever-present penetrating cold, the serenity of mind, the daily fight for survival. At night, my friends and I sat in our igloo, and slowly smiled. And the words formed in my journals, as I huddled inside my caribou skins, could not have been written in our suburbs.

Sitting on the komatik or running alongside, minute spots in a vast, drifting whiteness, a cold that froze our faces if only slightly turned into the wind, I yet felt a clarity of thought, of mind that I have experienced nowhere else.

There is a harmony in an igloo that is rarely equalled Outside. Children play together endlessly, at all hours and in all kinds of weather, and never quarrel—

"How'd you get into this sort of thing?" I'm often asked.

It all started with baby photography. While an X-ray technician, my spare time was taken up more and more with it.

author's preface

"Can you photograph my baby?" mothers would ask. The mothers always loved the result—the babies never objected.

I gave up my job. My wife and I began to make cautious bicycle trips to get photographs and materials for illustrated magazine articles. Like most beginners, we aimed high—the National Geographic Magazine. Instead of that, we got our first check from a Sunday School paper for $2.50.

But the trips became longer, better planned, more daring—and I had found my niche—free lance photography.

Where formerly I crisscrossed Canada "riding the rods" it was now by car; by canoe trips of many weeks, swallowed up by the wilderness of Northern Ontario; by tractor trains across Central Manitoba's winter bushland; by snowshoe through provincial parks and by packhorse in the Rockies.

In between Arctic trips came others to a dozen foreign lands, from Surinam to Timbuktu, from jungle to desert. But back again next winter to the land of friendly people —and frozen fingers.

note to the camera enthusiast

"How can you take pictures up there?"
"Doesn't your camera freeze up?"
"And what about your fingers?"
These questions and many others about technique, cameras, film, filters, meters, etc., are frequently put to me.

Well, I am sorry to disappoint the technique- and gadget-minded. On my trips I usually carried two Kodak Medalists and two Leica cameras, with an extra lens. Panatomic X film for the Leicas, and Super XX for the Medalists. Usually also a few flashbulbs.

On the sled, everything soon froze solid in my small

suitcase. Only the Leicas, which I carried in my fur pants and slept with at night, remained usable. The Medalists proved too large to carry under my fur clothes. They drew more cold than my body could counteract, and one of them on my stomach felt like a lump of ice. Also, they forever went out of order, and I lost some irreplaceable shots in that way. The Leicas kept on faithfully.

None of my cameras was ever winterized. (A seal oil lamp is ideal for thawing out frozen cameras slowly, without getting frosted over in the process.) A cold camera takes the skin off the fingers, and film becomes so brittle that I learned to put a fresh ice-cold spool into my sleeping bag at night. In the morning, I quickly changed film in the igloo, before setting out for the day.

Travelling at 40 to 60 degrees below zero leaves no time for technique. The exposure and the diaphragm would be pre-set. There is not time to put on a lenshood. Valuable seconds would be lost in fumbling with it. That gave me about two minutes for photography, before the shutter slowed down and my fingertips froze, leaving me howling with pain. With a last desperate effort, my numbed hands would push the Leica back into my pocket, and I stamped around to restore circulation in my chilled body. Many times I passed up excellent possibilities, because I was just too damn cold.

It would be foolish to attempt any developing of film during the trips, and toward the end, one always becomes a little anxious to see the results. No major disaster has ever taken place . . . and here are the results.

Richard Harrington

THE FACE OF THE ARCTIC

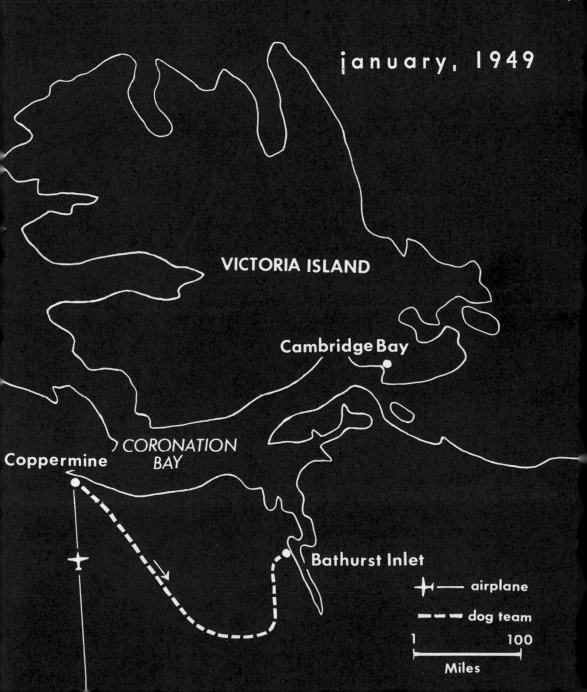

1. view of a typical arctic trading settlement: coppermine, on coronation gulf.

january, 1949

VICTORIA ISLAND

Cambridge Bay

CORONATION BAY

Coppermine

Bathurst Inlet

✈—— airplane

--- dog team

1   100

Miles

I

outside

WHEN THE BARBER IN EDMONTON ASKED ME WHERE I WAS going and I told him north, to Coppermine, a hundred miles beyond the Arctic Circle, he became careless. I let him do his worst. This was as good a way as any to kill time in the "Gateway to the North," where a Chinook blew, making the streets slushy, bringing a temperature unusually high for the season. It was January 5, 1949, and once more I was on the eve of a trip to the Far North— literally the eve, since the plane to Yellowknife, the first lap of my journey, would leave the following morning.

That warm wind blowing from the southwest may have had something to do with my restlessness. I felt tired, excited, impatient and doubtful—the way you feel when you are setting out, after an absence, to see a woman you have been in love with. Sitting there in the barber chair, I was afraid that memory had played me tricks, that things would not come up to expectations.

I had felt like this a year before, exactly, when I had flown from Moose Factory to Port Harrison for my dog-team trip down the eastern shore of Hudson Bay. And the

5

year before that it was the same thing when I travelled from The Pas to Churchill for my dogteam trips inland to the Chipewyans of northern Manitoba. I had made trips, by motorcar and canoe, to places like Fairbanks in Alaska and Moose Factory on James Bay. However, it was on my last two trips that I had really fallen in love with the North, for on these trips I had travelled the native way, by dogteam, living in tents and igloos, taking risks, enduring fatigue and cold. The Far North had sometimes made me whimper with cold and hunger and fatigue, but it had also, in a strange way, stimulated me. Back from those trips I felt like a changed man and was always surprised to find that I still looked just the same. Long ago I had given up trying to expain to myself or anyone else what kept pulling me back to the north. I simply accepted the fact.

And here I was, in 1949, facing another northern trip, again with my travelling equipment practically reduced to my cameras—two 35 mm. Leicas, two Kodak Medalists, and film for 1,400 exposures. It would be my first trip north of the Arctic Circle in the long black arctic night so much talked about, and for this reason, maybe, I was a little more than usually nervous. I was not thinking so much about myself and how I could stand up under the 50 below zero temperatures. I was thinking of those films and cameras, for at less severe temperatures than that my cameras had sometimes frozen. On the Port Harrison trip it had happened several times. In the past I had had good luck, but that did not guarantee good luck for the future.

Then, I was wondering about the Copper Eskimos. I was going to travel inland from Coppermine to see them, and hoped they would not disappoint me. I had heard that some of them still used bows and arrows. Not only would that make a good "picture story," but it would bring me in contact with a primitive people almost untouched

6

R.H. on Coppermine Trip

by white men's civilization. To date, I had preferred the Eskimos who had had least contact with white men.

Maybe it was as crazy as the barber obviously thought to go to Coppermine of my own free will. But the government at Ottawa had treated me like a sane man and had been cooperative. Letters had been written which would enable me to accompany a Royal Canadian Mounted Police constable on a patrol, by dogteam, of the very region I wanted to see. That region had not, in fact, been thoroughly patrolled for more than a decade, although the

7

Mounties patrolled hundreds of miles of their many thousand-mile sectors annually.

I had learned the name of the Constable-in-Charge of the Coppermine Detachment Area: Richard H. Connick. With an assistant, he was supposed to police some 200,-000 square miles of tundra, sea and islands, where lived about 600 Copper Eskimos and 29 white people, the latter traders, missionaries, and government employees—there was a weather station and a radio transmitting station now in Coppermine. I was wondering about Dick Connick. We would have to be night-and-day companions for weeks on end, share food, tents, igloos, fatigue and annoyances. That sort of thing puts character to the test, and in the back of my mind I was a little anxious. Supposing he resented having someone from outside along to share every minute of the trip?

The Gateway to the North had certainly disappointed me. It was a much more bustling town than when I had last seen it. The streetcars tooted like streetcars anywhere, the people looked like civilized people anywhere—slightly harassed and very hurried—and I had discovered, when I bought a last batch of magazines to take north with me, that they read the same magazines here as elsewhere. With the same advertisements, the same inducements for wasteful buying. Apparently I would have to go much farther to find the North I was looking for.

Yet the Arctic is less than a day away from Edmonton. In 1949, a daily flight took you to Yellowknife in five hours, ten minutes, including stopovers at Fort McMurray and Fort Smith. From Yellowknife, a monthly flight was made in to Coppermine, one hundred miles north of the Arctic Circle, in something like six hours, including a halt at Port Radium. In the old days it had taken months to cover that distance by canoe or dogsled. Now, one day you are "outside" and the next day you are "inside"—to

8

use the language of the Far North that makes the Arctic sound safe and cosy, like an igloo at night after a hard day of dogteam travel.

The interior of the plane to Yellowknife looked pretty shabby, the paint was worn and chipped. But the crew and the hostess wore uniforms, so you might have been going anywhere. We were grounded two and a half hours at Fort McMurray—the terminus of the railway from Edmonton, and so to a certain extent the farthest point of "civilization." There, the four other passengers—two miners headed for Yellowknife, and two women going back to their husbands there after a shopping spree outside—got into fleece-lined boots and fur-trimmed parkas. In the little depot, warmed by a sighing oil stove, one of the pilots dropped off to sleep at once on two chairs. It began to seem a little like the Far North.

While the miners were clearing off a table and shuffling a pack of limp playing cards, getting ready for a game of rummy, the co-pilot asked the usual questions: "Where to?" and "What for?" "To Coppermine, to take pictures," did not seem to make sense to him. Fortunately for me, a *Standard* was among the magazines that had been cleared off the table. I picked it up from the floor and handed it over, open to the rotogravure section.

"Those are mine," I said, pointing to some Eskimo shots I had made the year before at Port Harrison. There they were, and I was looked upon with new respect.

"So, you've been north before!" said the co-pilot, who had not been able to place me. I did not look like a fur-trader, a missionary, or a government official, and who else would go to Coppermine without being forced to?

We were soon flying northward again, this time through banks of clouds. Our halt at Fort Smith was only long enough to remark, "So that was Fort Smith!" The tiny

9

cluster of houses could not be called a town or even a settlement, but it is one of the many places in Canada that perpetuate the memory of the great Lord Strathcona who was once upon a time plain Donald Smith.

Yellowknife was reached in storm and darkness. A taxi took me to a hotel, and the hotel was new. In the lunchroom were twenty-two chrome and red imitation leather stools along a counter with the usual shiny dispensers and, in a corner, an unusually gaudy juke-box. However, the citizens wore parkas and fur boots, the women were in bright colored ski clothes and walked on tiptoe in moccasins, so there was some "local color," store-bought, and I will admit we had a good dinner of liver-and-onions.

The monthly plane to Coppermine would not leave till next day. So, after dinner, I did what you do in a small town. I looked up some people my wife knew, the Whyards—Jimmy a cartographer, Florence an occasional contributor to newspapers.

They lived in a new government-built apartment house that I was supposed to photograph but couldn't because of the storm. Jimmy turned out to be a camera hobbyist, and over our whisky and soda we talked shop. I learned I was lucky to have a government assignment, since a spy scare was on and anyone with even a baby Brownie might be suspect. A fellow had gone to Port Radium with $1,000 worth of camera equipment—which he had been persuaded not to use.

After looking at some of Jimmy's photographs of Bermuda—where he and his wife had spent their last vacation—our conversation drifted, as it always does in the Arctic, to the white people stationed there. Everyone in the vast region seems to know everyone else, whether they live in Aklavik or in Pangnirtung. To the white people stationed there, the Arctic is a small town.

They had seen some of my pictures of the Chipewyans,

printed in the *Beaver* magazine, and they asked me about people at Churchill, Moose Factory, and Port Harrison. Then they talked about the people at Coppermine. Miss Oldenburg, they said, had recently gone through Yellowknife on her way there; she had been at Port Harrison when I was there. Canon Webster, they said, had recently gone inland from Coppermine. He would be sure to have some fresh pictures of the very Eskimos I wanted to see and photograph. And of course the name of Learmonth came up, as it always does in almost any conversation up north.

I must explain. Miss Oldenburg is a "character." Middle-aged, hard of hearing, hard smoking, she is an ex-librarian from Minnesota who charters planes and flies everywhere in the Arctic simply because she likes to. Canon Webster is the Anglican missionary in Coppermine—or was, then—whose photographs appear in magazines. L. A. Learmonth is a kind of T. E. Lawrence of the Arctic. Formerly district manager of the Hudson's Bay Company and stationed at Coppermine, he stays on in the Arctic, lives near Spence Bay, Boothia Peninsula, because he likes the way of life in the North. The Eskimos like and respect him; he likes and respects the Eskimos. As we talked, I realized the Whyards could not quite understand why any white man should of his own free will face a life of "hardship." As with most white people stationed in the North, their life was rather sedentary, and they had little desire to know more about the "natives" than they could learn from printed pages.

When I went back to my hotel, the storm was still blowing, shaving away the snowdrifts, making flying hard for the dozen or so ravens that were fluttering about in the stormy darkness, picking up garbage. In the streets, snowed under, were lines of cars and trucks. I recalled what Jimmy had told me about the price of gasoline: forty-nine and a half cents a gallon.

In my hotel room I spread out the maps Jimmy had kindly given me. They were mostly blank spaces and dotted lines, indicating supposed contours and possible deviations of the magnetic needle. Most of the territory I planned to cover was unsurveyed and my route would take me in the direction of the North Magnetic Pole.

Sleep was out of the question. A radio was blasting away next door, and the walls of my room were of thin, unfinished wallboard.

I suppose my resentment against that noisy music bore my thoughts to a quieter and more serene world—the world of the Chipewyans that I had glimpsed two years previously. It was already in my mind, for that evening I had told Jimmy about my experiences in caribou hunting —me with a camera, Robinson Throassie, my Chip companion, a rifle. I had described the patient waiting, the long watch on the top of a hill. Anyway, as I at last dozed off, I was again in the tents of the Northern Indians of the edge of the Barren Lands just north of where the caribou winter.

Each day I had visited the tents. At first I had gone there to procure good clothing of caribou skins as soft as cloth and as warm as the tropics. I continued my visits simply because I liked the people. I had got used to the sight of the caribou heads ranged on racks outside the tents, frozen stiff, glassy eyed—at first they had given me a shock. I had learned to like the half roasted tongues that were the chief delicacy. I had observed and photographed all the processes of curing the skins. Gradually I had been accepted by the Chipewyans—oh, not as one of them, nothing like that—as a daily visitor, from whom, incidentally, tobacco could be cadged. I would arrive by carriole, flop down inside a tent, along with the scattered marrow bones, half cured hides, and drippy-nosed children. The

fire in the improvised stove—a gasoline drum cut in half
—glowed red. Constantly the women had to feed it with
the small wood that grew nearby, stunted spruce half buried in the snow. An old crone would be, say, rubbing
brains into a hide to soften it, her toothless mouth working in harmony with her knotted hands. We would all
smoke a while in silence, spit reflectively on the frozen
dirt floor. Then I would persuade one of the girls to start
up a song. After a while we would all be singing the monotonous chant . . .

Again I was on the shores of Duck Lake, which has
many other names: Lake Nejanilini on the map, but called
by the Chips Baralzoetui. And I remembered the fierce
storms, the brilliant sunlight, the ground-drifts, the solemn
people of the Little Sticks, the wild songs and drum playing; I was living them again.

There had been that day of storm, when the entire
landscape had been a mass of galloping white snow horses
blown by the wind across Duck Lake. Yet a warm April
sun had shone only the day before.

We—the children and I—were singing, a shrill, monotonous tune, which started gradually and after a while
stopped like a run-down phonograph record. Presently we
were all dancing around the stove together, in a slow
shuffle, our feet always on the ground, moving in a heavy,
short step. Around and around the stove we went, bending our heads so as not to touch the tent-walls of caribou
skins . . .

Early next morning I was out on the air-strip at Yellowknife, watching the ski-shod *Norseman* plane being loaded for our trip north to Coppermine. Ernie Boffa was the
pilot; I had met him still earlier in the Canadian Pacific
Airlines office. We talked, in a disconnected way. I told
him that if I had the money I'd like to charter his plane

Coppermine radio and weather station buildings, Northern lights and stars overhead

for some trips to outlying Eskimo encampments he had seen in some of his emergency flights. Slow-voiced, calm-eyed, with rumpled clothes and unruly hair, Ernie is small only in stature. He is in fact a big man, for he is of a disappearing profession, a bush pilot, the kind that takes to the air, no matter what. They are the ones that make the news occasionally when there is some kind of rescue flight on. The way Ernie flies, he deserves to make the news every day, for he will take his plane up when the average pilot prefers to stick to the good, safe ground.

There were no seats in this plane. The monthly flights out of Yellowknife to Coppermine are mostly for mail-carrying purposes. This time, the *Norseman* was stacked high with parcels, a lot of them overdue Christmas gifts and mail. We, the passengers, crawled in last, and sat wherever we could find room, on our bedrolls.

There were three other passengers. One was a wooden-legged man with a hangover, who was going to cook for a gang of miners near Contact Lake. The other two were going to Coppermine with me. Vernon Marsh, a young fellow who would be assistant at the radiosonde (weather) station there; the other an Eskimo lad who had been flown out for a t.b. checkup—results negative.

With a roar, the *Norseman* leaped into the air, like a kid bounding up a staircase. Ernie is famous for those take-offs.

The man with the wooden leg was set down at Contact Lake, and the plane took off again without delay. Then we came down at Port Radium long enough to read and digest the big sign posted up, warning what would happen to us if . . . and all about Atomic Energy Control. Ernie said about 400 men were employed there. It is a small place, but bustling, with steam hissing out of chimneys. A big company plane was unloading cargo. The whole thing depressed me. I wish they'd leave the stuff in the ground.

Then off again, this time over some sheer bluffs, hills, and little chasms to the east of Great Bear Lake. Trees gradually petered out as contours flattened and landmarks disappeared. We were at last in the clean, uncluttered Arctic.

"Feel that bump?" Ernie shouted at me. I hadn't. "That was the Arctic Circle," he said with a grin.

Taking altitude, we were enveloped in gray clouds for a while. Then, about a hundred miles farther on, we dropped slowly through the clouds. "That's Bloody Falls!" Ernie shouted again, jerking his chin down towards a landmark I could not see. Bloody Falls marks the place where Samuel Hearne's northern Indians massacred the Eskimos in 1771. Shortly afterwards, Ernie called out: "I think Coppermine's just about here!"

We dropped down still farther, circling a while over what looked to me like a rocky coast, and Coppermine came up to meet us, a string of low white houses on a white, icebound beach.

Almost the entire population came running out of their houses and approached the plane before the propeller had stopped spinning. They wanted to be on the spot for the monthly delivery of mail, and they wanted to get a first look at the strangers, Vernon Marsh and me. The scene reminded me of Port Harrison, to which I had flown a year before: a little crowd of smiling people in enormous parka hoods, stamping their feet, peering at us from beneath frosted eyebrows, all of them at first glance seeming to be Eskimos. But the crowd was divided into two groups—the noisy, shouting group in front were the whites, the shy and quiet group at the rear were the natives, who belonged there in the Arctic.

I was introduced to members of the first group, of whom I recognized one, having seen his portrait in magazines: Canon (now Archdeacon) Webster, of the Anglican mission. Leo Manning, manager of the Hudson's Bay trading post—Coppermine's reason-for-being—immediately came forward with an invitation to take all my meals at his house while there. Dick Connick, Constable-in-Charge of the Royal Canadian Mounted Police detachment in Coppermine, greeted me with the quiet remark: "So, you're to go with me on the inland patrol." He had received the messages from Ottawa, and all was arranged. **16**

R.C.M.P. barracks at Coppermine, N.W.T., from left to right: living quarters, wind charger, storehouse, special constable's house

a typical arctic trading settlement

Dick's looks and words relieved me, for I liked him at once—and I never had cause to change my first impression.

My travelling companion, Vernon Marsh, was taken in charge by Jack Scarlett, head of the radiosonde station. They went off, with a casual "See you tonight at the Mannings'!" Father Delalande, of the Roman Catholic Mission, then introduced himself and his assistant, whose name I did not get. A French couple, with a Quebec accent, then came forward, inviting me to dine soon "at the hospital." They were Abigail Dufresne, registered nurse, and her husband Emile, her assistant. Beside these, there was Johnny Jackson, head of the radio station and also postmaster and justice of the peace in the settlement.

It was impossible, in the confusion, to sort out who was who among the women and children. Anyway, they hurried off, shivering, as if unused to the out-of-doors.

The crowd dispersed, and Ernie Boffa, the mechanic, and I trooped off with Dick Connick to the R.C.M.P. barracks.

I kept turning round to have another look at the Eskimos, who had stood shyly by throughout the shouting and the introductions. The lad that had been flown out for a t.b. checkup was now lost in that group. They were real Eskimos, all right, and I felt I had seen them before. I had: their blood-brothers in the Eastern Arctic. Their skin-clothing was a little different in pattern. But they had the same dark shining eyes, the same broad smiling faces, the same look of being at home with themselves and their world. The icy wind whipped the women's cotton over-dresses. Yes, they wore them here, too, as did the white women, the wives of the men stationed in the Arctic. An old tradition, this, dating from the first missionaries, who were shocked at the idea of women in fur pants, and insisted on putting them into calico Mother-Hubbards.

1 8

ll

inside—but still in a
white man's world

It was all arranged, I would accompany Dick on that inland patrol. But we would not go for another two or three weeks, for several reasons. Dick's assistant constable, Martin Donnan, was away on a patrol to Read Island, to the north. We would have to wait for his return. In addition, what with the Christmas mail, Dick had a great deal of "paper work" to clear up. Then, supplies for the trip would have to be accumulated. I had to get new skin clothing, hire a dogteam driver, buy food and other supplies. While waiting to start, I would have time for the great winter occupation of the Far North—visiting. During the time the sun is below the horizon—for about fifty-four days at Coppermine—Eskimos and whites alike go visiting, and in a settlement as small and isolated as Coppermine, what other pastime is there?

At Coppermine there were, in 1949, eight white men's houses, snug wooden boxes kept at fever heat with big oil-burning stoves, double and triple doors, insulation, and blocks of snow banked almost to the eaves. Wind chargers provided nearly every house with electricity. There was no plumbing; collapsible rubberized canvas tubs and toilets of the bucket type took care of sanitation. The water supply, ice blocks, cut from a lake some miles distant, were stored in stacks at every doorway. A barrel was in every house, somewhere near a stove, where these blocks were deposited, for melting down.

The wooden houses and everything in them except those iceblocks had come from outside, being shipped down the Mackenzie River, deposited on the coast, and reshipped on a coastal steamer which reached Coppermine once a year, usually in August.

Coppermine, like most other settlements in the Far North, has no telephones, no roads, no wheeled vehicles, no garbage disposal, no domestic animals aside from the dogs bred for hauling sleds. There are no movies, and some of the government employees feel that the $50 "isolation bonus" they get each month for working in the North is not enough to compensate for the lack of such amenities. Every house had its radio, however.

With a population of nineteen whites and about thirty Eskimos, Coppermine had two "churches"—the front rooms of the rival missionaries' houses. The four-bed hospital with a registered nurse in charge was Coppermine's latest acquisition. There would soon be a school—the timber and furnishings had come down to the coast the previous summer and would be conveyed to Coppermine in the summer of 1949. Hospital and school alike were provided by the government for the natives. A doctor can be flown up in an emergency, but white people prefer to fly outside for treatment. As to education of white children, correspondence courses flown in by plane would take care of that.

At Coppermine were no snow houses—or igloos, although this word means only "house." On the fringe of the white settlement were a number of *tupiks*, caribou

20

skin tents, where lived the native population—always re-
ferred to as "the people"—an unconscious translation of
the Eskimos' own name for themselves, *Innuit*. This collection of skin tents and their inhabitants might correspond to city slums. Many natives in the settlement received "Destitute Allowance" from the government. From
this Eskimo settlement the white residents drew their
tinkers and tailors and dogteam drivers, as well as house
servants (called "native helpers").

That first night at the Mannings', the majority of the
white population had foregathered in the brightly lit and
overheated sittingroom. They put the usual question to
Ernie, Vernon Marsh and me: "What's new outside?"
And scarcely bothered about the answer. What interests
them is news about other white folks in the Arctic, and the
one subject they get excited about is "What to do about
the people?" Most white folks are convinced that the Eskimos must somehow be made to act and live more like us.

Coppermine, I decided, was not only a typical white
man's settlement in the Far North, it was a microcosm of
the white man's world. You might say it was a boil-down
of our civilization. You could not say it was a "trans-
planted" portion, for no one in the Mannings' sittingroom
had put down any real roots in the Arctic. They represented Commerce, Christianity, and Government, and
were here only temporarily. In a few years they would be
sent elsewhere in the Arctic—or would have realized their
dream to be outside again.

To my mind, the Arctic can never be the white man's
home, nor can he bend it to his ways. So, white men fly
in briefly, remain for a while, leave as quickly as possible,
and yap about it endlessly afterwards—including me, of
course.

In the old days, when trapping licenses were issued to

white men, you found individual traders who intended to spend their lives in the North. I have met some of those few remaining white trappers—all, now, well over forty—and none of them had really become one with the country. They had merely turned their backs on the outside world, for some reason or other. By inclination, they were hermits more than anything else. As for Learmonth, his case is so exceptional that he has become legendary in his lifetime.

I have spoken of "whites" and Eskimos. I must explain that Eskimos are not a dark-skinned race. They are weather-beaten, smoke-grimed, and, in summer, sunburned. But white folks in the North are usually very white-skinned. This is the result of the exceptionally sedentary lives that most of them live, especially the women. For months on end they scarcely stir out of doors, except to dash from one house to another, usually a distance of about a hundred yards.

As the conversation limbered up, I thought how suitable it was that we should be gathered in the residence of the Hudson's Bay Company post manager. Always in the Far North, that is the heart of the white community, which has usually grown up in this order: first the trader, then the missionary, then the government. Indeed the familiar "HBC" is waggishly translated as "Here Before Christ." In modern times you occasionally find visitors such as Ernie and myself. We were a typical gathering, and the talk was typical.

I tried to keep mum. I thought I was only listening to the talk about how the people must learn to take baths, to live in permanent wooden houses, and to read and write English. But apparently some words escaped me, for I began to hear a familiar refrain: "Oh, come now, Harrington! You can't turn back the clock!"

Yes, I had seen what had happened elsewhere. Learning to wash meant a dirty towel in every tupik, used by the entire clan until it was worn out—and until every one of the users had contracted the same disease. Learning to read and write English meant losing the highly developed native skills essential to the perpetuation of the race. The Eskimo boy and girl learn from their parents, by precept and example. Take them away from their parents at an early age, and who is going to teach the boys to stalk caribou, drive dogteams, spear seals, jig for fish? Who is going to teach the girl to use the woman's knife, that wonderful half-moon shaped *ulu* of so many vital uses? How and when will she learn to cure caribou skins and sew skin garments for the hunter?

"Oh, but," said someone, "the government intends to teach the Eskimos their native skills."

Maybe. I had also seen what happened when that was done. In the Eastern Arctic I had met some Eskimos who were induced to turn to some "industrial" account their ability as craftsmen. They had been told to carve out of soapstone and ivory little "souvenirs" for sale in the cities outside. And they turned out miniature walruses, *kayaks* and, oh ye gods, book-ends and ash trays. But they were neglecting to spear walruses and make real kayaks.

I defended myself from a friendly ragging—by denying I wanted to "put back the clock." Had anyone there ever tried to regulate a striking clock? If so, they must know you could not hurry up the works without jamming them, and having your clock strike two at half past four.

Tactfully, someone changed the subject to photography. They were all very kind and nice people. And after all, they had been in the Arctic longer than I had . . .

Several camera enthusiasts besides Canon Webster were there. Jack Scarlett was the proud owner of a 3C Leica with all the gadgets. Dick Connick was interested in photography, and even the usually silent Ernie Boffa joined in this talk. The women were left out of the conversation for the time being—there was Mrs. Jackson and her little girl, Mrs. Webster and the Websters' two grown girls, and our calm and beautiful hostess, Mrs. Manning with her two little girls. They busied themselves setting out evening refreshments—hot coffee and chocolate cake —to warm us up for our short homeward trips through the cold.

After midnight there was a great bundling up in parkas and furlined boots, jovial invitations to "drop in and see us"—then came the plunge into the icy darkness, our flashlights boring a hole of light into the whirling inferno of blown snow.

Before leaving the children, I managed to get on their good side with a parlor trick or two. I can wiggle my scalp and flap my ears, talents that had delighted the native children on both shores of Hudson Bay. These white children were immediately won over, and twelve year old Marguerite Webster shyly pulled me by the sleeve and said, "You must come to see my canary tomorrow. I have a canary, it's been here three years, and it sings!"

Jack Scarlett and Vernon Marsh accompanied Ernie, the mechanic, Dick and me back to the barracks, to go on with the camera talk. We kept it up until 2 A.M., lounging in the kitchen by the hot stove. The barracks had two big oil-burners, one in the office, one in the kitchen. The office was stacked high with papers, and the kitchen was the most comfortable room in the place. So the sign up at the door to the barracks had some point. It read:

ENOET POLAKTUN KUKIOVIKME KISEME.
—PALISMA.

TRANSLATION:
"People when visiting must stay in the kitchen.
—Police."

2 4

The boys asked me about some of my experiences with the northern peoples, who are frequently camera-shy. Had I had any trouble of the sort? I recalled the hard time I had in persuading the Chipewyans to let me photograph them. I managed to get my wants explained through two interpreters—my words passing from English into Cree and then into Chipewyan. What had I told the Chips? I told them I had come all that distance to take pictures to show the white man (that obscure busybody) what hard lives they led, how hard they worked to obtain food, how poor they were. I explained that the white man (there he was again) knew very little about them and wanted to know more; I said that personally I didn't give a damn whether they let me photograph them or not, but if they condescended to do so, I had some tobacco for them. Finally, for a few quids of tobacco, they were willing to pose for me as much as I liked. But they thought it was silly when I followed them around photographing them at their daily chores, the ordinary tasks of cutting up caribou, or preparing hides for skin-clothing.

Then I told the chaps in the barracks about the time my Medalist camera froze up, inside an igloo. It was near Port Harrison, when the temperature outside was about 30 below.

"We'll hit worse temperatures than that, inland," said Dick. "February is the coldest month, and that's when we'll hit the igloo country . . ."

That Medalist had given me trouble several times on the dogteam trip out from Port Harrison. There was that time I wanted to photograph the frozen Nastapoka Falls . . . As I talked, I could again hear, in imagination, the subdued roar of the falls, a roar that could be heard a mile off. The wind carried the spray,–freezing my eyelashes together. It had been a hard job crossing the sea ice through that icy vapor, and when I got there, the view was obscured by ice and spray. But I took several pictures just to prove that I'd been there, after managing to thaw out my camera in a nearby igloo. I froze my fingers, but I got the shots. One of them was of a woman with a baby in the back of her *artiggi* (a hooded tunic of caribou skin). She had watched with great interest as I thawed out the camera over her seal oil lamp.

I recalled the fatigue of those thirty-five miles, how hot I got in my skin clothing, how cold my fingers were. I remembered how the dogs, fan-hitched, had crept along, searching for a footing on the rough sea ice, slipping now and then, and raising a comic howl. I remembered the vapor that had hovered over the falls like smoke all day as we advanced.

"And was it worth it?" asked Ernie, puzzled.

I hesitated, realizing it would be difficult to explain my feeling of achievement that night.

"Yes," I said at last, "it was worth it!"

"Camera crazy," said Jack Scarlett. And all agreed that I must meet Paulette.

Paulette Anerodluk was a talented Eskimo girl living in Coppermine. She had been to school at Aklavik and spoke English perfectly. When Learmonth had been at the Hudson's Bay post at Coppermine, he had taken an interest in her, given her a camera and taught her how to use it. He had also employed her as bookkeeper at the post.

Dick, Scarlett, and Ernie all seemed to be enthusiastic about her. She was pretty, well behaved, bright, and the men treated her with respect, exactly as if she were a white woman. They opened doors for her, lit her cigarettes.

She was keenly interested in photography, for she now developed her own films, used a contact printer, in a 3 x 6 foot darkroom. She warmed up the dishes on an oil stove, then took them to the icy cold darkroom, where she developed the films see-saw fashion.

"And she has not forgotten native techniques, either," said Dick. "You'll see. When you get your skin clothing made, ask her to make your boots for you."

I agreed to do so.

They went on to say she was over twenty, which is long past the marriageable age for Eskimo women, but she was not yet married. Two Eskimo boys had been rejected by her. Were she to marry an Eskimo, she would lose her privileged position among the whites. As to a white man ever marrying her, I knew—and the others knew—how unlikely that was.

"Where does she live?" I asked.

Her parents lived in one of the skin tents on the outskirts of Coppermine, but she lived, they said, with the Jacksons, where she was employed as "native helper."

Well, this finished off the subject of Paulette, and I was glad when Jack Scarlett again put in a question about his camera.

About two o'clock I produced a bottle of rum and we had a round of "Boffa Specials." In case anyone wants to know, a Boffa Special is a two-way drink. First you put a jigger of maple syrup in your glass. Toss it off. Then you put the same amount or more of rum in the same glass and toss *that* off. The maple syrup coats your throat cooly against the burning rum and trickles down your gullet after it. Believe me, it's a pleasant experience.

"What would they say if they saw us now?" said Jack Scarlett.

By "they," he meant the white women of the community.

White women in the Far North seem to disapprove of a lot of things and maybe, I reflected, maybe the regulations regarding marriage, in force both in the R.C.M.P. and the Hudson's Bay Company, had a reason for being.

Bachelors are decidedly preferred. Dick Connick, for instance, was twenty-six but until he had done five years of service, he must remain a bachelor.

"Women!" I said, in a tone of voice calculated to convince them I was a woman-hater. They had been kidding about my reasons for liking Eskimos, talking about the wife-trading practices by which I might be expected to benefit, and so forth. "Women!" I said. "They are trying to introduce lace tablecloths into the Arctic! Watch out —with one lace tablecloth a white woman may upset the balance of civilization that is centuries old . . ."

We all laughed. I told them about a certain H.B.C. post where the wife of the manager had objected to my vocabulary. I had been talking at table about a wonderful lead-dog that happened to be a bitch. With lifted eyebrows the lady had informed me that in that household dogs were either man-dogs or lady-dogs, and had reminded me that children were present.

"I was glad you said what you did tonight about the family towel," said Ernie Boffa, as we prepared to break it up. "Usually we're blamed for bringing in disease."

That was so. Whenever a plane came, there was apt to be an epidemic of something or other, usually head colds or influenza, a few days later.

"We're all guilty," I said. "We're all enemy aliens here."

"Well, this enemy alien must go to bed," said Dick, good-humoredly. "I'll be away when next month's mail comes in. Tomorrow I have paper work up to my ears . . ."

Dick went off to his room, where he had a real bed. Another real bed was in the office, for Dick's assistant, Constable Martin Donnan. Martin might come back any night now, from his 250 mile patrol. So his bed was out.

Jack Scarlett and Vernon Marsh bundled up for the

three hundred yard trek back to the radiosonde station, making a great to-do about having to face the cold again—it was 20 below zero—such treks being about the limit of endurance for a sane white man, according to Jack.

It was almost three when Ernie, the mechanic, and I rolled out our eiderdown sleeping-bags on the floor of the livingroom and crawled into them.

Outside, the wind blew, rattling the stovepipe, shaking the windows. You don't hear the wind when you are inside an igloo, I reflected; it is the wind whistling round the corners of white men's houses that sounds so cold.

I was awake for some time after Ernie and the mechanic had dropped off. Not far from the barracks some huskies, tethered for the night, began their antiphonal chorus. Huskies don't bark, they howl, and in a peculiar way. Had those "nightingales of the Arctic" scented a wolf or a polar bear? It was comfortable to lie there in my warm sleeping bag, and as I drowsed off, I imagined I was once more in a snow house. . . .

The inside of an igloo is not dark, nor is it cold and drafty. There is a pleasant gloom, something like that of the inside of a tent, but more luminous. Sitting in your fur clothes or lying in your sleeping bag, you are cosy and warm. The wind does not penetrate, and at night the candle burns with a steady flame. Big shadows are cast on the snow-block walls by the candle, or by the roaring primus stove, or by the flickering *kudele*, a soap-stone blubber lamp that replaces the hearth for the Eskimo.

When those lights are put out, the thick snow sides of the house become gradually translucent, particularly on moonlit nights. This light that filters in is like the light inside shadows, and any painter will tell you that no shadow is completely black, that is to say, devoid of light. It is a twilight favorable to reverie.

a typical arctic trading settlement

An igloo is not cluttered up with useless things as are white men's houses. Everything inside it is useful and has its appointed place. From the sleeping bench of snow, you can reach everything you need, or your Eskimo friend beside you can reach it. From the head of your sleeping bench you can stretch out an arm from the sleeping bag and light the lamp or stove to boil your morning tea. You do not need to leave that bag to have your breakfast, nor do you need to leave it to use the chamberpot—usually an empty lard can. There is no privacy in an igloo except what your sleeping bag affords, but there is a feeling of

Inside this igloo an unusually long 'Kudele' seal oil lamp is used. Bannock, just baked, in foreground. Drying rack situated above flame

human closeness and mutual tolerance which is good. At night, inside the igloo, there is a faint smell of iron—if you have a primus stove that is cooling off—and of snow and fur and perspiration and urine. In the morning, these smells are covered up by the fresher smells of tea and tobacco. They are all good, normal smells, inside the snow house.

When the roaring primus stove is put out, silence descends. Not total silence, for there is no such thing. You can hear your own and your companions' breathing. Those are good sounds. If a storm is raging, you may faintly hear the seething of the ground drifts, but there is no whistling round sharp corners, for an igloo has no corners . . . Sometimes the huskies curled up outside, back to the wind, raise their voices in a weird howling, that stops as suddenly as it begins. And if your igloo is standing on sea ice, you hear the straining and cracking sounds of the ice as the imprisoned tides force against it. But wherever you are and at no matter what time of the year, one sound is missing: the sound of tree branches moved by a breeze.

There are no trees in the frozen lands. In the short summer there are flowers and birds, but there are no trees. In some parts of the land grow stunted willows and spruce. I like trees, but I do not miss them in the Far North, for there are so many other kinds of beauty. For instance, the beauty of northern lights over a snowy waste as your sled, which the Eskimos call *komatik*, plunges and bumps along, taking you apparently from nowhere straight ahead into nowhere . . .

I had dreamed that I was in an igloo—an ideal one, for some are uncomfortable. I woke to the welcome warmth of the big oil-burning stove. Dick Connick was making coffee; its smell had wakened me. The dream had been pleasant, but reality was not so bad either. Not, that is, until Dick reminded me, with a comical grimace, that we were going to church that evening.

Seeing my look of resignation, Ernie said: "I bet Harrington won't go!"

I assured him he would lose his bet. In the isolated settlements of the Arctic I make a point of church-going. It seems to me that is the least a traveller can do for the discouraged missionary who, more often than not, has to preach his sermon to his obedient family, if Protestant, or, in the case of a Catholic priest, to a row of empty benches.

III

mostly about mounties
and missionaries

THE WIND WAS STILL BLOWING LEVEL DRIFTS OF SNOW.
Dick lent me his artiggi that came down to below my
knees—he being more than six feet tall—which enabled
me to dash outside the barracks several times to get some
storm shots.

Even with the stormy sky, the Arctic night was not as
black as I had expected. It was more like the gloom of an
especially dark day farther south. The sun had set towards
the end of November; it would rise again in about two
weeks' time. Already, Dick said (looking at me above his
stack of mail) you could see reflected sunshine towards the
north if you climbed to the top of a low hill nearby. On
some days that sunshine was deflected by clouds out upon
Coronation Gulf.

While the mechanic worked on the plane, getting it
ready for the flight out next day, Ernie camped in the hot
sittingroom, yawning over the magazines I had brought
up. I spent most of the morning exploring the barracks.

a typical arctic trading settlement

The barracks consisted of a kitchen, a sittingroom. Dick's bedroom, the office, which was also Martin Donnan's bedroom, a workshop in a lean-to, and a lavatory (bucket-type) at the end of the workshop. Two oil stoves were kept going night and day—one in the livingroom and one in the kitchen, where the temperature was much too high for comfort.

In the office I noticed a large poster tacked up on the wall. It was issued from Ottawa, and it was in syllabics—that lettering that looks like shorthand and which was invented by early missionaries. I asked Noel Avadluk, the Eskimo Special Constable, what it said. "Family Allowance instructions," he replied. Could anyone read it here in the western Arctic? I asked. Noel said that no one could; but that everyone understood what it was all about. The instructions were there, and the women who came in each month got their $5 to $8 per month per child—the Canadian allowance for children under 16.

Issuing Family Allowance vouchers was one of Dick's office jobs. Cheques and money are, naturally, useless to the people, so they get their Family Allowance in trade at the Hudson's Bay Company store. It means a lot of bookkeeping, for both the trader and the Mountie. And things, said Dick, were getting into a fearful tangle because of the Eskimo practice of adopting children. "You never know who's the real mother or father of any child!" he said, exasperated.

I knew of the practice of adoptions, which held sway throughout the Arctic. A woman is pregnant, she gives birth to the child. Next thing you know, another woman is nursing and packing the infant. And maybe, later on, still another woman will have it. This is a big headache to the people who keep "vital statistics." It would simplify things if the Eskimos would change their point of view about children—to wit, that a child belongs not so much **34** to a couple as to the tribe. There is no such thing as bastardy among the Eskimos, all children are "legitimate" and all children are loved and cared for—by everyone.

The mixup at first confused the Eskimos, too. For the government put just as high a value upon little girl babies as upon boys. In their economy, based on hard necessity, it had always been thought unwise to allow too many girl babies to grow up. Infanticide was, in some cases, practised. A child must not, they thought, be allowed to grow up unless there was a good probability of her finding a mate. But now, with the Family Allowance, to destroy a girl baby meant losing the opportunity to cash in on her. I wondered what would happen to the superfluous little girls when they grew up.

Ever since I had arrived, I had noticed the quiet comings and goings of an Eskimo lad, who seemed to be occupied in shovelling snow, clearing a path from the barracks lean-to to the "john," a distant outhouse.

In a guarded way, I enquired about him from Noel Avadluk. I learned that he was Peter Meuk, who had stolen furs from a Hudson's Bay post and had then tried to sell them back to the trader. Avadluk tapped his head, and looked ashamed. I was to learn that all the Eskimos of Coppermine were ashamed of Peter Meuk.

From time to time Meuk would come in, help himself to tobacco from the tin on the table, roll a cigarette, hang round, pick up one of my magazines—say, *Esquire*—stare for a while at some picture, then ask Avadluk for further instructions. The instructions were always: "Go on shovelling." So Meuk shovelled through the deep drifts. But the wind soon filled up the path again. With Eskimo ingenuity, he solved that. He built a tunnel of snowblocks. He beamed—that job was finished for good. The pity was that the john was never used in winter.

It was very unusual to have a prisoner at the barracks, said Dick, looking up from his twentieth letter. This was the first time a prisoner had been at these barracks since Dick had taken up his duties in 1943. Peter Meuk had been sentenced to hard labor for two years. While confined—Peter lived in a canvas tent near the barracks—the prisoner received "single rations"—flour, milk, butter, canned meats, jam, tobacco, and coal oil—comprising, in fact, white men's luxuries. The Mounted Police furnished him with the tent, a stove, cooking utensils, and clothing. His treatment, aside from being confined to a restricted territory, was about the same as that of the Eskimo Special Constable. I wondered what the Eskimos made of this.

Meuk's real punishment would come later. When he had served his term, he would have a hard time rehabilitating himself as a trapper. His dogs were already gone—lost or dead. He would become another Eskimo "post lounger," probably.

When I presented Meuk with one of the wire puzzles I had brought up from Edmonton, he took it apart and put it together again in no time. That puzzle had absolutely stymied me, but I have yet to see a puzzle of any kind that will get an Eskimo down.

Noel Avadluk, the Special Constable, and his forty year old wife, Marie Kablunak, fourteen years his senior, lived in a shack nearby and they had two adopted children. Eskimos do not seem to be prejudiced against the older woman as a wife, since children can always be adopted. Another thing to note is that there are no family names among the Eskimos, and the woman therefore does not take the husband's name, but retains her own, the one bestowed upon her at birth. In addition, the baptized Eskimo has a Christian name; and by the way, you can

3 6

almost tell whether he is Protestant or Catholic by that name. It is easy to guess, since the Catholic missionaries are all usually French or of French extraction. So I realized at once that Noel Avadluk and his wife Marie Kablunak were Roman Catholics.

Their shack was furnished with a stove, a cupboard, a table, and two chairs. Two wooden platforms, covered with caribou hides, served as beds, remindful of the arrangement in an igloo.

As Special Constable, Noel's duties were to act as guide, interpreter, and caretaker of the dogs. It was up to him to keep the travelling gear in repair and to hunt for dog-feed. He also helped Dick and Martin with such jobs as painting and repairing the barracks and the police boat that was used in the short summer season. For these duties he received "single native rations" plus a salary of $55 per month and coal-oil for his stove.

Marie Kablunak kept busy, too, making and repairing the skin clothing used by her husband and by the two Mounties on their patrols. Her hands were always busy, her calm and smiling face was always bent over some kind of work.

Her face was tattooed in the old style. Blue lines formed a V on her forehead and were distributed on her cheeks and chin in parallel lines. Her hands and arms were also marked with blue lines. This custom is no longer practised among women in the Arctic, and therefore it is never seen among women under thirty-five. Marie Kablunak was a handsome woman. The tattooing was at least as decorative as lipstick, powder and rouge are on white faces of women outside.

It seemed a happy household—and this in my experience is the rule among Eskimos. Several times, as Noel Avad-luk passed near his wife, she would give him an affection-ate little kick with her soft sealskin-booted foot, and when they exchanged some infrequent remark it was always in a gentle tone of voice.

Avadluk had been employed at the barracks for four years, and the neatness of everything, the fresh paint, the snugness of the place, were greatly due to his efforts.

In prowling about the barracks, I ran across a washing machine, with which Dick and Martin did their weekly wash. The two Mounties had made it themselves, Dick told me, from parts they had scrounged here and there. The motor worked off a 32-volt plant, kept supplied by the usual wind-charger. The belt was a webbing of sealskin thongs, the kind used for dog harness.

These two Mounties could do almost anything. They barbered one another, I learned, and they prided themselves on their cooking. Every week they baked a batch of bread, and Dick was famous for his baked beans and doughnuts.

When I finally settled down in the livingroom with Ernie and became absorbed in reading some stuff I had picked up in the office, the Sabbath morning had passed.

"Anything interesting?" enquired Ernie, opening one eye at me. I told him I was reading up on the Royal Canadian Mounted Police. At which he promptly went to sleep again.

I had a 1948 report and a folder marked "G" Division, Coppermine Area. It contained various newspaper clippings, very informative. From this material I learned that the "G" Division of the R.C.M.P. takes in the Yukon and Northwest Territories and northern Quebec: of the total strength, only 96 uniformed men policed that vast area, aided by 32 Special Constables, natives such as Noel Avadluk. During 1947 that force had patrolled 411,513 miles by dogsled, boat, airplane, automobile, and on foot. The 232 dogs accounted for 45,695 miles.

Lead-dog and pup

a typical arctic trading settlement

As Constable-in-Charge of the Coppermine Detachment Area—200,000 square miles, 629 population, of which 29 whites lived at Coppermine, Read Island, Holman Island, and Bathurst Inlet—Dick Connick loomed in my mind as someone quite important. In the past winter he and Martin had covered close to 3,000 miles by dogteam and during the past summer had covered by boat more than 500 miles. They certainly did not lead sedentary lives!

Consulting my printed matter, I learned that the Mounties, in addition to the usual police duties, serve as game wardens, assess the fur tax, issue game and business licenses, supervise liquor shipment . . . Oh, my two undeclared bottles of rum! They also registered vital statistics —births, deaths, marriages—and issued relief to destitute people in their area. Beside the routine patrols, they must stand ready for emergency calls—famine, epidemics, accidents, and crimes.

"The Eskimos have as usual been very law-abiding during the past year," one report ended.

I had heard about a murder that had taken place near Bathhurst Inlet in 1947. A woman had helped her arthritic husband commit suicide. Tired of life, he had tried to shoot himself, but his fingers and arms, stiff with arthritis, had not been able to manage the gun. He called to his wife to help him. She had obliged—and was charged with assisting in a suicide. They gave her a sentence of one year and nine months. She served it at Coppermine, having quite a social fling. A mild sentence? But it had to be taken into account that, from the Eskimo point of view, this was no crime. Suicide in such cases is commended: when a man can't pull a trigger, he is pretty useless.

I was still thinking about that case of the murderess during the midday dinner at the Mannings'. By the time we had pushed back our chairs and were drinking our last cups of coffee, several people had dropped in for a chat and the conversation had turned upon crime among "the people." It went something like this:

"You may be right, Harrington, it's amazing how law-abiding the people are, considering they have no form of government among themselves. But suicide must not be permitted, no matter what the excuse. Surely you agree." This from one white.

"And surely you wouldn't condone the cannibalism they sometimes practise?"

I had heard of those rare cases that still occur when, in time of famine, a family had managed to survive by using a corpse as food. A blood-curdling idea. But—

"Cannibalism has been known to occur among some of our past expeditions. It was strongly suspected of the Franklin expedition, to name only one . . ."

"And surely we must punish incest when it occurs . . ."

On this subject I had first hand information. "I knew a case, that one at Port Harrison," I said, and I went on to give what details I had learned about it while there.

Kalakaluk was his name. He was living as a prisoner in an igloo behind the walrus shed when I was at Port Harrison. He had committed incest with his daughter, after the death of his wife. There had been no other woman for him in his little community, and in such cases the Eskimos more or less condone incest. Their idea is that every man has a right to a mate and every woman has a right to a mate. Well, the R.C.M.P. constable heard of it, arrested him, and held him for trial. That was early in 1947, I believe. The *Nascopie* that carried the trial lawyer and judge sank that summer, and I do not know how the case ended.

"Maybe he is still being held, for all I know," I ended up, "and is getting single rations all this time. How can we hope to explain such things to the Eskimos?"

Mrs. Leo Manning, wife of H.B.C. man at Coppermine, and her daughter speak over the air to friends at Bathurst Inlet

"We can't explain," said one of the visitors. "But the Eskimos have jolly well got to learn our point of view on such things!"

And that was that.

Every Sunday at 3 P.M., or almost every Sunday, the people in Coppermine, whites and Eskimos alike, have a chance to broadcast messages to their friends at other posts. The program is broadcast over VBK, is called

"The Voice of Eskimoland," and the folks at Read Island, Holman Island, Bathurst Inlet all listen to it regularly. Tune in on 4.455 megacycles, short wave.

That afternoon we were about thirty people, of whom about sixteen were Eskimos, crowded into the radio station room, over which Johnny Jackson presided. Canon Webster led off with a little sermon to his distant flock. Then the microphone was turned over to anyone who had anything to say.

The messages were for the most part simply greetings to distant friends—"I am well and hope you are the same" sort of thing. On occasion, however, these messages are of some importance; for instance, when someone is starting out on a dogteam or boat trip, the people along the route may be advised of his coming. (By the way, if you want to hide or lose yourself, the Arctic is not a safe place since radios came in.)

After a few of the white population had their say, some Eskimos stepped forward, with obvious eagerness. Smiling broadly, as they always do out of good manners when they converse, they chatted away unselfconsciously into the microphone.

Jackson told me afterwards that some of the Eskimos had addressed friends in distant igloos and tupiks devoid of radio receiving sets. They had great confidence in white man's magic.

After this, I went to the St. Andrew's Anglican Mission. For me, this Sabbath day held two church services, for I wanted to get some pictures of a baptismal ceremony. Canon Webster was to baptise a child after the usual service for his Eskimo congregation that afternoon. Manning had told me that the happy father, Peter Kamingoak, owned the best dogteam in Coppermine, recommended him to me, and I thought I might look him over before hiring.

About a dozen Eskimos comprised the congregation, and

they sat smilingly and meekly on benches drawn up in four rows in front of the bare altar of the Anglican "church" —a room in Webster's house. I noticed that the baptismal font had the date 1915 carved into it.

As I followed the service in an English prayer book, I wondered what Webster could do with such phrases as "remission of sins" and the "cross of Christ." I had found the Eskimos singularly devoid of any notion of sin. And how could you explain the cross to a people who had never seen a full-grown tree in their lives and had no tradition of cruel punishments?

Leafing through the prayer-book, I studied the text of the Ministration of Holy Baptism to see what problems Webster would encounter there. The parents would have to renounce, in the name of their child, "the vain pomp and glory of the world." That would be a hard thing to put across! It all seemed pretty hopeless to me. Here was a people who used water—melted ice, rather—exclusively for drinking purposes. How could the idea of being made "regenerate and born anew of Water and the Holy Ghost" be grasped by them?

Apparently it had been, for a tremor of excitement ran through the little congregation as Peter Kamingoak and his wife Cecile Nalvana advanced towards the font, she bearing in her arms their third child and first son, an infant a few days old. They were smiling broadly, proudly . . . Canon Webster, in rather rumpled vestments, carried out the ceremony with as much dignity as though a hundred well-dressed people had been present in an echoing cathedral.

I was so busy getting my flash bulbs ready and posing the family afterwards for a couple of pictures that I forgot to ask what was the child's name in Eskimo. Its name would not be that of its father or mother, that I knew. Canon Webster had said solemnly: "I name thee Arthur William and commend thee to God . . ."

As we started out from the barracks for the evening service, I asked Dick what in the world he did about Eskimo names? He flung up his arms in mock despair. "We just register as many of them as we can find out," he said, cheerfully. "It's up to Ottawa to untangle such mysteries."

I knew that not only did Eskimos have no "family" name but that frequently for some reason or other they might change the name they had started out with. It was almost usual after some accident or some close shave with death for an Eskimo to take a new name. No one would think of preventing him from indulging the whim. And now, on top of all this confusion, there were the baptismal names, given by the Catholic or Anglican missionary . . .

And I kept thinking about little Arthur William, son of Kamingoak.

For the evening service, seven chairs were arranged in three rows for the white congregation. The benches used by the Eskimos that afternoon were pushed against the wall.

The sermon was painless and brief, but even so, my mind wandered. I recalled my Chipewyan friend, John Duck, who had told me that his clergyman preached sermons of inordinate length. "He talk, talk, talk, maybe three hour," said John. "Many people, they go to sleep." I added fuel to the fire by telling him that the sermon in The Pas never lasted more than an hour and sometimes only a half hour but that, even so, "many people, they just go to sleep."

All this took me back to Duck Lake. I was there again, in a tent with John and his son. We had had a good meal of bannock, dried meat, backfat, cheese and jam. The spruce sticks roared in the stove, a candle on a stick cast a flickering light. The dogs had been bedded down for the night on spruce boughs outside and given their fistfuls of frozen caribou meat. It was almost time to crawl into our sleeping

bags . . .

Dick nudged me, I woke up, and followed the others into the Websters' sittingroom, where Mrs. Webster began setting out cups of coffee and home-made cake.

Sure enough, as Marguerite Webster had said, a canary was there. It began singing as soon as we arrived and nearly burst its throat in an effort to be heard above Lili Pons when Canon Webster put on some new records he had just received. After the soprano, there was, of all things, a good recording of the *Malagueña*. I smiled to myself, as that sensuous music, even more out of place there than the canary, unwound in the bright livingroom of a missionary's house.

Then Canon Webster began talking about the inland Eskimos. He was about to set out on another dogteam trip inland, having returned from one only a few weeks before. As he talked about the drumming he had heard, the teeth he had pulled—he always carried forceps along with him, as well as a medicine kit—his quiet enthusiasm for his work and his obvious love of his scattered flock (how did you explain the word "flock" to a people who had never seen sheep in their lives?) made me begin to understand and like him.

The sky was flooded with pulsating Northern Lights, pale blue and green, when we dashed back to the barracks. No one even stopped to watch them. For one thing, Mrs. Jackson was suddenly stricken by the cold, and we had practically to carry her home, staggering over the drifts and supporting one another under the unexpected load.

That night, Ernie announced that he must snatch some sleep. "Got to get up early," he said. But he said this several times before 3 A.M., when we finally ran out of talk. And he told the mechanic to set the alarm for seven, since he intended to take the plane out "about nine."

The alarm went off, but serenely we slept on. About nine A.M. I heard someone moving, then the roar of a motor

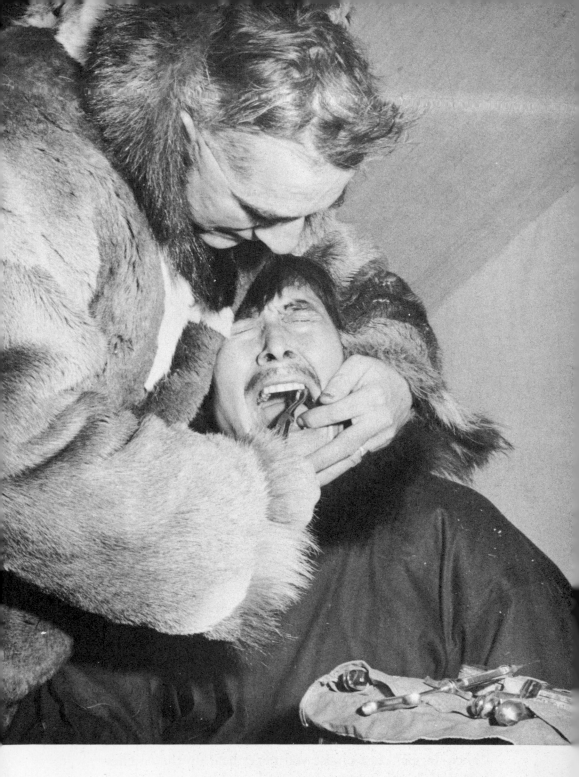

Canon Webster of Coppermine also pulls teeth

somewhere in the distance. It was the mechanic, warming up the engine. We, bleary-eyed, fumbled about the house, pulling on our clothes, doing our morning chores. At last Dick had breakfast ready, coffee, toast, oatmeal porridge with condensed milk, and as we sat down he began the usual subject: "Say, if you can use an f3.5 lens . . ."

Outside, the wind had dropped, and the silence was almost something you could touch. It was an unbelievable 6 above zero, too, and my store-bought clothing was warm enough.

Visibility was low, but Ernie seemed confident the sky would soon clear. Gradually the population, white and Eskimo, trooped down to see the departure of the plane. They stood about, waiting . . .

At last the *Norseman* roared, stamped its ski-feet, bumped to the natural runway facing the wind, and with a deafening howl took off.

"Good old Ernie!" said Dick and I to each other, as proud as if we ourselves were piloting that plane.

An hour later, sure enough, it cleared. By noon there was a gentle display of colors, and a low sun-dog. The sun still hid behind that hill, but to the north on an outlying island, it glowed red.

I strolled down to the H.B.C. store with Manning, to see if there might not be some ready-made artiggis that would fit me. As we passed some tethered dogs, they stood, stretched out their front paws, arched their rear ends high, and shook the snow from their thick fur, yawning widely, showing their red mouths and long pointed teeth.

It was a friendly gesture. But in the Far North you let it go at that. Huskies are considered dangerous animals, and "Nice doggie!" is a phrase you never hear up there. They have killed and at times eaten little children, and mauled at least one white woman to death.

IV

Adeeliorli acquires new clothes

THE INSIDE OF A HUDSON'S BAY COMPANY STORE IN THE Arctic is usually like a refrigerator, and this one was no exception. The nail heads on doors and walls were thickly frosted, and from experience I knew that you could not pick up a thing with bare hands without risking freezing your fingers. I almost froze mine just trying on some mitts.

We spouted jets of steam as we spoke and the floor echoed with our stamping feet as Manning showed me some ready-made *kulitaks* (outer coats) and *artiggis* (inner coats), boots, pants, and mitts, all of caribou skin. Nothing fit, and the mitts I thought good split open at the seams when I thrust my hands into them. The design of the clothes was different from what I had worn in the eastern Arctic. The hoods were rounded instead of pointed. Also, the skins were not as soft as those of the Chipcwyans.

Clothes would have to be made for me, and they would be all the better for it. An Eskimo woman puts her best work into the clothing her husband wears, the next best work into the clothing to be worn by someone known in her community. The more indifferent work goes into clothing for white men in the settlement, as is well known.

"We'll get Martha Alonak to work on your clothes," said Manning. "She's our best sewing woman here. And she'll want to choose the skins herself."

Manning would take me over to Martha Alonak's tupik and would arrange everything for me. I would pay the sewing woman according to the rates fixed by the H.B.C. and she would receive her payment in credit I would establish for her at the store.

"She'll be proud to make clothes for Adeeliorli," Manning added.

"For who?" I asked, throwing grammar to the winds.

"That's you. They call you *Adeeliorli*— 'The Picture Man.'"

I was glad to hear this from such a good linguist as Leo Manning. He was in fact one of the best linguists in the Arctic. And I told him about the army chap in the Eastern Arctic who bragged about *his* Eskimo name. According to him, it meant "Great White Father." In reality, it meant "Squint-Eyed One." The Eskimos usually bestow descriptive names, and they have a good sense of humor.

We were on the point of leaving, when some Eskimos arrived to trade. The trapper, a young fellow, had brought with him his wife and child. Trailing after them came some of their local friends, who did not want to miss the show. This is a peak event in the lives of the inland Eskimos.

The trapper had brought 12 fox skins and the price that year was a fair one, $10. (Sometimes the price falls as low as $3.) One at a time he put the soft fox pelts on the counter. Manning put out a corresponding value in metal discs.

First of all the trapper, without hesitation, bought staples: tea, tobacco, and ammunition. Manning took back

Inside Hudson Bay Company store at Coppermine—Leo Manning trading with Eskimo, Arctic Fox furs on counter. Store is unheated, temperature Arctic low

the discs, one by one, until they all had disappeared. Then onto the counter went another fox pelt. And more metal discs, which disappeared quickly as the trapper bought a plaid shawl, a blue beret, and a baby rattle. After which, a chuckling conference with his wife.

With the last fox on the counter, excitement ran high, among everyone present. Nervously the young man stepped outside the door, had a leak, returned, and scanned the shelves . . .

Sardines were only 10 cents a can. He asked for some, they were produced. He would probably taste canned sardines for the first time in his life.

The young man's wife had been looking covetously at a portable sewing machine. When nearly all the discs had gone, she pointed to it. Alas, there was no possibility of buying it now. They would have to wait until next year to acquire that luxury.

As Manning and I walked along the frozen shore in the direction of Martha Alonak's tupik, I had my first good view of Coppermine. The air was clear and still. Eskimos could be seen trotting unhurriedly from house to house. Some children set out towards the hill with toboggans. One Eskimo native helper carried a toilet bucket out of a house, to empty it at a distance. Some dogs were at his heels to devour the excrement as soon as it had been emptied—the native economy allows for no waste and incidentally takes care of hygiene.

I asked Manning a few haphazard questions. The shelves of the store were, I had noticed, half empty. What would happen, if the annual boat failed to bring in supplies? He said that, to begin with, it could hardly happen. Supposing against all odds that it did: emergency supplies could always be flown in. He was confident that the white man's world would always be there, with planes and factories. But as we walked along in the milky whiteness, past the little white wooden houses that looked as though any wind could pick them up and blow them away, I wondered . . .

The houses in Coppermine are set out on a windy beach, at intervals of a hundred or so yards. This is the usual way of settlements in the Arctic. The snowfall in the Arctic is much less than in some of the more northern states.

I asked Manning about the lad who had been flown out for a t.b. checkup and had returned with me. Had he said anything about the sensational things he had seen outside?

"Not a word," said Manning.

I had heard other white folks speak almost indignantly about this singular lack of response on the part of Eskimos who had been privileged to see the wonders of the outside world. So I chuckled.

"Of course not," I said. "How could he explain such things as revolving doors, lawn mowers and elevators to his friends?"

The language needed to explain would not make sense to his listeners. I myself had sometimes been guilty of using senseless phrases when talking to Eskimos. For instance, I once caught myself saying something like this: "Look through this view-finder. See! the image is reversed. Don't drop it, the thing cost a hell of a lot of money, and money doesn't grow on trees . . ." This, to someone who had never studied optics, never seen a real tree, and never handled money in his life!

Having bought fourteen caribou skins for $1. to $1.50 each, which were being made up into clothing for me by Martha Alonak and her daughter Grace Hayokhok, I visited their tupik almost daily. Soon I felt at home in their caribou tent which was about eight by ten feet in size and at its highest point barely six feet. Outside, it was densely banked with snow. Inside, a camp stove kept the place reasonably warm. It was fed with branches, procured from a stand of stunted willows growing about ten miles from Coppermine. A kerosene lamp cast a yellow ring of light. For hours I would sit on the bed platform, watching Alonak and Hayokhok at work. They sat in the usual Eskimo posture—legs straight out in front of them. I doubled my legs under me, white man fashion.

It was good to be with them in the quiet gloom of the tupik. We smoked, and spat reflectively towards the stove.

Talk was not needed. Occasionally the two women exchanged brief remarks in a gentle undertone.

Visitors constantly crowded into the tent—to look at me, to watch the progress of the work. Many of the women were back-packing children. This was a world of women and children, the men were away on their trap lines or somewhere off the coast, seal hunting. It was a quiet world. The children were never scolded. The Eskimos are a people who, for thousands of years, have done very well without tribal organization, rulers or chiefs. They are used to commanding themselves, and one of the first things white men had to do when they came in contact with them was to explain the idea of rules, regulations, government, and of men vested with power.

The infants rarely cried. Cosy and warm, they rode naked on their mothers' naked backs, inside the artiggi. When an infant whimpered ever so softly, it would be shifted around to the front to be nursed, still warm and secure and out of sight. This had nothing to do with modesty, for when a tent or igloo is warm enough, the mother's breast is displayed without shame.

How do the babies remain clean, without cloth diapers? On the Barren Lands grows a moss soft and absorbent, and excellent for this purpose as well as for menstruation. Nature has provided the Eskimos with all they need.

I watched every stage of the preparation of the skins, as I had done with the Chipewyans two years before. The Chips had rubbed caribou brains into the skins, to soften them. Here that was not done. Only the interminable scraping of the skins softened them. For to begin with, the skins were hard as boards. Deftly scraped with a semicircular shaped knife—that useful *ulu*—the fleshy substance was gradually removed. Gradually the skins became soft and pliable.

54

Adeeliorli acquires new clothes

In a few days' time, my garments were cut out. The women did not measure me, their eyes were sufficiently trained. And their hands were equally expert. How deftly they wielded their *ulus* to cut out my garments! How skillfully they used the sharp 3-sided needle and how small the stitches of pliable sinew, stronger than any thread!

My mittens were made first—two for each hand. The inside mitten, serving as lining, would be worn hair side in, and was of fawn-skin. The outer mitten was a little harsher, made from two-year-old caribou, and was to be worn hair-side out. They reached only to the wrist. (For a man intending to build snow-houses, they would be provided with a gauntlet and worn outside the sleeve of the tunic.)

Then the socks were made, soft as silk, with the fur in. On top of them would go the slippers, which the old woman crimped with her teeth. And on top of these would go the boots, which Paulette was making in her father's tupik.

Paulette, whom I also visited at her work, told me about my other garments. The *artiggi*, or undercoat (shirt or tunic, however you wish to describe it) would be, she said, of fawn-skin. It would be worn fur turned inward. The outer coat, called the *kulitak*, would be of older caribou, and would be worn hair outward. Wolverine had been bought to border the long sleeves and the hood. It is a fur from which snow and frost can easily be brushed or shaken. The underpants, cut only a little less voluminously than the outer pants, would be worn hair side inward, the outer pants hair-side outward. The artiggi would come down almost to my knees. It would be loose, without fastenings, and the hood would be big, sheltering my face, but not too closely. A hood too close around the face may frost up from the breath, which condenses and freezes—something greatly to be avoided.

The soles of my boots were made of imported moose hide, which Paulette said was more durable. They should last out 1,000 miles of travel over snow—we did not expect to travel over sea ice which is rough. For travel on sea ice, the skin of the *ugrug*, or bearded seal, is preferred.

My caribou skin sleeping bag was made large enough to fit inside my eiderdown bag. Paulette said that the older the caribou the thinner the skin and the longer the hair.

She spoke English perfectly, and helped me acquire a larger vocabulary in the difficult Eskimo language—believe me, it is difficult. As with our own language, there are many names which differentiate the caribou—chief subject of our conversation. These names identify the animal as to sex and age. *Tuktu* is the generic term, and it means simply caribou. The adult bull is *Pagnirk*, the adult female, *Kullavuk*, and *Nowak* is the fawn. I wrote these down. But I made no effort to learn the different forms of these words, when they are used differently in a sentence.

I doubt if many white people ever master Eskimo grammar. Fortunately the Eskimos are polite. They listen respectfully to our efforts at communicating . . .

I shall never forget the alarmed look in Martha Alonak's eyes when I tried on some of the garments in the presence of visitors. Laughing as I did so, I stretched the seams with all my might. She would have felt eternally disgraced if a seam had split. None did. But I noticed that her stitches from then on became even smaller.

By January 15, my new outfit of skin clothing was ready. At once I put it on and strutted around for everybody's admiration. I was told I looked like a brown bear. It did not matter: I felt like a complete man again, secure and at home in a world no longer hostile. The temperature was 10 below zero, and I was too warm after awhile, so stripped off my kulitak.

Dick Connick on hill south of Coppermine settlement, watching returning sun at noon, January 15

a typical arctic trading settlement

For one thing, in skin garments, you have to adopt the Eskimo tempo, which is slow and unhurried. With fast movements, you work up a perspiration—than which nothing in the Arctic is more fatal, for it may freeze upon you. Eskimo dress is so designed that you can cool off easily, either by ventilating at the neck, or simply by taking off a layer, as I did.

No people anywhere at any time have ever evolved a mode of dress more adapted to their needs. You feel completely at ease in skin clothing, there is no dragging or pulling at any point, no buttons to slow up dressing and undressing. And the entire outfit weighs less than ten pounds. It seems to be weightless. As to warmth—at a 15 below zero temperature you can sit in comfortable warmth on a block of snow, if no wind is blowing.

Next day, with Dick, I climbed the nearby hill and saw the sharp edge of the sun rise above the horizon. Looking back at Coppermine, you could see the long level rays streaking across the snow to within 400 yards of the store. It was a cheerful sight.

Everyone seemed to be glad of the approach of the dawn after the long period of gloom. But, discussing it with the experienced men in Coppermine, I learned that this coming of sunlight was not, to their knowledge, celebrated in any particular way. It merely meant that soon seal and caribou hunting would be resumed. Conversely, no one there had run across any case of the "Arctic hysteria" that is supposed to occur in the period of darkness.

Once again I was made to realize that more myths have been embroidered on the Eskimos than the Eskimos ever embroidered for their own amusement.

On Friday nights everyone stayed close to the radio sets, listening in to the broadcast of the Northern Messenger

Service, sponsored by the Canadian Broadcasting Corporation. For over half an hour we listened to personal messages read out in monotonous voices. These are recordings of brief notes written by relatives of people stationed in the Far North—a good idea, maybe, for people who suffer from a feeling of isolation. The messages are read off in alphabetical order, and most people listen in only long enough to find out if there is any message for them.

Most of the messages ended with "Love from Mom and Dad," and some were full of Bible quotations. One message was a recipe that had been asked for in a letter, and there was some conjecture afterwards as to whether it was for a soup or pudding.

I heard some messages for people I knew elsewhere in the Arctic, but none came through for Coppermine the night I listened.

Before leaving Coppermine, I had to pay a few calls and accept some invitations. When Jack Scarlett had said one night, "Come over for breakfast some morning, we have it at eight," Dick and I replied: "Pi-shuk!"—Nothing doing! No one in the Arctic ever thinks of getting up before ten.

However, one morning we went over, shook him awake, and helped cook breakfast. After which, we watched Jack and Vernon send up the morning balloon for their weather-forecasting.

I had seen these gadgets and had had them explained to me at Port Harrison. A radio transmitter is attached to the latex balloon and sends down spluttering signals about the weather in the upper atmosphere. I had looked at the radiosonde station graphs and had tried in vain to understand them. Well, about all I know for sure is that the boys spend their time working on the information, coding it, and sending the results by radio to weather men in Washington.

Aside from furs, about the only thing exported from the Arctic is the weather.

And I visited the Dufresnes. The registered nurse in charge of the hospital had invited me to dinner. I had already photographed Abigail Dufresne several times, on her visiting-nurse duties in the tupiks and at the barracks. But this was the first occasion I saw her at home—her home being likewise the hospital and dispensary. And it was the first opportunity I had had to talk with her husband, Emile.

He was a great talker, full of anecdotes, some of them not fit for drawingrooms. He and Abigail both hailed from Amos, Quebec. Religion rested lightly on his shoulders. He told me with a straight face some far-fetched tales about the cut-throat activities of missionaries, who would go to almost any lengths, he said, to secure converts. I had heard similar stories from the Anglicans, told with less humor. According to Emile, the rival missionaries kept their ear to the ground and whenever they heard that a woman was pregnant, they got the data on it and each hurried to harness up the dogs to be on the spot for the happy event. The object was, of course, to baptize the child. This was the logical way to acquire "converts," and the easiest. Emile hinted that something of the sort was at the bottom of Canon Webster's present inland trip.

I asked him how he explained the fact that the native population of the Coppermine area was 85 per cent Protestant, though the Roman Catholic missionaries outnumbered the Anglican six to one.

"They had a head-start, the Protestants," said Emile. "Just you wait. Look at the Roman Catholics now. They say there are 40 priests now in the North. New missions are springing up all over the place. Why, they even have their own air-line . . ."

I knew about "Arctic Wings."

Adeeliorli acquires new clothes

The Dufresnes, typical rural French-Canadian people, were economical and obsessed with the high cost of living. They still used kerosene lamps, not yet having put up a wind-charger. Kerosene—called coal-oil in Canada—was $2 a gallon. And coal was $220 per ton, delivered. Who could afford to pay such a price? Not they . . . Beer was prohibitively expensive. Delivered on the annual boat, the freight cost $3.50 a case of 24 pint bottles. And by monthly plane, it was $42.00. Clearly you had to do as the Eskimos did: drink plain water or tea.

Emile's chief chore was to carry the blocks of ice into the house and melt them down in the big barrel.

They proudly showed me two oil barrels in which they kept frozen meat and fish outside. I noticed in the kitchen two big frozen fish, a salmon and a whitefish, standing near the stove, to be thawed out slowly. My hopes rose. Perhaps I would be offered some fresh food. My hopes were dashed: it was the usual meal of canned goods. Madame Dufresne may have thought I shared the prejudice among whites against eating anything in the Arctic except canned foods. On Hudson Bay I had eaten caribou and seal meat, learned to relish the liver of both caribou and seal, but when I mentioned this to my friends in Coppermine, they shuddered. As to fresh fish (which is frozen) I had tasted it only in tupiks. The deficiency of fresh food in the diet of the white population was compensated by vitamin pills. Usually a bottle of them stood on every dining table.

Naturally, in the presence of a nurse, the conversation turned to the people and projects for improving their hygiene. The Dufresnes seemed to think the only solution for the people was to make them all live in permanent wooden houses, where they could be taught how to live like white folks, and keep themselves clean. What could you do about improving a people who lived in tents or snow houses? They admitted it *was* a problem, when I pointed out that houses and everything in them would have to be imported from outside. But they thought it could be done. The Eskimos must become more like us. The trend was in that direction. More and more the people were depending upon our food, fuel, utensils, and clothing. Dick had told me that the number of "Destitute Rations" issued was on the increase.

We discussed disease. I was able to report on an epidemic of measles that had wiped out a Chipewyan settlement just before I reached Duck Lake. The infection had been brought in from The Pas by two Brochet natives who had come visiting. It had wiped out, according to my Chipewyan friends, 62 people.

Yes, conversation at the Dufresnes' was in the usual groove: "What to do about the people?" My nose looked for a clothes pin.

The same thing happened when I went to pay my respects at the Oblate Mission.

Father Delalonde, O.M.I., was from France, a witty talker in a cultivated vein. He offered me a glass of something that may have been sacramental wine, quite good, and put me at ease at once, discussing my forthcoming trip, the route I would cover, the people I could expect to meet.

He said I must meet Father Lemer, of Bathurst, who spoke Eskimo fluently. Father Lemer might be able to render us services. I was also told about an interesting Eskimo heretic, Koikhok, who had invented a "new religion" with himself as chief prophet. We would stop for awhile at Koikhok's camp, I would have a chance to see him. Webster had mentioned this Eskimo to me, as had Emile and others. Apparently it was the only time Roman Catholics and Anglicans had ever got together and cooperated. For when this heresy of Koikhok's had drawn too many

62

followers, Christianity had seem really to be threatened.

I risked telling Father Delalonde that I had heard of some fanatical priest among the Chipewyans who forbade his flock to eat meat on the usual fast days. This, to a people who eat meat exclusively, seemed to be a hardship. Father Delalonde did not commit himself, merely said that I would run across narrow-minded servants of the Church in all places. Smiling, he added that he did not think one fast day a week would be a great hardship to a people who sometimes fasted for days during famine, yet managed to survive. Did not these caribou-eating Chipewyans also eat flour? I had to admit that they were beginning to consume flour, usually in the form of half-cooked, sticky, and almost indigestible "bannocks." (A Scotch word that some writers list as an Eskimo word!)

A distribution of vitamin pills might help, said Father Delalonde. There was a twinkle in his eyes, as he spoke, which showed that this weather-beaten, rugged priest did not hold much with such solutions. He looked more like a fur-trapper than a priest, and indeed, like most R.C. missionaries, he had a trapping license, used it, and traded his furs in at the H.B.C.

The moon was at its full now, and for several days circled above the horizon, without setting. As I walked back to the barracks, snugly warm in my new skin clothing, the moonlight cast my long black shadow before me on the snow. So bright did the moon shine that you could read a book out of doors at night. But no one would want to read out of doors at 40 below zero.

In the moonlight, the snow-banked houses and tupiks, almost invisible in the dimness of the days, were etched blackly. Far off on the frozen sea showed some snowy ridges of islands. The ice below the settlement made cracking sounds as the tide moved. Nearby, a dog whined. Another dog in the distance took it up. Then there was complete silence except for the crunching of the snow beneath my feet.

Some light smoke trailed out of several tupiks into that dark blue silence. It made an interesting pattern. I hurried towards the barracks, with the idea of getting out my camera for a time exposure. By the time I had everything ready, the fires were out, the smoke was no longer there, and my picture had vanished.

On the porch was stacked a great accumulation of travelling gear that I had not seen before. Light streamed from the office in the barracks. Martin Donnan had returned from his 250 mile patrol. I went in to meet him.

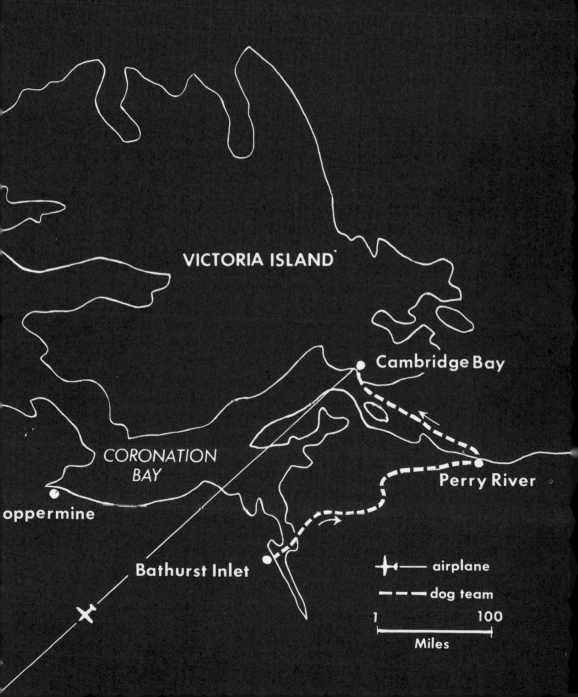

2. close-up of an r. c. m. p. arctic winter patrol

february, 1949

VICTORIA ISLAND

Cambridge Bay

CORONATION BAY

Coppermine

Perry River

Bathurst Inlet

✈—— airplane

----- dog team

1   100
Miles

Dick Connick in kitchen, having prepared for patrol—doughnuts, biscuits, frozen cakes of beans

V

preface to a mountie arctic patrol

Now the sun was coming into coppermine. At first, sunrise and sunset were all one; the great red disc of the sun remained above the horizon only briefly. Each day, however, it remained longer, until finally you saw that it was describing a low, ever-widening arc in the southern sky. We hurried our preparations for departure.

Dick, now that Martin had returned, was free to concentrate on preparations. The paper work now fell to Martin. It was Martin, now, who sat in the office issuing destitute allowances and family allowances, and making an official report on his patrol, while Dick performed culinary wonders in the kitchen. For days on end doughnuts were fried, baking-powder biscuits were baked, and pork-and-beans were cooked in the pressure-cooker. I learned a lot from Dick.

The cooked foods were put outside to freeze instantly. The beans were first spread out in pie-plates, then put outside to freeze. Knocked out of the plates the 20 bean-cakes were stored in bags, as were the 350 biscuits and 220 doughnuts, hard as rocks. It would not be too much, for

Dick Connick knocks the frozen beans out of the pie plates before putting them into a bag for journey

Dick and Noel Avadluk would cover 800 miles in something like six weeks' time. And, for the first part of that patrol, as far as Bathurst Inlet, they could count on me to make inroads on these things, for I had no intention of being bashful, especially in regard to doughnuts.

I had already purchased my supplies at the Hudson's Bay Company store. Now, I watched Dick gather his stores from the bountiful R.C.M.P. barracks larder. He intended to take along a quantity of pilot biscuits (hardtack), tea, sugar, powdered milk, dehydrated soup and fruit, spaghetti, corned beef, and so forth. Some of the camps were very far apart, and we could not rely upon getting caribou meat at them.

Peter Kamingoak, whom I hired as dogteam driver with the aid of Manning, had studied to be catechist under Canon Webster. He had given up his career in the Church for the more remunerative one of trapping and dogteam driving. I'll say it was remunerative! Never before had I paid a dogteam driver as much, $10 per day. That is to say, I paid him $10 per day to take *me* as far as Perry River and to take *himself* back to Coppermine, meanwhile providing him and his abandoned family with food during his entire absence. By the time I had finished negotiations, I had used up $550 of my credit at the store, part of the amount in provisions, but most of it for Kamingoak.

"He has the best dogteam here," said Manning.

"Travelling by plane is much cheaper," was Dick's comment. I agreed. But you don't see a country when travelling by plane, and I wanted to see the country.

Kamingoak was a bumptious, conceited and noisy fellow, very different from any dogteam driver I ever had. His dogs, though, were good. He had eleven of them, all well fed, thick furred, with massive heads and backs. That he was proud of them could be seen by the smartness of the harness and their jingling bells. I hoped Kamingoak's pride in his team would prevent him from gambling it away on the trip. I heard he was a great poker player, and I knew what that might mean.

Meanwhile, Dick hired a special guide to guide our guides as far as the first native encampment on our route —the heretic Koikhok's camp. This guide, Okaitok, had six dogs and would be paid $7 a day and food. We would therefore set out as a caravan of three teams—maybe more, for, with the coming of the sun, I noticed many sleds and dogteams were being made ready for long trips. On the way, heaven only knew how many other teams would join us, for Eskimos like to travel in company.

From Coppermine, westernmost point of Coronation Gulf, to Bathurst Inlet, an arm of the eastern end, I would accompany Dick on the first portion of his patrol. Our route would take us inland in a southeasterly direction to about 100 miles south of the Arctic Circle. This would bring us to tiny clusters of stunted spruce and ground-willows. We would then strike eastward, crossing the Barren Lands for more than a hundred miles, when gradually we would move towards the northeast, following a wavy line towards Bathurst Inlet, which we should reach in three weeks' time.

At Bathurst, Dick and I would part company. He would return to Coppermine along the coast—there was one camp to visit on that route—and I would continue in a northeastward direction to Perry River Post on Queen Maud Gulf, a trek of more than two hundred miles. From that point onward my plans were vague. With luck, I might be able to go southeastward from there, across the Barrens to Garry Lake and Baker Lake. This would give me a glimpse of the Arctic Spring I had heard so much about, and of the more remote bands of Caribou Eskimos.

Noel Avadluk was interested in the maps I spread out on the floor. Some of the maps I had brought in from Ottawa, others came from Yellowknife, and a sketch map Canon Webster had kindly given me. Noel Avadluk, like all Eskimos, understood maps. But I soon learned that the place-names marked on mine meant nothing to him. He knew Bathurst Inlet, for another trading post was there. But Queen Maud Gulf? Perry River? September Mountains? The Willingham Range? These names were to him and all Eskimos of the region sheer jabberwocky. For that matter, they even had another name for Coronation Gulf and for themselves. The phrase "Coppermine Eskimo" meant nothing to them. They had many names for themselves, depending upon the part of the Coppermine area that they inhabited and their way of life. It would take an anthropologist to list them. But I wrote down some of them: the Pallirmiut, the Kogluktogmiut, the Utkusiksaligmiut. Yes, despite the maps, the Eskimos go on using their own language to designate places, and who could blame them? The names on the maps make sense only to people acquainted with the early history of English explorations.

This mixup was only one of many that would complicate the trip. For in that land without roads or signposts, sometimes without any landmark visible to a white man's eye, a compass is practically useless—the North Magnetic Pole is too near. My projected trip with Dick to Bathurst Inlet and the trip I would take beyond, to Perry River, led towards that ever-shifting Magnetic Pole. We would go blindly into an immense white space, trusting to the sixth sense of an Eskimo guide . . .

Of course, this is not so. Our Eskimo guide would follow boundary lines laid down by nature—valleys, bluffs, frozen rivers, windrift patterns, and would seek out with a keen eye the almost obliterated sled tracks that led from one

Martin Donnan, R.C.M.P. constable, in his Coppermine barracks registering the new baby of Nelvana for Family Allowance

camp to another. Noel Avadluk pointed out to me on the
maps the probable locations of the inland camps, named
them in the order they would occur, and I wrote them
down. Each encampment bore the name of the most respected man in it, and they were: Koikhok, Natiak, Aiyaligyoak, Ivagluk, Papik, Negak, Taipana, Aviak, Katik, and
Otokiak.

During these last days, I got some pictures of Dick as cook and Dick as barber, with Martin the barbered one enveloped in a R.C.M.P. tablecloth. I also got one of Martin in uniform, issuing Family Allowance. And then, when almost everything was ready for our trip, a wish I had often expressed was granted.

Before leaving Coppermine, I wanted to get some pictures of the seal camp about twelve miles distant to the northwest, off Cape Kendal. Dick agreed to accompany me, and Jack Scarlett also decided to go along. We waited for a calm, clear day, which arrived—Jack, our weather man, claiming all the honors.

I watched with interest as Noel Avadluk made the R.C.M.P. sled ready for the little trip, and as he hitched the dogs, for in this part of the Arctic there were methods I had not seen before.

Getting a sled ready for a trip means chiefly re-mudding (or re-icing) the runners. Centuries ago, the Eskimos found a way to make wooden runners (from driftwood) glide over snow. They did this, and still do, by applying thawed black muck from the muskegs. The mud is patted on the runners, perhaps two inches thick. It soon freezes solid, and is then smoothed down with a home-made plane. It is a skilled procedure to the last detail. A mouthful of water is spit along the mud, and is immediately smoothed by a piece of polar bear fur. The Mounties' sled was partly shod with oatmeal porridge (cooked without salt). They found it tougher for going over small exposed rocks. And I guess if it came to the worst, you could always eat your sled runners.

Another wrinkle in sled travel, new to me, was the snow anchor, a pronged iron attached by a length of rope to the tow-line. When not in use, it is carried on the komatik. It is invaluable on steep slopes, to brake the sled.

The dogs watched Avadluk prepare the sled, trembling with eagerness. As he hitched them, one at a time, they let out loud yelps of impatience—they wanted to be on the trail again, as much as I did.

In Coppermine, the "Nome hitch" is used. This, too, was new to me, since in the Hudson Bay region the dogs are usually fan-hitched.

The lead-dog is at the head of a long tow-line, in the Nome hitch, and the remaining dogs are paired behind him. For some reason the dogs nearest the sled are called "wheel dogs." Because we were travelling light, Avadluk hitched only nine of the thirteen R.C.M.P. dogs that day.

Dogteams are not controlled by reins. They obey spoken commands and the crack of the long whip—which is rarely used except as a threat. Huskies *like* to work.

They like to work and they love to fight—the husky is the toughest fighter, the hardest worker, and the most unfriendly member of the *felix canis* tribe. Where their ancestors came from is a point still being argued. They seem to be related to the Samoyed dog of northeastern Siberia. How and when this dog reached the American continent is as big a problem as are the origins of the Eskimos. The Eskimo economy is dependent upon the huskies and might well perish without them.

No other domesticated animal in the world could stand up against such a tough life. They sleep outdoors, even at 60 below zero and are fed rarely in summer. They can pack a weight of thirty pounds in the summer. Depending upon how they are hitched, they can haul a weight of between 150 to 200 pounds per dog for thirty or more miles. The thirteen R.C.M.P. dogs on the inland patrol would be put to the test, for the sled, eighteen feet long, would carry at the start a load of 1,500 pounds in addition to the weight of two men—Dick and Avadluk, who would ride part of the time. They would be fed once a day, after the day's run, with three pounds of meat or fish and a hunk of tallow. These dogs in Coppermine were fortunate. I had

Chained down for the night, police dog chews up fish in a few seconds

seen many less fortunate in my travels. Sometimes they
have to go days without any food at all. In those circumstances, they keep on working, getting thinner and weaker,
and drop down dead in their tracks. I had seen this happen.

Peter Kamingoak arrived with his team—he had hitched
only six of his dogs that day. With a cracking of whips,
we were off, the level sunlight casting long shadows ahead
of us.

For me, that visit to the seal camp was a heartwarming renewal of old experiences. Again, at the approach of dog-teams, I saw children pouring out of snow houses, and again the women were eager to offer us tea. My only disappointment was in not seeing the seal hunters. All the men were miles out on the sea ice, looking for seal breathing-holes. Dick's time was limited, we could go no farther that day. "Oh well," said he, "you'll see plenty of seal hunting near Bathurst."

The igloos were set out on a crescent beach. Each igloo had a long entrance tunnel, perhaps twenty feet long, having a sharp turn near the outer end to provide a kind of shelter from the wind. Inside the houses there was the usual seeming clutter of meat put there to thaw out gradually: dead, frozen seals, standing upright like giant ninepins.

I went from one igloo to another, getting my pictures. The children followed, and I behaved like an electioneering politician, making myself popular. I sent the women into stitches of laughter when I offered to buy their offspring for $5. Quite a wit, me! But for a minute I was scared, when it looked as if my proposal might be taken up.

After mugs of good hot tea in one igloo, we returned to Coppermine. As we rode homeward through the milky whiteness of the afternoon, I felt happy as I had not been since my last trip to the Arctic. There is something about sitting on a veering, bouncing komatik that fills my soul with serenity. More and more I was looking forward to the long trip, impatient for the next few days to pass. Dick said we would start within a week . . .

Towards the end of the month, the barracks were in a commotion. All kinds of things were strewn over the floor. You had to clamber over grub-boxes, medicine chests, lanterns, primus stoves, harnesses, and tentpoles, to get anywhere. Yes, we were carrying a tent—as Martin Donnan had done on his recent patrol. This, at a time of year when igloos could be built, seemed superfluous to me. Tents flap in the wind, are difficult to anchor down. True, they heat up quickly; but they also cool off quickly, as soon as the camp stove is put out. I'll take igloos every time.

By January 31, all was ready. With a great going to and fro and some ear-splitting hammering, all the provisions were packed and carried out onto the porch, to be ready for loading in the morning. As Avadluk carried the gear out, Dick read off his inventory. It went something like this: "7 bags of fish for dogs; 3 bags of frozen foods; 3 grub-boxes of tinned and packaged food; 1 case of tallow for dogs—Damn it! where is it? Here you are! 10 gallons of coal-oil; 2 thermos bottles—Did you test them? Yes? All right. 1 lantern, 1 package of candles, 2 snow knives; 2 primus stoves; 1 tent; 2 bed-rolls; one sled-wrapper, caribou skins for ground sheets; 1 30-30 rifle; repair gear; 2 bags of mail. . . ."

The bags of mail were for the two H.B.C. men at Bathurst Inlet. With luck, they would get their 1948 Christmas gifts and letters by the end of February, 1949.

I crawled into my sleeping bag before midnight, for I wanted to be wide awake for the early morning start.

The police dogs hitched Nome style, resting while we have tea. Dogs frosted up from their own breath—temperature probably 30° to 40° below zero

VI

southeast by dogteam

WE LEFT COPPERMINE ON A BEAUTIFUL, CLEAR MORNING, following the frozen Coppermine River inland. On the first stretch, while we were running beside the frozen rapids and falls, the blinding whiteness made sense. I could visualize my map, I knew where we were going. I still knew more or less where we were when we swerved slightly towards the southeast and followed another frozen river for a spell. It was the Kugaryauk, and the snowy landscape was cut up into gullies.

Here and there stood abrupt cliffs, and occasionally the land was strewn with big glacial boulders, brown and naked on the windward side. After that, I lost track. The country was lifeless for miles, it was just a white galloping landscape without a single landmark and without even a clear delineation of horizon until the sun made its brief appearance. Then, it must have been towards noon, you could see some miserable stunted willows thrusting their topmost twigs above the hard packed snow. About that time a wind rose, blinding us with driven snow and obliterating the sun that had been our bulls-eye for awhile. Okaitok's komatik, only 200 feet ahead, became utterly invisible.

"It takes an Eskimo guide to find the way through this," I shouted at Dick, as I ran beside him for awhile to warm up. We seemed to be driving ahead into nothingness, but the nothingness was threatening to freeze my nose.

Apparently it would take a guide other than Okaitok to find the way, for soon he had led us smack into a dead-end canyon.

Getting lost in the Far North is a not unusual experience, so we calmly took advantage of our temporary shelter from the wind to have a snack. As we drank our tea out of the thermos bottles and ate some of the frozen doughnuts, Avadluk and Okaitok had a discussion, and the dogs wisely lay down in their tracks for a short rest. The going, thus far, had been hard, and some of the icing had worn thin on the runners, but they would have to wait till we made camp to be put into condition again.

So we sat there, huddled in our furs, two helpless white men, waiting for two Eskimos to get us out of trouble . . .

I had been lost before—exactly a year before—and had felt helpless like this. That had been on my trip south from Great Whale River, when I was heading towards Fort George. Commonplace though the experience had been, I could not resist telling Dick about it.

We had been following the shore of Hudson Bay, over the sea ice, and somewhere north of Cape Jones we had turned inland, following a well-marked track, across what must in summer be muskeg, lakes, and sloughs. Just then a wind rose and soon, with darkness coming on and the drifting snow, we could not see to go farther, so camped for the night. Next day, the wind still blew, but our provisions were running low—I had expected to reach Fort George sooner—so we pushed on in what seemed to me a circle. Through the darkness we tracked over what must have been portages. The dogs stumbled. I stumbled and

80

Dick Connick, constable in charge of Coppermine, R.C.M.P. detachment, —ready to start on his patrol

shivered. Charlie, my dogteam driver, ploughed ahead. My flashlight seemed only to accentuate the darkness beyond its cone of brightness. We camped again, erecting our tent in waist-deep snow. Charlie was sure we had overshot the mark, were beyond Fort George. Next day on again we went—or cruised round and round—the whirling snow settling on our faces, frosting our eyebrows, sifting into our neck openings. The dogs whined and refused to pull, sensing our uncertainty. For three nights on end we camped like that. Then, on the fourth day, I sent Charlie back to find the last Indian encampment to get someone to show us the way to Fort George. He went off with the dogs, and I stayed there with food running low, for the better part of a day. Charlie returned with an Indian guide. We had got lost only about 10 miles from the Post!

Dick said the nearness to or farness from a post had little to do with it when you were lost in an Arctic storm. Canon Webster, for instance, had a bad experience on sea ice only a few miles from Coppermine. His lead-dog had broken loose, just as a storm came up. Webster did the wrong thing: he ran after the dog to catch him. But then his entire team broke away—he had not thrust in the snow-anchor strongly enough—and there Webster was, alone, lost, in a swirling snowstorm. He was found two days later, with some bad frost bites, and nearly dead . . . The dogs had found their way alone to Coppermine.

While Dick and I talked, Avadluk and Okaitok had continued their patient search for sled tracks. They now came up to us and announced that a track had been found which was clearly the right one.

Hurray! All was well—so why not celebrate? Jimmy, a Coppermine Eskimo who had followed us thus far, to get some meat he had cached nearby, flung himself down a smooth slide of hard snow. Head first, sliding on his stom-

8 2

ach, he landed in the ravine. Roaring with laughter, Okai-tok followed. Then Kamingoak, and then Avadluk! Not to be outdone, Dick and I joined in the foolishness. I found that caribou skin clothing slides very well . . .

It was great fun and, as we kicked the dogs into action for a new start, our blood was racing.

The celebration was a little premature, it turned out. For as we once more pushed ahead in the storm, Okaitok was still uncertain. We lost the tracks again, and darkness was gathering.

Hours passed, during which we retraced our way several times. I tried to doze, but woke up with cold feet. Getting off the sled I ran towards Dick, who was bending against the wind, beating his arms and stamping his feet.

"We're lost again!" I called. You have to speak loudly to make yourself heard when you are talking to someone in a caribou hood, even when there is no wind blowing.

"Looks like it," Dick called back. Then, trying to be gay, he twisted up his face, stiff with the cold, into a grin. "Lost on the Barrens! Why don't you take a picture of us? It might make a good news-picture!"

He knew very well that to use a camera in those circumstances was out of the question.

"What're we going to do?" I shouted, feeling cold and hungry. We had travelled more than 30 miles, fatigue was setting in, and one of my cheeks was frozen.

"Camp. Wait out the storm!" Dick called back. And he ran ahead to tell Noel.

The sleds halted. The dogs lay down in their tracks, back to the wind, their noses tucked beneath their plumed tails. Avadluk walked about, looking for a suitable camp site. He found it, and the men began to tether their dogs and unload the sleds.

8 3

Exchanging scarcely a word, the boys all sprang into action—I was merely an admiring spectator. Maybe, since camping in the Arctic is quite a trick, the procedure is worth recording. First of all, Noel Avadluk and Dick unlashed the tarpaulin sled-cover, shaking it free of snow and folding it up carefully. Then Dick anchored the dog chain at both ends. Unhitching the dogs one by one, he secured them to short lengths of chain at just the right intervals to prevent them from fighting. Even after a 35 mile run on an empty stomach, huskies will fight if they get a chance. Then Dick straightened out the dog-harness of canvas webbing, so that it would be ready for use next day.

Meanwhile, Avadluk set up the tent with its poles, and with stakes driven into the hard snow. This done, he dug a small trench about a foot deep inside the tent, to serve as refuse pit. Next, the primus stove box was carried in and the stoves put on the boxes. Caribou skins used as ground sheets were spread upon the ground, hair-side down, next layer hair up, covering everything except the pit. As things were unloaded, great care was taken not to carry in any snow with them. In the warmer atmosphere of the tent, the snow would melt, then on the road or later at night it would freeze again, causing discomfort if nothing more. Next, our sleeping bags, crackling with frost, were beaten free of snow and inside the tent they went. After that, I helped carry in some grub-boxes and settled down myself, as Avadluk started the primus stoves, using methyl hydrate to first heat the burner. It was a welcome sound, that roar, and in almost no time the air at the top of the tent was quite warm—you could feel it when you stood up. It then took no courage to slip out of our fur things and get into lighter weight store-bought parkas. Carefully we folded up our caribou garments and laid them back in the tent.

It is a matter of comfort and hygiene to keep the ground inside a tent frozen. You can always insulate against the cold by means of caribou skin ground sheets. In the tupiks of the people, where improvised stoves cast some heat, a frozen ground is maintained by making a small hole in the tent-wall close to the ground.

When Okaitok and Kamingoak had tethered their dogs for the night, they came in to sit down with me, as Dick prepared supper. The *menu* that first night was:

> dehydrated soup—diluted with snow-water
> frozen beans—warmed up in melted fat
> frozen biscuits, with butter and jam
> tea, with powdered milk.

"This tea has a burnt-snow taste," Dick said apologetically. And he explained. When you put snow into a pot to melt down, you must take care not to heat the pan too quickly, or the snow will stick to the sides and the pan will heat without any liquid in it. The tea did have a burnt-pot taste—or burnt-snow, if you like.

After our meal the boys went out to feed the dogs— each husky got one dried fish (Arctic char) weighing three pounds, plus a third of a pound of tallow. Only Avadluk came back, for Okaitok had erected his own tent, which he would share with Peter that night.

Dick and I made short work of washing up. I refer to the pots and pans, which we sloshed out with warm tea and wiped with one of the towels Dick had brought along for the purpose. What refuse there was went into the pit, where it instantly froze. We made no pretence of washing ourselves—nor did we on the entire trip. One of the things you learn on a long dogteam trip is that man isn't the dirty animal he seems to think he is. The height of absurdity was the white woman who attempted to take a bath in an igloo, shooing out her husband and a baffled Eskimo.

Letting the primus stoves continue to roar for awhile, we sat round talking, until late, luxuriating in the relative

Dick Connick inside the double canvas tent melting down ice for tea

warmth. Then we took off our boots and parkas and crawled inside our bags.

It was that night that Dick told me the story of the Eskimo heretic, Koikhok.

Some years ago, Koikhok, one of the best hunters on the northern plains, had a dream, in which he saw his son, re-

cently dead, go to Heaven. The son commanded his father
to teach the old beliefs to the people, who were being drawn
away by Christianity. They must hunt caribou and give up
trapping fur-animals for the white man. They must respect the old taboos, say the old prayers, and throw off the
white man's taboos and laws.

Koikhok, who was respected not only as a hunter but as
a medicine-man—he could predict weather, foretell the
routes of the migrating caribou—soon had quite a following. He and his adherents even went so far as to wear
distinctive clothing—two white tassels of deerskin, from
the caribou's belly, hung at the side of their artiggis. And
they staged a passive resistance to the white man. Their
children went unregistered and unbaptized. They themselves offered up the old prayers for caribou, and forgot
about the Christian calendar.

It took some time to stamp out the heresy, which threatened to spread over the Barren Lands. But eventually the
missionaries of the rival denominations joined forces and
used some kind of threats against Koikhok and his followers.
The R.C.M.P. intervened with effective admonition, and
everything settled back into a law-abiding routine—the
white man's.

All this had happened years ago, before Dick arrived in
the Arctic. Koikhok was now a middle-aged man and had
behaved himself for many years. The new religion was no
longer practised, but Koikhok was still the most respected
man in his band, and his encampment—which we should
reach in another three sleeps—still bore his name.

"And is Koikhok now a good Christian?" I asked. "Is he
one of Canon Webster's flock? Or is he a Roman Catholic?"

"No, he stuck to his guns. Koikhok is still a pagan. And
I don't believe anyone will ever succeed in converting him
to Christianity."

Getting up in the morning is no joke in sub-zero weather. After breakfast—reaching out for my cup of hot tea which somebody makes for me—I drink it half inside my sleeping bag. Then I pull myself out, gasping with the cold, shiver over the primus stove, grab my fur garments that are folded nearby, pull them over my head . . . And in two minutes am warm again. For you are in a well-insulated house when you are inside caribou skin clothing. No wonder the Eskimos can manage with most perishable kinds of habitations: they carry their houses on their backs.

But as I face the outdoor cold, I gasp again.

Outside, the boys are working on the sled runners, re-icing them for the day's run. At night, when the sled is unpacked, it is propped up, overturned, on blocks of snow, to be ready for this morning job. The dogs, shaking themselves free of their snow blankets, stand watching the proceedings with great eagerness. Those brutes can't wait to be off again. It is a kind of fever in their blood.

Huskies, unlike their petted brothers outside, do not have anyone to take them out for their "morning constitutional," so necessary to the digestive functions . . . They must wait until, harnessed, they are on the track again. And then it is up to the dogteam driver to swerve his sled back and forth to avoid running over the dogs' excrement, for the poor brutes must squat and run, at the same time.

Repacking the sleds is a meticulous business. First the caribou skins that serve as ground sheets are folded the exact width of the komatik. On top of these go the heavier articles, the heaviest case being set in the middle, the highest at the front, to serve as the driver's box. Then come the lighter articles, then the tent, then the tarpaulin, which is carefully lashed down.

The dogs are harnessed. The whip cracks. We are off with a lunge, the dogs' feet twinkling ahead. The komatik swerves and creaks, as the driver holds it back from one or

Dick Connick and Avadluk lash down load to komatik on trail. Note: front of sled runners are covered with frozen porridge instead of mud

another of the squatting dogs. Then on we go again, into the pearly whiteness . . .

The only thing that was clear that day was that we were lost. The wind had dropped, but the air was full of tiny ice particles which hid the sun during its brief appearance, and there was no horizon, sky and snow-covered land were one. Okaitok continued to be puzzled about what route to take. We came upon some sled tracks, but they criss-crossed in a confusing way, and we decided they must be the tracks of trappers. Perhaps one might come along?

One did. Peter's keen eyes were first to see signs of him. "A komatik!" he called out, pointing ahead. We looked, but could see nothing at first. Then, in the whiteness we descried a black dot. The black dot grew—at first slowly, then rapidly. It was, yes, a komatik. The Eskimo driver was someone Peter knew. He was a trapper, making the round of his lines, and was as amazed to find us there as we were to meet him. We had come too far south, much too far. He

Eating methods become greatly simplified

put us on a trail which, after hours of travel, brought us to a small encampment of caribou hunters, where we spent the night.

There were only three tupiks, and they were so banked and splattered with snow that they were almost invisible until we reached them. The encampment was not on Dick's list, there would be no work for him to do. We were unknown, but we were received with great hospitality. The women had seen us in the distance and had at once thrown some extra hunks of meat into a vast caribou stew that was simmering on a stove improvised from a gasoline drum and burning small willow branches.

We ate with the Eskimos and as they did, holding chunks of meat in one hand, cutting off the pieces close to our lips, risking shaving off our noses in the process. We did add salt—a thing the Eskimos go without.

After the usual gallons of tea, our party of four bunked down in the biggest tupik, made of twenty caribou skins at least, and possessing a sleeping bench of snow, as in an igloo. We were all exhausted—being lost on the Barrens had worn us out more than we let on. Anyway, almost immediately after our meal, we fell asleep, as relaxed and content with our lot as the huskies were with theirs, outside in the snow.

Next day we were put on the route to Koikhok's camp by one of the people. Our way led through treacherous hill country, all the hills sloping gently to the north, and ending abruptly in a sheer cliff. Boulders lay scattered about on the ground. Dick said the shape of the hills probably indicated the movement of the ice-cap in the glacier age, and we let it go at that. All we knew was that these hills were risks, in a country almost without shadows. Before you knew it, you would find yourself at the bottom of a ravine, with a broken neck.

Police dogs on the march again

On one downhill run I scraped my leg with the snow anchor, but not seriously. On another hill, Peter's sled overturned—some 1,000 pounds of weight, with him half under it. Luckily, I was running at the time, and he got off with a bruised hand, caused again by the snow anchor, which had caught in his artiggi hood. The dogs continued dragging the komatik with Peter still under it, and it was a miracle there was no more damage.

Inland patrol on a "milky" day

While the boys were picking up the pieces and putting the sled to rights, Dick told me about a chap who, one of these milky days when everything is invisible, had gone over a small cliff with sled and dogteam. He landed at the bottom under his komatik. Said Dick: "I don't guarantee this, but they say the chap urinated his way out of the snowbank."

Kamingoak, grimacing with pain, laughed loudly. For

Dick had not used the genteel expression when telling the story. In fact, when we turned our backs on Coppermine we left behind us our polite vocabulary. Our talk now contained a great many four-letter words. Kamingoak knew enough about white men to realize how shocking these words were. We were violating a white man's taboo— so he laughed loudly.

Eskimos have no words that are considered obscene. They have only one word for an act, and so all words are entirely respectable. A Mountie in the Eastern Arctic had told me this and had recounted a story that was a propos. I passed it on to Dick, as a warning. It seems the Mountie asked his Eskimo Special Constable every night, "Did you feed the blankety-blank dogs?" Then the Mountie married a pretty girl of delicate breeding. The Eskimo, to put his best foot foremost, and make a good impression, came to the house, and smiling widely, reported, "Tonight I fed the blankety-blank dogs." My Mountie friend was so shocked at the crude language that he nearly threw the Special Constable out.

"Lots of fun, this trip!" said Peter Kamingoak, as he climbed onto the komatik, nursing his wounded hand. "Lots of dirty talk! Canon Webster—he would say to keep quiet!"

Zoological note: the third day out, we saw three white ptarmigan, one raven, one wolf, one fox, and ran across some recent caribou tracks. For those interested: they say over one hundred different kinds of birds nest north of the Arctic Circle.

We passed several meat caches, marked by stacks of caribou antlers. The third day out we did 40 miles.

On the fourth we met with intensely cold, windless weather. The result was that we travelled in a cloud of mist, leaving behind us a long vapor trail. The dogteams ahead

R.C.M.P. patrol going inland, across hard snow, down a slight grade

were enveloped in mist so that they were a moving cloud.

It takes a trip in Arctic weather to make you realize that living animals are living engines, pumping away, exuding heat which turns to steam. We forget this in our air-conditioned and centrally-heated civilization.

Another thing you realize on such a trip is how pleasant human beings can be. Dick and I, even in times of stress, enjoyed being together. At least, I enjoyed his companionship, and he acted as though he enjoyed mine.

Dick would swear and groan over little miseries, but he always ended up with a laugh. That day, for instance, we stopped about noon for a snack—pilot biscuits and tea from our thermos bottles. From the way our eyebrows were frosted up we decided the temperature that day was 50 below zero or even lower. So Dick cautioned me: "On a day like this, be careful. Don't take your mitts off, even for a split second. And watch that mug of yours, slosh the tea around in it before you drink from it . . . The cold enamel cup sticks to your lips."

I cautiously sloshed my tea, to warm the cup.

"Damn it!" said Dick. "There goes a piece of my lip!"

In the midst of advising me he had forgotten to take the very precaution he had warned me about! The accident was painful, but Dick laughed, turning the whole thing into a joke.

Following a gentle valley upward for several miles into the September Mountains, we reached some straggly timber—stunted spruce, scarcely more than three feet high, black against the grayish whiteness. The sun made a brief appearance, and, while it shone, the shape of the rocks and the curves of the hills became visible. It was like looking at a flat picture through a stereoscope: the third dimension was suddenly restored. It was lost again, as soon as the sun vanished.

We were travelling briskly, now, for Okaitok's dogs realized they were going home. They strained on their harness, they could not go fast enough, and they let out joyful howls. At the end of a run of twenty-five miles we reached their home—the camp of the famous heretic, Koikhok.

During extreme cold a vapor trail forms and stays behind us

A typical caribou skin tent encountered on inland patrol. It has a large ice slab for a window. On the lines a few rare wolverine skins

VII

koikhok's camp—and on to the next

THE SMALL, GRIZZLED ESKIMO WHO WELCOMED US TO HIS tent was Koikhok. The smiling woman with the tattooed face was Kabunak, his wife. At first I was disappointed: Koikhok's looks did not correspond to "the noble savage" I had built up in my imagination. But as the first greetings were exchanged and as my eyes became accustomed to the brown light inside the tupik, I was impressed.

His serene dignity and his hospitality were no more than I had expected. What surprised me were his features. They were strong and fine; he had a good profile, with a straight and jutting nose. It was not the usual Eskimo profile nor were his eyes the usual impenetrable black. They were a bluish gray. Nor was his face nearly hairless, like the usual Eskimo's. It was covered with a stubbly beard, as might be any Caucasian's. I was in the presence of that rare physical type that Stefansson has called the "blond Eskimo." On that subject has been poured a flood of ink to which I do not wish to add. Much better to get back to Koikhok's tent and to Koikhok, the man I knew and photographed.

It was a prosperous and tidy tent. An ice-window was

set to one side, resting on the floor. Portions of the caribou hide of the tent had been scraped clear of hair to let in still more light, and an improvised camp stove, fed with ground willows, glowed red. There was an appetizing odor. A huge piece of freshly roasted caribou was on a board beside the stove, and the appetizing odor was enough to make men hungry if they were not already so. A sleeping-bench had been contrived at the far end of the tent, a platform of snow on which were spread caribou hides. A *kudele* stood in front of it, made of soapstone, burning backfat, the wick of Arctic cotton. This stone lamp was of ancient design, half-moon shaped. And the wick was strung along the straight side. Arctic cotton is a sedge grass with a plumy seed head. A stone lamp, to burn well, must be kept full of melted fat and the wick constantly trimmed. The woman's place within an Eskimo habitation, is always in front of that lamp, and Kabunak, after greeting us, sat down before it, putting on a kettle of tea.

We sat down on the floor with Koikhok and ate the appetizing caribou roast. By this time I had acquired some skill at wielding a pocket knife close to my lips, but admired the confidence with which Dick whacked away with a butcher knife, which must have been even harder to manipulate.

Some children had entered the tent behind us. They stood quietly watching as we ate. And as we drank big mugs of tea, more people drifted in.

Dick talked quietly with Koikhok, Noel Avadluk interpreting. It was simply a routine enquiry into the affairs of the community: the general health, the traplines, the prospect for caribou hunting, marriages, births and deaths. Dick did not throw his weight about, he was in no way the officious policeman. Nor did Koikhok speak as if with any authority. He was no "chief," he was merely the man-most-responsible in this camp.

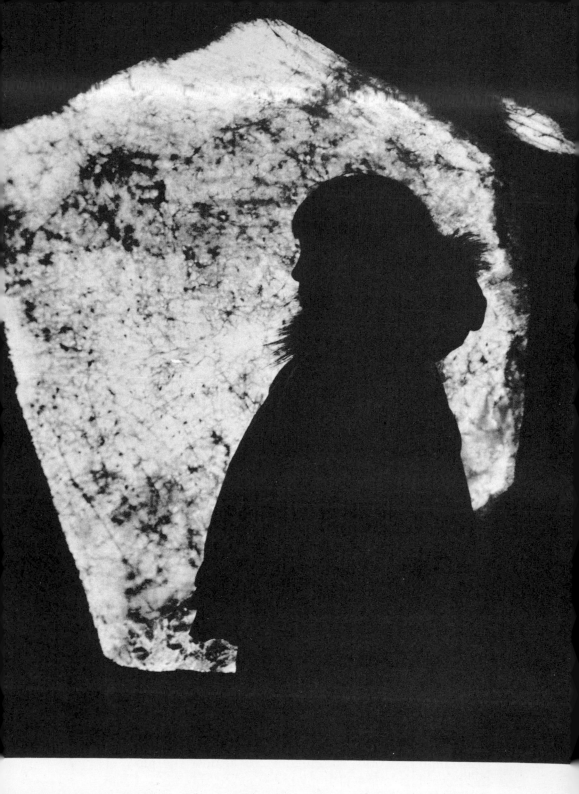

Inland people sometimes use a scraped skin window, which lets in a brown light

There had been, since Dick last heard from this community, several deaths and marriages and births, which he would register in his books next day. No misdemeanors or crimes had occurred, and there were no complaints or quarrels to be investigated.

Having exhausted the conversation for that night, Dick then turned to me and asked if I would like to hear some good drumming. "It all sounds alike to me," said Dick, "but I'm told this man is good."

I then spoke directly to Koikhok for the first time—if you can speak directly to anyone through an interpreter.

In answer to my eager request, Koikhok reached up from the sleeping bench and took down a round frame of willow that hung to one of the tent poles. Then he spoke in a gentle undertone to his wife, who handed him a piece of scraped caribou hide. She then helped her husband to stretch this tightly over the frame.

As he worked, the atmosphere grew hot. Other people had come into the tent, and stood watching intently. Among these were women with babies on their backs under the artiggis, and a number of men. One of the men was presented to us by the name of Puniak, a likeable fellow who, said Avadluk, knew many of the old chants.

No one in this encampment had Christian names. Did this mean that all, like Koikhok, were pagans?

Koikhok, as he worked, had stripped to the waist, showing a fine-muscled naked torso, shining with sweat.

At last the drum was ready for playing. Puniak stepped forward, standing motionless as Koikhok bent towards the drum, lifted the thick wooden drumstick, and closed his eyes intently. From where I sat, his beautiful profile, a face from another world, was silhouetted against the glow of the stove. His long hair hung to his naked shoulders. From the expectancy in the tent and from Koikhok's withdrawn look, I realized that this was going to be no ordinary drumming.

Holding the drum in the left hand, by a short handle, Koikhok struck the frame. With swift, sure movements of the wrist, he moved the drum back and forth, striking the rim at different angles, evoking an astonishing range of muted sounds. They and the strange rhythm were obsessing. You could think of nothing else. You wanted to shout,

Koikhok beating his drum, Puniak dancing and singing with abandon

to let yourself go in some kind of wild singing, you wanted to dance. Puniak did just that.

"I will dance the hunt!" he cried—Noel interpreted for us.

Then rhythmically he recited a tale, with eloquent gestures of arms and hands, but barely moving his feet from the floor. In the story-dance, Puniak imitated the hunter, taking aim, then cutting up the slain animal, carrying it on his back. He also became the *tuktu* itself, fleeing the hunter, brought to bay, slain at last.

The men, women and children in the tent sat round on the floor or on the sleeping bench, exchanging remarks among themselves, clapping out some of the rhythms, encouraging the dancer.

Among the crowd, the women with babies would from time to time make a movement, switch the child round in front or lift a breast, then would sink back somnolently as the child was suckled.

The fire in the oil drum and the fire in the stone lamp cast the shadows of Koikhok and Puniak upon the dark walls of the tent, gigantic, grotesque.

I thought of the violent land, of the pulsating and throbbing Northern Lights. Everyone there partook of Koikhok's visible ecstasy. The drumming went on and on, the dancing continued. . . .

Then abruptly Koikhok stopped. Without a word, he handed the drum to his wife Kabunak, who hung it up on a knob of one of the tent poles. Standing, Koikhak put on his artiggi. He did not say a word or even look in our direction.

Neither Dick nor I made any gesture or comment. You cannot applaud a thing as moving as that.

Dick and I spent the night in Koikhok's tent, our dog-team drivers sleeping elsewhere. It was not until next morning that I learned how they had spent their night. Kamingoak had played poker until six in the morning—and had lost all his dogs before dawn . . .

Whereupon, I behaved like a white man, bawling him out. He deflated like a punctured balloon. At the time I became aware of the shocked and embarrassed silence of the onlookers. Too late I realized that I had violated their code.

For they have some rules of social usage which must be observed: (1) it is polite to smile when speaking; (2) to show rude anger is undignified.

My behavior was infectious. Peter Kamingoak took it out on the dogs, cursing and kicking them. Noel Avadluk looked on, with a subdued expression on his face.

Later on in the day, Kamingoak came to me apologetically and promised that there would be no more poker-playing this trip. I afterwards learned, from a hint Avadluk gave me, that Kamingoak played poker again that very night—to win back the dogteam. And he won.

Since we left Coppermine, I had kept the shutter of my camera clicking as steadily as weather conditions would permit. I had slept with my camera. I found it was the best way to keep it from freezing.

Before reaching Koikhok's camp I had used up a number of rolls of films, got some good shots of the sleds tearing down hills, of the dogteams leaving long vapor trails behind them, of us all (except me) lost on the Barrens, tiny helpless little people in a vast white wasteland, and several pictures of Dick. He had posed for me standing beside one of the tangled bunches of antlers that marked a cache, and again in a tent, making supper, in a cloud of steam. I would have to wait till I got back to civilization to find out how these pictures turned out.

Now, at Koikhok's camp, I was all set to make a record-

Dick Connick taking down vital statistics. The women wear their cleanest Mother Hubbards. Behind them is an ice window

ing on my films of Dick, the Mountie, in action. I thawed out a frozen Medalist and followed Dick from one tent to another, succeeding now and then in getting an interesting picture.

Mounties, nowadays, are armed with briefcases, and the routine duties of a R.C.M.P. constable on patrol are registering births, especially for Family Allowance, deaths, and marriages. "Native marriage" is recognized by law, and is the same thing as common-law marriage. Usually a missionary persuades the couple to have a religious ceremony when he makes his parochial visits by dogteam. The Mountie also issues vouchers, where necessary, for Destitute Allowance. And, on this trip, Dick urged the people to come in to Coppermine April 15, when a doctor would be at the hospital to make t.b. checkups by X-ray.

At Koikhok's camp were no families to be put on Desti-

Caribou antlers piled up, a landmark designating a caribou meat cache nearby

tute Allowance, several marriages to note and brand-new Eskimo babies to be registered. They would be given a plastic disc with numbers on it. Each Eskimo wears, like a religious medal, a plastic disc, the size of a 50 cent piece, with "Eskimo" printed on it, along with a district number and a registration serial number.

All this information had to be entered in Dick's books and would eventually be filed somewhere in Ottawa.

The people at these camps usually made an annual trip to Coppermine. The Family Allowance vouchers, $5 per child per month, which Dick was issuing, would then be handed in at the H.B.C. trading post, and in exchange, the parents would secure supplies—dried milk, Pablum, baby clothes and so forth. The Eskimos cause both government and trading company a great deal of bookkeeping!

As I was taking my pictures, I listened in on some amusing interviews, Noel Avadluk acting as interpreter. This one, for example:

"How many children do you have?"

After some deep thought, the native brings out: "Three."

"Are they all yours by this wife?" (She is present.)

"Yes." Deep frowning, and eventually the native adds: "One is by Panningabluk."

"And have you adopted children?"

The native's brow is now *very* furrowed, he exchanges glances with Avadluk and with his wife. They all know how the white man objects—inexplicably—to adoptions. It makes such a lot of work for the white man! But truth will out, and at length the native says: "Yes, two boys are adopted, but one lives elsewhere, now adopted by my brother."

"Ye gods!" says Dick, pushing his cap back with an exasperated gesture and then erasing something in his books and writing again. Avadluk does not interpret the ejaculation, for nine times out of ten it is something more emphatic and untranslatable than that.

After the natives leave the tent, Dick and I talk about these eternal mixups.

"Adopting children and wife-trading gets me down!" groans Dick.

"Yes," say I, "it's a big headache for you and the missionaries. One was holding forth about the nefarious wife-trading habits of Eskimos. I think maybe I gave him a new slant. I said to him, 'Have you ever thought about it this way? Maybe it should be called husband-trading? Maybe the woman likes the idea of borrowing a new husband, for a change?'"

"And what did he say to that?" says Dick.

"Nothing. But he turned purple."

My private opinion is that the open adultery of Eskimos is better than the furtive and frequent adulteries of white men. And as to the rare cases of bigamy and polyandry I have run across, the practice is open and unashamed, usually being accounted for by the infertility of one of the spouses and the natural desire for offspring.

At Koikhok's camp there had been no breaches of the law to investigate, no family quarrels to be decided, and no complaints of the trader's injustice to hear. So we prepared to leave.

Before going, I persuaded Koikhok to pose for me in his best clothes. Inset into the kulitak were white bands of cloth and, on each side of the hood, two white bands which strangely recalled those white tassels that he and his followers had worn in the bygone days of the famous heresy. Perhaps it was only a curious coincidence.

As he had bent towards the drum that night, I got a flash-bulb picture of him, bare to the waist, his hair hanging down to his shoulders, his profile mysteriously lit up. The two photographs would help me preserve a memory which at the time seemed unforgettable.

Our dogteams were again wreathed in mist as we once more pushed on across the Barrens to the east. The air was windless and the temperature was 50 below zero. Tiny snow crystals had formed on the snow, glistening in the sun.

We now had a new guide, James Hala, since Okaitok had remained behind at Koikhok's camp, which was his home. Hala was a cheerful fellow and promised that we would reach the next encampment before night.

He kept his promise. But the next camp, Katiak's, was overflowing with visitors when we arrived. Though a small encampment, there were a number of sleds around the place, and a horde of people flocked out of the tents as we appeared. It looked as though everyone in the Barrens had decided to go visiting that night and had made this camp their port of call.

The result was that all five of us crowded together in one of the filthiest caribou skin tents I have ever seen. Because of the crowding, the air was almost suffocating and the frosting inside the roof of the tent constantly melted and leaked down upon us, soaking our furs. A man who seemed to be dying, of t.b. or rheumatic fever, was also billeted in that tent. He kept coughing and spitting throughout the night. The floor below his part of the bed-platform was a sheet of filthy and slippery ice. Everyone else present seemed to do an unusual amount of coughing and spitting that night: I had noticed that I too, after coming in from a 50 below temperature, always had a congested feeling.

"I predict there'll be plenty of work for you in *this* camp, tomorrow," I said to Dick, as I crawled disgustedly into my sleeping bag.

Eskimos are as a rule polite and hospitable. Fatal as all generalizations are, I believe this one can stand up. But the conditions I saw in this tent at Katiak's camp did not

110

conform to the rule. I never saw a more untidy and apathetic bunch of people anywhere. Indifferent to their own comfort, they did nothing for ours. They were out of tea, so we gave them some, which they accepted with an apathy bordering on rudeness. I was thoroughly glad when Dick had finished his paper work and we had left the place behind us.

The only thing of interest at Katiak's camp was the framework of an inland *kayak*, the small type of skinboat which lay outside one tent, propped up on ice-blocks. This kayak under construction was a portent of spring, for the boat would be used on the many inland lakes of the region, which in four or five months' time would be almost free of ice.

A sick, semi-conscious Eskimo in a caribou skin tent. Dick Connick studying his condition

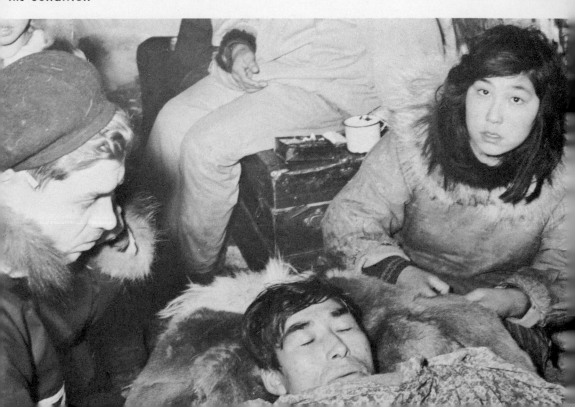

VIII

"tea-to-witchee!"

THAT AFTERNOON, AS WE SPED EASTWARD ACROSS THE
Barrens, we saw another cloud of vapor on the horizon.
James Hala called back, pointing: "Dogteam!"

It was Canon Webster's. He had been away two weeks
on another round of his parish, and was now on his return
journey.

We stopped in our tracks to have a "mug-up" with him
there in the white wastelands. Dick handed out some of
his good doughnuts to celebrate the occasion. Then, camera fans all of us, we took each other's pictures.

It always seems fantastic to meet people like this on a
limitless and roadless plain. But it is understandable when
you realize that all travelling is done between camps, usually following the most suitable topography—gullies, valleys, smooth slopes. Sled tracks are usually in evidence if
you look sharp. Even after a big storm, detached raised
fragments of track can be found here and there.

It was not long after this unexpected meeting with
Canon Webster that we again had to stop. In going down
one rough slope, the mudding on the big police sled

113

runners got badly damaged. There was nothing for it but to stop, unload the komatik, and shave the runners smooth for the time-being with a home-made plane. At camp they would have to be re-mudded—with oatmeal porridge. We carried with us, for such emergencies, a thermos bottle of hot water, which obviated the necessity of using the primus stoves except in camp.

That night we did not reach the next camp on Dick's list, but had to pitch our tent again. We spent a miserable night. The tent was meant to hold only two men, but all five of us crowded in together. No one could turn or bend to get warm or find a comfortable position. I lay awake most of the night, pulling my frozen and crackling eiderdown behind me to keep the cold out. But then I suffocated and had to open my sleeping bag for ventilation. We are all wakeful. But when, in the night, I exclaimed: "Hell, Jesus Christ, I am goddam cold!" Everyone roared with laughter.

At any rate, we were a good-natured bunch.

We did not reach the three-family encampment of Aiyaligyoak until next evening, when we were given a cordial welcome. The natives there were out of practically everything except caribou meat, but of this they made a good stew for us, which we ate with chunks of frozen back-fat. Seeing they were short of tea, I made them a present of a half pound from my supplies. Aiyaligyoak put his hands behind his back. "Cannot pay for it," he said shyly, refusing to accept. "It's a gift," Peter Kamingoak said. The tea was then accepted with a display of gratefulness. I put the whole performance down as an indication of contact with white men and their ways. For it was certainly unusual in these people, who share everything and are in the habit of regarding anybody's property as belonging to everybody.

Here and at subsequent camps, we delivered messages that had been given us. The messages were written in the Eskimo language, but printed in Latin lettering—syllabics not being used in this part of the Arctic. The notes were on small pieces of paper, carefully folded. Kamingoak took charge of them, for he knew to whom they were to be delivered.

Often, when outside, I had raised a hymn of praise to the Eskimo child and the attitude of parents—their devotion without fussiness or sentimentality. How many times had I said: "I never have seen a spoiled Eskimo child!" Well, on this trip, I had to reverse my opinion in one case. It was at Ivagulok's camp, our next stop.

The child was five-year-old Martha Ihumnitak, the adopted child of George Ivagulok and Alice Kabgalyok. Her foster parents were her absolute slaves. Dimpled and adorable, in her pretty outfit of ground-squirrel furs, she was the ruler of the household. When she issued an order, her parents stepped lively. I felt like reprimanding her, but instead took a few pictures of her, one of them with a drum, which she was learning to play.

I have been told that when you find a spoiled child like this among the Eskimos, it means that she is "inhabited" by the "spirit" of a respected ancestor. Not knowing the language sufficiently well, and not being an anthropologist, I would not swear to this.

Another little girl in this community set the usual example of good behavior. She was Annie Tadedluk, and I ended up by getting on the bad side of her. Seeing her play with a doll—an Eskimo doll dressed exactly like the child herself, in ground squirrel furs with wolverine tags—I asked her mother where I could get one like it. The mother politely offered me Annie's. Seeing this, Annie's eyes clouded and she wrinkled up her nose at me, then hid behind her

A young Eskimo girl, dancing with her drum, inside a caribou skin tent. Dick Connick still wears his fur pants

mother, sulking. I declined the gift, but Annie still held it against me that I had coveted, as she thought, her precious doll.

That gesture of wrinkling up the nose is a typical one in Eskimo children, when they are put out at something. It is brief—so fleeting that I was delighted to succeed in getting a photograph of Annie making that grimace—and it reminds one of the twitching of a rabbit's nose. I have seen little babies still being packed by their mothers express disapproval like that.

I asked the child to stand alone

Coppermine Eskimo child with doll. The mother had offered me the doll—
hence the woebegone look

Speaking of typical gestures, nose-rubbing is not generally indulged in, except between older women and small children. It might be called a grandmother-gesture, and is utterly charming.

Before the coming of white men, Eskimos did not know the ritual of hand-shaking. But since that contact, they have adopted it wholeheartedly. Indeed, when we arrived at a camp, we were expected to shake hands with everyone, including the unweaned babies!

George Ivagulok's camp was a prosperous one. Great hospitaility prevailed, every pot had its caribou stew, marrow bones strewed the floors, caches of meat were all around the neighborhood. Ivagulok was a superior trapper, but he confessed that so far that year he had caught only two foxes. It looked like the beginning of a bad year. One bad year of trapping means privation the next, for without foxes to trade, the people have no means of obtaining ammunition. A fox is the equivalent of money to the Eskimo. It represents so many "sticks"—as the numbered discs now given him by the trader are still called, in remembrance of the old days when sticks of differing lengths were used. It represents food and clothing for the people since without ammunition they cannot shoot the caribou.

Several things at this camp indicated contact with the white man—an alarm clock and Ivagulok's wrist watch. The wrist watch ran, although it kept no kind of time. The alarm clock was frozen and did not go at all. Once Ivagulok thawed it out while we were there—we spent two sleeps —and the infernal thing rang for hours.

Clocks in the Arctic are mere ornaments and toys. Who cares what hour it is in that timeless land? No matter what the time of day, however, tea-parties go on, almost continuously. I noticed this particularly at Ivagulok's camp.

Solid comfort in this igloo near Bathurst Inlet. Drying rack is also baby's crib

"Tea-to-witchee-ee-ee!" some woman calls out at the door of her caribou skin tent. "Come and have tea" is a general invitation and is quite irresistible. The population flocks there. Then, an hour later, another woman stands at the door of her tent and makes the same broadcast: "Tea-to-witchee-ee!" And everyone flocks there, for another mug-up.

We began referring to all our meals in the same way. "Oyok-to-witchee" was cooked caribou-feed; and nothing prevented us from announcing to each other: "Doughnut-to-witchee!"

The night was glorious with Northern Lights, and I wanted to get a time-exposure. An idea had been in my mind for some time. I now decided to put it into action.

Snow houses are translucent, as I have already said. When you are inside one, light filters through the snow. In the same way, an inhabited igloo glows for some distance, like a great pearl set in the velvety darkness. If there is an ice-window, as in a permanent dwelling, and if a candle is burning inside, the light streams warmly out. I had often watched a man building an igloo—he builds the igloo around him, gradually disappearing from sight as the snow-block walls grow higher. He usually puts the last blocks in place by lantern or candle light and I had noticed the beautiful effect, especially before the snow blocks were chinked. At Ivagulok's camp I persuaded a man to build an igloo for me and leave it unchinked. He was glad to satisfy the unusual request for a package of tobacco and some cigarette papers.

When the work was done, I carried down four candles which I placed in the snow house.

The effect was astounding. It was a conflagration, a burning symbol of human life in the midst of that vast dark emptiness. I took several time exposures on ordinary film and also some in color. Tramping round on the crunching snow, alone in the enormous clear silence, I forgot all the disagreeable incidents of the journey, the weariness, the biting cold, the lack of privacy, the occasional filth, the cramped sleeping. I was filled with elation, hard to explain. I felt small. But it was good to be a little man alive there on the great curve of the world, which I seemed to feel turning under me, slowly.

When at last I had taken my pictures and had returned, shivering, into the tent, Dick looked up smilingly.

"Well, was it worth it?" he asked, meaning was it worth facing the cold.

"Yes," I said, thinking of something more than that, "it was worth it!"

Papik's camp, our next halt, was situated in a tiny grove of stunted spruce trees, about four feet high. We spent the night here in Peter's mother's tent.

Peter Kamingoak had not seen his mother for many months, but the two met without any display of emotion. He slept in another tent—where he probably played poker. However, he had brought her some gifts of tea and tobacco and a few other luxuries.

A visiting doctor had seen her a year before at Coppermine and had given the old woman two years to live. He had advised that she be flown outside, for care. She had refused. She did not want to go outside. So here she was, gradually rotting away, among her own people.

Our caravan, from Ivagulok's camp onward, had grown and continued to grow. At every camp, as we started out, some Eskimos decided that this was a good opportunity to go visiting. So they trailed along, behind or ahead of us, camping when we camped, invading no matter what tent we happened to be in, helping themselves to our tobacco and tea. The Canadian Arctic may be thinly populated with Eskimos—there are only a little more than 8,000 —but they certainly do, upon occasion, crowd together.

We began to look with some misgivings upon our shrinking stocks of food and tobacco. We also began to hoard, feeling guilty. For these people were ready to share all they had with us, and did. Dick carried dried fruit, which he now hid out of sight. "Why should I give a dried peach to some Eskimo who wouldn't even like it?" he asked.

During extreme cold inland dogs froze inside their thighs—had to be given belly bands, to keep tender area warm

"They prefer their own food. But I wish they'd stick to it," he ended morosely.

By the time we reached Negak's camp, I had become a real addict of marrowbones. I preferred them cracked, split, still warm from the fire. Nothing better when you are hungry than to suck out some good succulent marrow!

The people in this region looked well fed and well dressed. Their tents were in excellent repair. All this with caribou, exclusively! Said Peter Kamingoak: "It takes 200 caribou a year for a family and their dogs." That is, used for food, fuel, tents, rugs, bed-rolls, and clothing.

This was the second week of our travels and we were all a little fatigued. With weariness came irritation. I was annoyed at myself—having neglected to change my socks as frequently as I should, perspiration had made my feet colder. But I was chiefly irritated at Kamingoak.

With the natives, he behaved like a city slicker among yokels, showing off, making them roll his cigarettes for him, boasting about his prosperity, and about his knowledge of white men's ways. When he interpreted for me and asked people to pose for me, I was infuriated at his officiousness. Then, he was bold and conniving. A couple of times he succeeded in billeting me in one tent while he went off to sleep elsewhere—taking the grub box with him, pretending that his tent was more convenient for cooking. My supplies sank visibly. We had prolonged our visit at Papik's camp—Kamingoak wanted to stay an extra day. His excuse was that the dogs needed rest. This was true, but it made further inroads on my supplies.

One of Kamingoak's dogs had developed bad feet and was leaving bloody tracks in the snow. Peter provided that dog with some sealskin "boots." Two of his dogs needed bandages. Sleeping, as they do, when cold, with their nose under a hind-leg, thinly furred flanks frost up and freeze, becoming very painful. Peter Kamingoak put soft caribou skin bindings around the dogs' loins, when travelling.

An escort had come to meet us from Negak's camp, having heard of our approach from one of the dogteams that had gone ahead. By this time, our caravan had become a triumphal march across the land.

We were now in the Willingham Mountain Ranges, to the north of the Thelon Game Sanctuary, the breeding grounds of the caribou. Going was slowed up by the terrain, long detours being necessary and the sleds having frequently to swerve to avoid glacial boulders, left there in the ice age. Our direction, from Papik's camp onward had been generally northeast, but it made a very wavy line on my sketch-map which now and then I tried to fill in as best I could.

As the sleds ran and bumped along, the drivers encouraged the dogs with talk about caribou. "Tuktu," they would say, and the dogs pricked up their ears, yelped joyfully, and gathered speed.

Our arrival at this camp again caused them to let out little howls—at the sight of the stunted trees.

Most of the trees here were only six to eight inches through. But some dead trees had been brought in from a little distance and they were a foot in diameter. I tried to count the rings, but they were so close together that, towards the center of the log, it was impossible without a magnifying glass. I counted up to 400 rings, when I had to stop. This means that those trees, despite their small size, were over 400 years old.

Our night at this camp was very gay, with crowds of visitors, drumming, and dancing. Negak sang well. His ballads were apparently about people present, for one after another the guests burst into self-conscious laughter. After the singing and drumming, various men and women present showed off their talents at the famous string-game we call cat's cradles. Peter explained their meaning to me. Each cat's cradle is representative of something: a caribou, a fox, a wolf, a trapper, a raven, a man dancing, a flame, and sometimes portions of animals, the teats or the anus. Laughter followed these demonstrations, but never was it salacious. And considering that a large portion of the people's time is spent at the rear of a dogteam, the predilection for depicting a dog's hind end with strings was understandable.

It was at Negak's camp that I noted most carefully the work of the women and secured some pictures of it. A prosperous camp of many tents, the women and girls were particularly busy. Home was the hunter! Evidences of his success were everywhere: marrow bones strewed the ground of every tent, hunks of meat were thawing out by every stove, great lumps of backfat were being rendered, bundles of wood had to be carried in, the pot was kept boiling with caribou stews, and the teakettle was constantly emitting steam and the odor of boiled tea.

The man traps or shoots game. It is the woman who takes over then, cutting up carcasses, scraping skins, and all the rest of it. Fresh hides were being scraped to make new clothing. Boot soles were being chewed and crimped. Caribou backfat was being pounded with a musk-ox horn on a block of ice. The killing of musk-ox is forbidden by law now, but apparently a number of them obligingly die to furnish tools for the Eskimos! The backfat was then thrown into the stone lamps—there were several *kudeles* of the old kind at this camp—and, gradually dissolved, would furnish both light and fuel. It was the woman's job to gather firewood and keep the improvised stoves going.

Smilingly and quietly the women went about their work. As I photographed them, I noticed their characteristic gestures. Walking all their lives in heeless shoes, they all seemed pigeon-toed. Their clothes being full and loose, they moved their legs and arms with great ease. When they bent, it was from the waist—it seemed as though their torsos actually rested on their thighs in that position. When they sat down, it was with their legs thrust straight out before them. And the movements of their hands were deft and swift.

They always seemed relaxed, but they kept eternally busy. Our coming increased their work, for with true Eskimo hospitality the women saw to it that our clothes

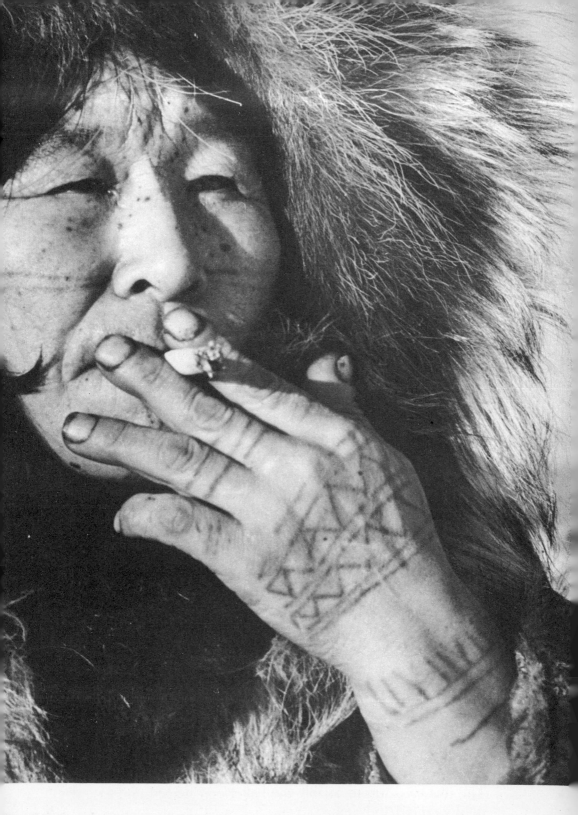

Inland Eskimo woman

Tending a caribou fat lamp. In this case an upturned piece of tin is used

were looked after. A good beating removed the snow from them, then they were placed on a rack over a *kudele*.

The ice windows of the tents were scraped from time to time, to clear them of hoarfrost. And the frozen snow floor was also scraped clean by these good housekeepers. The tool used was invariably the half-moon shaped *ulu*, so rightly called "the woman's knife."

As the women worked, their little daughters followed them about, learning, imitating, and sometimes lending a hand.

There seemed to be a great many children in this camp. Many of the women had that hunch-backed look so familiar in the Arctic: they were packing infants. Small children trotted around, looking for all the world like little brown rabbits.

It's because the cut of their pants between the legs is an opening that closes when walking but opens when squatting. In the standing posture, this makes an amusing projection to children's clothes, almost like a bunny's tail.

These little tailed creatures were sometimes a nuisance, crowding over each other into our tent, and at meal time, standing so near us that their faces were right over our plates. No begging—these children were plump as partridges —just sheer curiosity. They could not get enough of staring at us with their big black eyes.

Some puppies were at this camp and they, too, were a nuisance. They were always getting into our grub-boxes and following us around, with a guilt-complex look on their faces. They had only recently been weaned, and the bitch was no longer there to maintain order. (The only adult husky ever allowed indoors is the bitch with young.) The pups were certainly a hazard when we were doing our morning chore behind some tent or other.

While I am on this subject: going out of doors in Arctic weather is not the cold operation you would think. The artiggi and kulitak are loose above the pants and reach down almost to the knee. In a squatting posture, therefore, you are in a kind of fur tent, which is quite comfortable—if you don't have to kick a few pups out of the way.

During our stay at Negak's camp we more or less sorted out our grub-boxes which had got into a terrible mess. Not

129

Coppermine Eskimos, showing fly-opening of children's pantaloons

only were there biscuit crumbs in the sugar and tea, and caribou hairs in everything, but some of the boxes had been damaged in our rocking and bumping journey over rough terrain.

We congratulated ourselves that our thermos flasks and snow knives had held up. Travellers in the Arctic, whites and Eskimos alike, are sometimes let down by careless manufacturers. The blades of snow-knives break like glass in 50 below temperatures unless they are of finest steel. Often the manufacturers palm off as Swedish-made some pretty rotten imitations. Thermos bottles, too, are sometimes shipped in, all those thousands of miles, without being tested, and prove useless. The same with primus stoves. If you have defective things of this sort, you are just out of luck. Refunds? Impossible. It would take a couple of years to receive the "satisfaction guaranteed" on these packages shipped in from the outside.

As we packed our things to leave Negak's camp and push on, this time northward towards the Arctic Circle, Noel Avadluk gave me some news that he was well aware I would like to hear.

"Soon—next camp—we will be in igloos," said he.

Guesthouse à la Arctic

IX

all kinds of igloos

OUR ROUTE NOW LED AWAY FROM THE LAND OF STUNTED trees. Going in a northeastward direction, we followed a small river course, full of rapids in summer, for here and there the ice had been pushed up in hanging arches, which the level sunlight revealed in prismatic colors. The tracks in the snow and even the dogs were of a rosy hue, and a white ptarmigan that sprang up at our passing seemed to have its wings lined with pink. Here and there were tracks: of lemming, fox, Arctic hare, and caribou. Caches of caribou meat, usually marked by a tangle of antlers, were seen more frequently. Who said the Arctic was without life?

The cold was intense, the dogs were frosted up to their shoulders. Going was hard. For some reason, intense cold seems to make the snow grittier and the drag on the sleds is worse. I simply could not generate enough warmth, and I felt cold all day. I tired easily. And twice we rested to warm ourselves with tea.

Dick was glad of these stops. He too was feeling none too well. He was chiefly troubled by pain in his eyes, which were red-rimmed. We were all beginning to suffer from the level rays of sunlight.

But the pictorial effects were sometimes wonderful. Looking back, the white land was scrawled with glistening serpentine trails of the sleds. Clouds of vapor left by the dogteams was golden. Then it turned gray as the sun set. Now the full moon rose, startlingly large, but throwing only a little light.

I felt stiff and lifeless as we descended a last hill to a lake, in the middle of which Dick and Avadluk pitched our tent. I walked up and down, stamping my feet, beating my arms across my chest, longing for feed-time and the warmth of my sleeping bag. I knew in advance how long I would have to wait for these comforts. It usually took about an hour to unload the sled, erect the tent, and get the meal.

I looked at the dogs that had philosophically, as usual, curled up in their tracks to snooze away the waiting time until they got their daily meal, envying them their acceptance of their hard life, their patience, their endurance—and their thick fur.

We reached Taipana's camp next night. It was a settlement of snow houses, and a tiny igloo was turned over to us.

The igloo was barely large enough to accommodate three people. Avadluk, Dick, and I, were all travel-weary and needed a good night's sleep. We were delighted, then, to see our guide, James Hala, and Peter Kamingoak make off to another igloo. But our satisfaction was short-lived. As we ate our meal—it happened to be spaghetti full of caribou hairs and tea leaves, since the borrowed teakettle had not been emptied of the latter. Dick, in his haste to get through supper, had not noticed it. Crowds of visitors arrived. They kept coming in. They stood on each other's feet—and on ours. Our tobacco can was freely used. We were smiled upon, and eventually had no elbow room.

At last Dick managed to shoo the visitors away and we

134

Arctic winter patrol. Dick Connick in foreground, heavy ground-drifts around us, going south in a small valley

crawled into our sleeping bags. There was just room for us three to lie on the sleeping bench.

Then James Hala returned. Not finding room on the sleeping bench he cheerfully announced he would spend the night in the refuse pit. He crawled in there.

Typical tracks made by sled and dogs

We snored, pretending to sleep. Then Kamingoak came back—apparently his poker game had gone against him. He tried to squeeze in between us, failed, and settled down with James Hala in the refuse pit. After awhile he gave it up and once more tried to crowd in with us.

The night was intensely cold. But at length, in despair, Dick sat up and said: "You two boys must make yourselves a snow-house. It's impossible for us to spend the night like this."

To my amazement, both boys willingly bestirred themselves, took a snow knife, and went out into the moonlit night to obey Dick's instructions . . .

Next morning I woke up totally uninterested in any-thing—igloos, Eskimos, cameras, Avadluk, Dick, myself. Only hot tea. I craved that.

As we all squirmed around, getting into our clothes, hav-ing the first cups of tea, we exchanged the remarks usual to such occasions.

"I didn't sleep a wink."

"You did. I heard you snoring."

"Impossible. I heard *you* snoring all night long."

We grouched, but finally grinned. Dick, there was no doubt, was an ideal travelling companion.

"But gosh," Dick growled, "what I'd give for a little privacy! I'd swap a year's salary for just one good night's sleep."

He looked done-in. His eyes were bloodshot, a growth of stubble and brown patches from frostbite on his face did not enhance his appearance.

"What about a bath?" I asked.

"Seven sleeps more . . ." said Dick, almost drooling at the thought.

Following a natural valley, enclosed by high bare hills, we made good speed, reaching the first Bathurst camp to-wards nightfall. This was Aviak's camp, a cluster of rather odd looking igloos, some of them very large, with long tunnels and niches we called "blisters." These nooks were used for storing gear, for dog-nurseries, and one was al-ways "the çan."

Waiting for us at Aviak's camp was Father Lemer, O.M.I., to guide us to Bathurst Inlet. He had heard on the radio that we could be expected about the middle of Feb-ruary, and had set out to meet us. On the way, he had again heard of our approach from some Eskimos who had

Dick Connick just before arriving at Bathurst Inlet, near end of patrol

Portrait of a people, way inland, southeast from Coppermine. Special Constable Avadluk, second from left, my guide, Kamingoak, sixth from left

accompanied us and then gone ahead. Our party sometimes numbered as many as eight dogteams.

Father Lemer was from Normandy, and he looked more like a peasant than a priest. He needed to be rugged and good natured, for there were no Catholics at either this or the next camp, and there was some curiosity about his presence. What was this medicine-man doing in someone else's bailiwick? Peter told me this in great glee.

With Father Lemer, who knew the region as well as anyone, I discussed my proposed trip to Perry River and my hoped-for trip from there to Lake Garry. By doing the trip to the southeastward—Lake Garry, Baker Lake, Churchill—I would more or less repeat, in 1949, the overland journey made by Samuel Hearne in 1771, when he returned from Coppermine. He had gone there in 1770 to search for "northern Indians" and persuade them to come down to Churchill to trade. He had also been in search of a probable Northwest Passage to the western sea, and had returned to Churchill saying there wasn't any.

What was *I* searching for? I wanted to find Eskimos who still led the life their ancestors had evolved through countless centuries, the one most fitted to those latitudes. I had faith that they still existed somewhere. They would most likely be found in the little-travelled region lying between Perry River and Baker Lake, at the western end of Chesterfield Inlet, Hudson Bay.

As we set out for Kautik's camp next day, I was full of these dreams, and sat on the komatik, snug in my warm furs, looking out of my hood upon the world contentedly, like a commuter from his train window.

Kautik met us on the way. He had come out to meet us, in the manner of Homeric patriarchs. Every kindness was extended to us. But by this time we were too weary and irritable to appreciate it.

Dick was bitching a lot at inanimate objects. I was vexed at a number of things. At Kautik's camp my big camera was almost put out of commission. This happened when a woman poured out a cup of tea from a kettle held too close to my camera, which, as usual, I was trying to thaw out gently. The camera survived, as I had survived my nights with my cameras in the sleeping bag. But many a time I woke up resting on their sharp edges.

At Kautik's camp another accident befell me. Drinking my tea "in bed" I carelessly jogged my elbow and spilled a little into my sleeping bag. It was only a thimbleful—but it was enough to make a soggy patch in my sleeping bag which would later freeze and lose its insulating quality.

These were minor catastrophes. What worried me also was that on this trip I had not been able to get close to the people. Travelling with an arm of the law, even with as pleasant a one as Richard Connick, made me an associate of the law. The people—who have no form of government themselves—have learned to accept the Mounties, but never do they feel exactly affectionate towards them.

At any rate, I had been able to get some camera shots that had not been made before of a Mountie on an Arctic winter patrol. I would have to wait till I got outside, however, to know how good or bad they were.

Our last native encampment before reaching Bathurst Inlet was Otokiak's camp, a huddle of big igloos in a wide valley enclosed by tall cliffs.

Nearly all of the igloos had stovepipes projecting above the domed roofs—a new one on me—stoves in igloos. Ground willow grew not far off, and the people took advantage of it, not wishing to abandon snow houses. To compensate for the constant melting and icing that takes place in an igloo with a stove, the sides and domes had been banked and rebanked with snow, until their original pure form had been obliterated. They looked more like snowbanks into which the people burrowed than like igloos.

The nearness to a trading post showed in other ways. Here, again, the women wore Mother Hubbards. One woman wore hers inside her artiggi. She had cut slits in the front of it over her breasts to accommodate her nursing baby.

At this camp, too, a number of the women wore tartan shawls or knitted sweaters. And, despite the comparative

The igloo is not all darkness inside—the mother has taken the child from under her artiggi

abundance of caribou meat, bannocks seemed to be a daily part of the diet.

Before leaving Otokiak's camp, I bought two caribou carcasses, without legs, insides, heads or skins, for $3 each. Otokiak would not go to Bathurst Inlet for four months, but the transaction was conducted as usual: I simply wrote an I.O.U. for $6, which he would present at the Hudson's Bay store and use up in trade. The meat, frozen solid of course, would provide Kamingoak's dogteam with food while we were visiting at Bathurst.

On the last lap to Bathurst Inlet we were on the way to the sea. We started out early. The sharp edge of the sun rose above the horizon as we made off, throwing the dogs' shadows long and low across a smooth and seemingly flat countryside. But it was obvious, from the way the dogs flew along and the way the sleds had often to be braked, that we were constantly going downhill. The curving sled tracks were thrown into high relief in the sunlight. Ahead of us and to one side, bare cliffs and rolling hills, range after range, seemed constantly to grow higher. On some of the descents the snow anchors had to be used to keep the sleds from running over the dogs, which let out loud howls of fear and excitement as we raced down the sharp slopes.

Sometimes, for miles, when my sled was at the rear of the caravan, I sat there looking back at the receding white landscape, happy, but without a thought in my head. Once Dick joined me, and we trotted together for a while, to warm up.

"What's wrong?" he asked, surprised at my silence. "Why don't you use your camera on this—" His hand stretched out towards the track we had left, the great emptiness behind us.

"Nothing wrong," I said. "But as to photographing

143

that sort of thing—no market. Those are shades and forms that you must just carry in your head."

The landscape became steadily more stark, more severe. The cliffs, gray and serrated, reared higher. We were going through a landscape that looked prehistoric. It was like being on a dead world, or on the moon.

That was our longest day of travel—we made more than 40 miles. But Bathurst was too far away, we would have to wait till the next day to reach it. So, late at night we sweated and steamed through the darkness, until Father Lemer found an igloo that some natives had built on their way out from Bathurst Inlet. It was as good a place as any to spend the night. Dick and I decided to put up the tent. The others bedded down in the igloo. But before turning in, we all crowded in there, singing, joking, and drinking tea.

Our plates and cups were by that time crusted with dirt, grease and caribou hair. Our clothes and sleeping bags were again frosted up from dampness. We were all looking forward to the end of the journey when our clothes could be dried out and we ourselves could use the razor and soap once more. I was willing to admit that such things maybe had some value.

Next day we ran into bad weather. A wind blew, hiding upturned rocks with drifted snow, obscuring the sleds ahead, making going difficult, as we raced downhill. We tied ropes around our waists to keep the wind out, but the drift snow penetrated everything. Occasionally the dogs whined as the sled threatened to run over them. At one point we half-flew over a frozen waterfall about ten feet high, without breaking anything, not even our necks.

Majestic cliffs towered. And ahead of us, quite near, was another settlement of white men. I thought: how far apart are these pinpoints of warmth which men make for themselves in these vast spaces! How small we are, how enormous this world!

144

Bathurst Inlet settlement, consisting of Hudson Bay Company buildings and Roman Catholic church at the right. Igloos in foreground

I was also thinking, with a twinge of regret, that soon Dick's way and mine would part. From Bathurst, he would return westward along the coast to Coppermine, while I would soon be going eastward to Perry River. Already, this R.C.M.P. patrol seemed a thing of the past.

We made Bathurst Inlet on February 20, having travelled inland more than 520 miles since the first of the month. With wild enthusiasm we swung down the last slope . . .

"There it is!" called out Father Lemer, pointing.

Through the gusts of snow could be seen some distant cliffs, and huddled against them, it seemed, were the white and red buildings of the trading post.

Soon we were near enough to read the familiar sign, always heartwarming at the end of a trail:

"HUDSON'S BAY COMPANY
Incorporated 2d May, 1670."

X

bathurst inlet—hail and farewell!

OUR PARTY DISSOLVED, FATHER LEMER GOING OFF
to the mission house, Kamingoak and Avadluk trailing
along with our Eskimo travelling companions to nearby
igloos—there were only about four—where they would spend
the night. Dick and I were welcomed to the post by two
tall young bachelors, D'Arcy Munro and Sid Morris. They
had had no visitors for five months.

"Yippee!" said Sid, when he saw the two bulging mail
bags we had brought all the way from Coppermine. But
then his face fell. Upon examination, one of the bags
proved to be destined for Cambridge Bay. We had been
given the wrong bag in Coppermine. When Sid had re-
covered from his own disappointment, he exclaimed: "Poor
sons-of-guns in Cambridge!"

Then Dick and I washed up. After which, with our faces
burning from the unaccustomed use of razor and the overheated house, we sat down to an excellent meal of caribou
steak and all the trimmings—canned peas, beets, dehydrated
potatoes, followed by canned peaches and cupcakes. D'Arcy
had reason to be proud of his cooking.

We opened the bottle of Canadian whisky that had come all the way by dogteam. It was frozen almost solid, but was all right once it had been carefully thawed out.

The total white population at Bathurst Inlet was four men: these two "servants" of the Hudson's Bay Company and the two priests at the Roman Catholic mission. The only thing that recalled Coppermine to mind was the overhead whirr and whine of the wind charger.

We tilted back our chairs and talked. First there was the usual gossip about the people we knew in the Arctic. Then we discussed the world news the way men do who, without newspapers, try to arrive at their own conclusions in such matters. These things disposed of quickly, we recounted the mishaps of our trip and talked about the weather. As we had expected, it had been the coldest February, they said, since heaven knew when. The temperatures, during the patrol, had varied between 20 and 60 below zero at Bathurst Inlet, which would mean lower temperatures than that, inland, where we had been.

I asked about the sheer cliffs nearby, and was told they were perhaps 1,500 to 2,000 feet high. Then, of course, the conversation settled on "the people," and the same things were said about them that I had heard before. In the course of this discussion, I asked about the husband-murderess who had served a term of imprisonment at Coppermine.

"You'll meet her if you go to Perry River," said D'Arcy. "She lives at the only encampment between here and there. Has a brand new husband, younger and handsomer, and in much better health . . ."

We went to bed early, overcome with drowsiness in the overheated house, although I dreaded a little the night ahead of me. Sleeping on snow-benches in igloos is not at all uncomfortable. Snow floors and furs "give" more or

148

less to the weight of the body, whereas a wooden floor is obdurate . . .

"I'll bet you'll be glad to get back to civilization," said Sid, as he helped me bring in my things and arrange my sleeping bag on the kitchen floor.

"He—glad?" said Dick. "Why, he's not going back till he has to! From Perry River he hopes to keep right on going. Wants to go to Baker Lake, if he can. You'll have to send a radiogram out tomorrow for him. He can't get enough of it."

"Sure must like it," said D'Arcy.

"Sure do," I said, yawning and crawling into my bag.

Next day both Dick and I were suffering with sore throats. It never fails: you can sleep in drafty tents, face sub-zero weather, freeze your cheeks, get utterly exhausted on the trail. But you don't catch a cold. Then you reach a white man's overheated house, and there you are, with snuffles and a sore throat.

Dick sent a radiogram to the R.C.M.P. station at Baker Lake:

> Photographer Richard Harrington who is taking pictures for several government departments has accompanied me on patrol from Coppermine. He intends to continue trip to Baker Lake by dogteam via Perry River, hoping to arrive Baker Lake end of March. If possible, please arrange to have guide meet him in Lake Garry area or nearer Perry River, and please advise within a week arrangements made. Later please advise date of Harrington arrival. Munro and Harrington send regards.

Yes, we were once more in an outpost of civilization, with a spluttering transmitter and a radio that went almost continually, vomiting forth disaster, disagreement, demands for help in this and that public endeavor, and dear little bedtime stories for children and people who refuse to grow up. Whenever I was near the thing I took a fiendish joy in turning it off.

That Friday, when the Northern Messenger broadcast came through, we all listened intently, and whenever a message came through for someone we knew, we exchanged significant glances. There was only one message for "us" that day. It was for D'Arcy, from an uncle, and was a Scripture quotation . . . and D'Arcy tried to sink out of sight.

Two days later a message came through from Baker Lake:

> Due to severe dog sickness in this district including Back River camp, it is not possible to arrange for guide as requested. Have had no contact with Perry River or Lake Garry this winter, owing to dog shortage. Sorry we cannot offer assistance for Harrington's trip. Regards to Harrington and Munro. (Signed) Cp'l. McLaughlin.

That was a blow! The trip to Garry Lake and Baker Lake was off, at least for this year. I decided the grapes were sour, anyway, recalling something Father Lemer had told me. At Garry Lake, in that inaccessible part of the Northwest Territories, a new R.C. mission was being established, by Father Buliard, a relative of the pioneer missionary who had been for many years at Holman Island. I would not find at Garry Lake the pagan Eskimos I was looking for. The missions were the spearheads of our civilization and soon what I was looking for would have vanished from this earth. At Eskimo Point, Padlei, Baker Lake, Repulse Bay,

Bow with snow knife and block of snow, to be melted for tea

Pelly Bay, Thom Bay, and now Garry Lake, missions held sway. The Anglicans would have to step lively to keep up their end of the fight for the natives' souls.

I turned my attention to re-outfitting for the journey to Perry River, and to finding a guide to take me there.

While buying food supplies at the H.B.C. post, I purchased, for $15, a bow and arrow. It was beautifully made— but then, there is no craftsman better than the Eskimo on the North American continent. The bow was of musk-ox horn, spliced and bolted, strengthened by a wrapping of braided caribou sinew. The bowstring was also of braided sinew. The arrows were tipped with iron, procured from scraps salvaged around the trading post. Some of them were barbed.

We all tried my bow and estimated that the pull was close to thirty-five pounds. It took all our strength to pull it. But the Eskimos pulled those bows with amazing ease. I saw one lad give a demonstration. To him it seemed as easy as operating a slingshot.

At the native settlement several men had double-curved bows larger than mine. They used them when short of ammunition or to save ammunition when close to game. I was told that in summer they always took out their bows and arrows when hunting from their kayaks on the nearby lakes. And I persuaded some of these hunters to pose for me, pulling a bow.

Angligoitok, in a wolfskin kulitak, really looked like a stone-age man. He went down on one knee, bracing himself with the other leg extended stiffly, in a graceful though fleeting gesture. Old Peter Nokudluk did not bother to kneel, but aimed standing, admired by his son Kokagun, who was looking on.

152

An expert with musk-ox horn bow and arrow near Bathurst Inlet

The igloos at Bathurst were like those at Otokiak's camp. Banked with snow, they were provided with stoves, and stovepipes stuck out of their domes. The usual small wood was burned; larger pieces of wood could not have been used in a snow house, which soon would melt with continuous heat.

The women went out with U-shaped forks made of caribou antlers, to dig up the ground willows from beneath the snow. You saw them going and coming with great bundles of the stuff on their backs. D'Arcy said there was quite a stand of willows not far from the post, an amazing thing, considering that they grew practically on the Arctic Circle.

One day an Eskimo hunter came in from the east, bringing, among other things, a perfectly white caribou skin. It was from an albino caribou, which is almost unheard-of. The value of an ordinary caribou hide was $1.25. I bought this one for only $2.50, and felt like an exploiter. But the thin-faced, long-haired Eskimo smiled delightedly. With this unexpected wealth he was able to acquire many more things at the post than he had anticipated.

His name was Iksik. He lived at an encampment two sleeps away to the east—on the route to Perry River. When D'Arcy said that Iksik had once acted as guide for Learmonth, years before, I made a deal with him. He agreed to act as my guide to Perry River for a flat sum of $50. He would supply his own food and dog-feed. His wife and little daughter had accompanied him on this trip and would therefore be with us as far as their igloo. That would mean I would have to keep Kamingoak and his dogteam.

Kamingoak, who acted as interpreter for me when I was talking with Iksik, tried to prejudice me against him. "He's light-fingered," said Kamingoak. "He's not to be trusted."

"I forgot to tell you," D'Arcy put in, "that he's the son of that husband-murderess . . ."

154

A different type of igloo. A stove inside burns only a handful or so of willow branches. Reason: if more were burned—house melts down

Nothing could turn me against Iksik. I liked the man— he must have been about thirty. Maybe it was his profile, that recalled Koikhok's just a little, for he had a prominent nose and a smiling face.

"How far is it to Perry River?" I asked him.

"Five, maybe six sleeps," said Iksik.

Satisfied with our deal, I hurried preparations. Kamingoak loaded up our sled and on February 26 all was ready.

Dick was planning to leave Bathurst Inlet that afternoon on his return trip to Coppermine, westward along the coast. So we could literally be turning our backs on each other, since my way led eastward.

We said farewell with the usual gestures and emotions of white men, who on such occasions are always aware of the bigness of the world and the perishability of life. Eskimos part with far more dignity. They go away silent and solitary into the emptiness of their frozen land.

XI

postscript to the mountie patrol

IKSIK, FOR THE GREATER PART OF THE TIME, HAD TO RUN beside his team, for his wife and little daughter were riding on his sled. His wife wore a ribbon around her head because she had headaches, Kamingoak volunteered.

Also running beside Iksik's team for part of the way were some pups, only a few months old, but eager to imitate the older dogs, anxious to prove that they were able to run and were ready for harness. Those pups had a self-conscious look, trotting along like that beside the harnessed dogs. They were a nuisance. Since they were never tied up at night but were allowed inside our igloos, they got into everything.

The first day out was bright and clear and we sped swiftly along on the sea ice at some distance from shore, to avoid the pressure-ridges. At a distance of eight miles from Bathurst Inlet, we could still see the rugged hills around it, when we looked back. There was little wind, but a slight ground drift made the snow seem to flow over the ice. Now and then the komatik slipped up small ridges and bounced down. Some of the pressure ridges that had to be circumvented looked like volcanic eruptions of blue ice.

The dogs' feet twinkled ahead, and they seemed glad to be on the trail again. But something they had eaten at the post had given them a greater thirst than usual. Time and time again they picked up snow on the run, pushing their open mouths into it and gulping it down thirstily. The pups almost upset themselves following the example.

Kamingoak whistled softly to the dogs, a single encouraging note, as he ran beside them. He was proud of his team, which did make a good appearance, especially in comparison with Iksik's scrawny dogs.

For a time we travelled along the the base of high bluffs of yellow sandstone. We reached Gordon Bay at nightfall, where was a tiny empty igloo that Iksik had built for himself and family on the way to Bathurst.

We all crowded into it for the night. All five of us slept on the sleeping bench—Iksik, his wife, his little daughter, Kamingoak and I. You don't travel in the Arctic if you can't stand lack of privacy.

We shared the same bed and the same chamber-pot (the usual empty lard-can). After Iksik and his family had used it, without any embarrassment, it was passed on to me. When it came Peter's turn, he shocked me by behaving exactly as some white men would: he laughed loudly and obscenely . . .

We spent a cold night, because an old igloo ices up quickly at that time of the year. This one had to be scraped inside and chinked outside a bit before we could settle down. The newer and fresher an igloo is, the warmer it is. Snow is an insulation against cold, whereas ice seems to transmit it.

Next day I was weary and moody—partly the result of an uncomfortable night, partly the result of the cold I had caught in the warm trading post.

"What kind of medical kit did you take along on your

dogteam trips?"—is a question people often ask me. I reflect. "Let's see . . . well, I had a couple of aspirin somewhere."

Out of Gordon Bay we struck inland, following a frozen river at the base of some rocky cliffs. Then uphill, along rough gullies, and we came out on a white, featureless plateau. I was in no mood to see pictures that day.

Actually, I, who was fleeing white men's society, was missing Dick's.

The constant jingle of the dog-harness bells was already annoying me, when Peter Kamingoak suddenly burst out in loud singing. What he sang was evidently much favored by missionaries: "Jingle Bells!" Then, to disturb the great silence still more, he yelled: "Hi-yo, Silver!"

Late at night we struck another tiny igloo that Iksik had built on the outward trip. I decided not to share it, and asked Kamingoak to show me his much-boasted skill as an igloo builder.

Kamingoak walked a distance from Iksik's snow house, which glowed palely for awhile, then became dark and invisible when they put out their primus stove. Evidently they, too, wanted to get a good night's rest.

Now that the jingling of the bells and the creaking of the komatik had stopped, all was quiet. A few yards away from me I could hear a faint crunching as Kamingoak, with his snow-knife, probed the snow, searching for the right kind of building material. I could see his shadow faintly. The sleeping dogs nearby looked like rock outcroppings in the darkness.

Then Kamingoak cut his snow blocks and placed them in a spiral line around him. He was a snail-creature building his shell. I ploughed across the drifts and gave him a candle, which he lit. And again I walked up and down to keep warm.

Slowly the blocks rose around him, enclosing him until he sank out of sight. Slowly and carefully he laid one block against another and one row of blocks upon another. The candle light showed through the wall of snow. I could see Kamingoak's dark silhouette bending and stretching, scraping, lifting the blocks of snow around him. At last the dome was in place. I chinked the cracks from the outside.

As soon as Kamingoak had unpacked the caribou skins and spread them over the snow-bench, I went inside and sat there, still feeling miserable, and helpless. But when the primus stove and the grub-box had been brought in, I got busy, cooking supper, while Kamingoak fed the dogs. At last he crawled through the small opening on his belly and sealed us in for the night.

In Bathurst I had followed Dick's example, with variations, when I laid in provisions for this trip. Canned foods are difficult to handle in sub-zero weather. So I had emptied the cans, cut up the contents, and let them freeze solid again in blocks and cakes. Melting and cooking them over the primus stove was an easy matter.

Finally, warmed by the food we had eaten, we crawled into our sleeping bags. And long before midnight our two shapeless and prostrate forms were spouting little jets of steam into the darkness.

Next day, we did not travel, but slept late and rested. My cold left me, and with it my depression. By nightfall my mind was active with ideas—for new picture-stories, new dogteam trips to unknown parts.

We got an early start on Monday and reached Iksik's camp in a few hours, while everything was bathed in a rosy light from the rising sun.

As we sped along, we twice saw a small cloud of vapor on the distant hills.

"*Tuktu!*" Iksik said, pointing. At the magic word, cari-

Hair on back standing up with excitement, husky swallows chunks of frozen caribou meat

bou, the dogs leaped ahead. But they needed little encouragement, they realized they were going home.

There were only two large igloos. In one of them Iksik lived with his family: his wife, little daughter, and two adopted sons. The boys had been baptized by the R.C. missionary at Bathurst and their Christian names were Etienne and François.

The other igloo belonged to John Ohina and his wife, Lucy Anagaik. Kamingoak and I spent the night with them.

I looked at Lucy Anagaik with more than usual interest, for before me was the notorious husband-killer, the murderess I had heard about.

Now she had married John Ohina. While she was over forty, he seemed 10 years younger. Her kind, smiling face was tattooed.

Her movements were unusually alert and supple. The igloo was bright and clean. I noticed that her ulu, with which she scraped the ice window, had a handle of musk-ox horn.

Anagaik's second husband was a good hunter. The pot was kept full of caribou stew. Their dogteam looked well fed. Ohina was smart looking, with a trimmed moustache and with well made caribou clothes. I was in the presence of a happy couple, devoted to one another. Probably she had been as devoted to her dead husband, and it must have cost her some agony of spirit to carry out his wishes when she pulled the trigger which his arthritic fingers could not manage . . .

We consumed vast quantities of tea and meat while there. All the meat is eaten and not a vestige of the caribou is wasted, ever. When the hide has been stripped off for clothing, the carcass is cut up for food. The meat is eaten raw or boiled; the broth is drunk. Sometimes the blood is stirred into the broth, to enrich it. The marrow bones are sucked dry. The intestines go to the dogs. The stomach, containing half digested lichens, is boiled and eaten—it is not unlike Scotch haggis. The back-fat provides fuel and light and is also eaten raw and frozen. I have heard tales of the wasteful slaughter by Eskimos, but I have never seen any signs of it. There is no waste in their economy.

With Iksik and his two sons I went next morning to look for his meat caches in the neighborhood. It was amazing how easily he found them—there was no mark I could see, only a slight swelling in the snow.

Anagaik, the husband killer, attacks a caribou leg with her ulu

With Iksik the old skills would die. For his two sons, who had been to mission school, actually boasted of their deficiencies. In fumbling pidgin English they said they had almost forgotten the Eskimo language, and asserted that they could not build a snow house or drive a dogteam. Iksik told me that the boys did help him on the traplines. They did this for the white men's luxuries they could obtain at the trading post in exchange for the fox pelts.

Soon we were off again towards the northeast—in the direction of Queen Maud Gulf, although my Eskimo friends did not know it by that name. For the remaining hundred and fifty to two hundred miles, we would be on a deserted white plain where no people lived.

We were a small company of three, for Iksik had left his family behind. However, the first day out from Iksik's camp, we were joined by a strange dogteam—three mangy dogs and one pup in harness, doing its feeble best. The young man was apparently from Bathurst, and Iksik knew him. His name was to me quite unpronounceable, and I ended up by calling him "Useless."

Useless was the most worthless Eskimo I ever met. He had been to the mission school with Iksik's sons Etienne and François. He was wearing a wornout suit-coat, a stinking artiggi that was almost hairless, over which he had a ragged store-bought parka, evidently a mission cast-off. The harness of the team was broken and badly mended. Useless seemed to own nothing in the world except his mangy dogs, a torn and dirty Prayer-book, and an empty gasoline drum on his sled. Where he was going and why remained to the end a mystery. Evidently he had set out after us with the hope of being fed and housed, for until we reached Perry River he clung like a leech.

I could not talk to him. He seemed neither to speak nor understand English. For that matter, he talked little, and

Iksik and Kamingoak simply grunted good-naturedly at him. They regarded him with tolerance, this vagabond Eskimo. But I was irritated, and showed it when he hung round that night and crowded into the igloo Iksik built.

I asked Kamingoak about him, when we were settled in. Where was Useless going? What did he do—where live? And why was he so poverty-stricken? On his right hand he wore a silver ring—as some Eskimos do who have been married by the Church. Where was his wife? I was told that Useless had been married, but his wife's parents had given the girl to someone else. As to where he was going and why, Kamingoak simply shrugged and smiled. Who knew? Who cared?

Useless stood around like a whimpering pup. He helped himself to our tea and tobacco, pilot biscuits, and the remains of our evening meal. He was always hungry.

It was the climax when I woke up in the middle of the night to find him sitting over our roaring primus stove, using precious fuel. Why had he not gone to sleep when we did? I shook Kamingoak awake, and had my answer: Useless did not own a sleeping bag!

At length he turned off the primus stove, wrapped himself up in the ragged caribou skin upon which he had been sitting, and crowded in between Peter Kamingoak and me for warmth. It did not improve my peace of mind, that I still resented his infiltration.

The flat, featureless country sped away behind us, and more flat, featureless country came towards us. My map was of little help. There was a dotted line showing "Ellice River." I asked Kamingoak about it. He gave me an Eskimo name about a foot long, but said it could also be the Ellice River.

We were still going roughly northeast. The direction was shown by the ripples of snow sculptured by the prevailing winds.

Numerous tracks were now to be seen, mostly of fox. Also a wolf and a caribou track. Both excited the dogs.

We were crossing numerous lakes which must turn the country into a swamp during summer.

"You first white man here," said Kamingoak.

The idea that I was perhaps the first white man to venture into those parts somehow did not make me feel like Balboa. Who cared? Certainly not the wolf or the fox that had made off in haste at the sound of our coming.

There was daylight now from 7.30 in the morning until 5.30 in the afternoon. The level rays of sunlight sometimes played strange tricks with shadows. In a certain light the dogs' legs looked as though bent backward, as though refracted in water.

From the way the shadows slanted it was obvious that Iksik was still leading us towards the northeast. Before we set out, I studied my map and estimated that Perry River post was about 150 miles away, due east. I wondered why Iksik had swerved again slightly towards the north, and I found out when, that first night, we reached a deserted igloo, just big enough to hold us.

As usual, I was struck with admiration. I can never get over my wonder at how Eskimos hit these isolated igloos, finding them with apparently no trouble in the great white wastes.

For supper that night, we had caribou meat that Iksik had dug up from one of his caches. He had cut it into steaks with an axe. Here, for the cooks and gourmets, is how Kamingoak prepared those steaks, which we will call caribou steak à *la igloo*:

> Put steak into a hot frying pan with a lump of backfat. Fry quickly on both sides. Remove it and put it into a pot of melted snow. Add mixed dehydrated vegetables, a can of noodle soup, and a

spoonful of Bovril. Let all simmer together gently for 20 minutes.

Useless, our faithful companion, ate his share on a borrowed tin plate—he had none—and shovelled it down with a piece of wood taken from a grub-box. For dessert we all —including Useless—had pilot biscuits and jam, washed down by mugs of tea, black and strong.

As we left that camp next day, the hills ahead loomed ever higher. Hours afterwards, I suddenly realized they were islands. We were on sea-ice again. You could tell by the cracking and groaning noises made by the ice.

We were on Queen Maud Gulf, all right, but we had overshot our mark by several miles to the north. I had been right: we should have struck more directly to the east from Iksik's camp. But I was also wrong, as I learned later in discussing the trip with experienced Arctic travellers. In such a featureless landscape, it is dangerous to aim directly at your goal. Nine times out of ten you will miss it. Then you will not know in which direction to look for it, so you turn and turn and lose your bearings. Experienced travellers—and Iksik was one—intentionally aim to the left or right of their goal. They overshoot the mark in a pre-determined direction. Then, from that point onward, they know in which direction lies their objective.

We turned slightly southward, now, following the coast, crossing some pressure ridges, which were occasionally pushed up in strange forms resembling stalagmites. The dogs had a big time with these ice pinnacles, using them as lamp-posts.

How the boys found that night's camp I will never know. They had a conference, and struck out determinedly in a certain direction inland as though they knew where they were going. And sure enough, at nightfall, we reached something that looked like a big snowed-under igloo. The boys dug the drift-snow away and lo and behold! There, in the wilderness, was one of the tidiest little wooden shacks you could imagine.

To find, in the middle of nowhere (or rather, somewhere near Great Bear Point, Queen Maud Gulf) a little wooden house, with floorboards, a tar-paper ceiling, a tiny window, a wooden bed-frame, chest of drawers, and table, all home-made, and all startlingly clean by Far North standards, was nothing short of amazing. It may have belonged to a white trapper once; or it may still be inhabited occasionally by a prosperous native family. Who knew, and who cared? We settled in. But I was more than usually particular in my housekeeping that night. I wanted to be sure that the little house was left as neat and clean as we had found it.

I have no idea why Iksik was, that night, suddenly filled with religious fervor. It was a Friday, I believe, and early in March, 1949, for anyone with a church-calendar handy. Did he hope to convert me, a pagan, to his Roman Catholicism? I could never make it out, but in that strange house this is what happened.

Iksik asked me for three candles. These he lit and placed in a row on a low shelf in one corner. Then he drew an empty box up in front of it. I gradually realized he was fixing up a chapel!

He then handed Useless a tin can and a knife, and muttered some instructions to him. After this, he gabbled some prayers, in mixed Latin and Eskimo, genuflecting, chanting, standing and turning. All the while, Useless banged the tin can at appropriate intervals.

Peter snickered. Useless looked sheepish. I stared, in astonishment. And Iksik remained as sober as a judge—I mean, priest. At the end of the performance he said the Lord's Prayer in jumbled English. Then, looking pleased with himself, he got up from his knees.

168

A storm raged outside, whistling around the corners, rattling the window. After dinner—more caribou again—we talked about religion. Iksik wanted to know why I was neither an Anglican nor a Roman Catholic. I said—through Kamingoak—that I had my own religion. Iksik wanted to know what kind of religion was mine. I said I was something of a medicine-man, I had cured some babies in the Eastern Arctic, who had bad eyes. (As a matter of fact, near Nueltin Lake, two years before, I had bathed out some babies' eyes with boracic acid.) Iksik asked whether I could predict the weather. I said that, to do so, I would have to get into my sleeping bag. Iksik said he would like me to tell him what kind of weather we would have next day: would the wind drop, and would the sky be clear?

It was all too funny, and I decided to enjoy myself. So, deep inside my sleeping bag I let out some wild whoops. Everybody became hushed. You could hear nothing but the wind. Then, after a pause, I put my head out of the bag and said with great seriousness that the wind would drop in two or three hours and that tomorrow the sun would shine.

Iksik and Useless looked much impressed. Kamingoak seemed not to know what to think. Then Iksik, who had left his wife behind, asked: "Will I find a woman at Perry River?"

I dove back into my bag, wriggled violently, let out a few more whoops, emerged when I sensed the deadly silence in the room.

"Yes," I said, "you will get one, if you look around."

Iksik wanted to ask more questions, but I said my exertions had exhausted me, and that he should wait to test my prophetic powers.

Everything about that little lost house, and everything that transpired that night remain in my memory as strangely improbable. But it really happened.

The wind did drop during the night. What matter that it started up again next morning? My reputation as a prophet was saved, particularly since the sun was shining brightly.

A steady wind blew, there was a strong ground-drift, and we were soon plastered with snow, travelling into the teeth of the wind. But gradually the wind shifted, the sun shone brightly, until we sped along with a good tail-wind, enjoying it and the seething sound of the snow blown before us.

With a little effort, by travelling late, we could have reached Perry River post that night. But in the Arctic, dog-team drivers like to make a grand entrance into a settlement. Usually, therefore, a camp is made the night before not far from the goal, so that the teams can start out fresh and arrive at their destination in fine fettle.

We camped that night very early—it was not much after four, I imagined, from the position of the sun. A deserted igloo, a little old and a little cold, was our habitation for the night.

It was a rather dirty one, as well, and Useless, with his eternal nose-blowing (nose held between thumb and finger, snot flying) did nothing to improve the place. However, freezing temperatures take care of hygiene in the Arctic . . .

We sat about after supper smoking and drinking tea; Iksik respectfully asked me if it was going to be a good caribou year. We had seen many caribou tracks that day and some fresh droppings. So I confidently predicted a very good year . . .

Next morning the sled-runners were carefully re-iced, for our triumphal dash to Perry River post. While the boys were working, I strolled in the bright sunshine, in which every grain of snow, every crystal of ice glittered.

170

postscript to the mountie patrol

I was in a thoughtful mood, and walked with my head down, like a man searching for something. In fact, I was searching, for we were now in the part of the country where Sir John Franklin's party had abandoned their ships a hundred years before and had wandered in despair to their mysterious death. Supposing I found some tiny relic of that lost Franklin expedition? I knew Learmonth never made a dogteam trip in this region without keeping that expedition in mind, that he was always searching for some sign of it.

Suddenly some reflection of light attracted my eyes. I bent to see what bright object had been struck by the sun. It was a sharp-edged rock, standing on end. A hunter or trapper may have placed it like that as a landmark. Looking closely, I saw that it was heavily streaked with ore, alternating with quartz. Gold? Copper? Or maybe only fool's gold? Supposing it were valuable metal . . . In imagination I could visualize newspaper headlines: a strike, a discovery in the Far North. And I could imagine the sequel: a mine, white men pouring in, greedy for fortune, the land upheaved, the sparkling stillness disturbed, black chimneys rolling out smoke. . . .

Carefully I put the stone on its side and with the toe of my boot covered it with a blanket of snow. Then, feeling rather satisfied with myself, I returned to camp, where the sleds were being loaded.

Exactly a week and a day had passed since we had left Bathurst Inlet. Now, with smooth runners and over smooth sea ice, we sped towards Perry River post. Sled tracks crisscrossed in all directions. The lead dogs kept their noses to the main track, straining at the harness, and the other dogs let out yelps of joy. Then we entered a small horseshoe-shaped cove, and the trading post on Flagstaff Island came into view.

an r. c. m. p. arctic winter patrol

It was with a great cracking of whips and jingling of bells that at last we drew up before a small cluster of buildings, typical of Hudson's Bay Company structures of bygone days, but without the usual Company signboard. Several women and children ran out to see us. Then the trader himself appeared. He was an Eskimo.

XII

eskimo trader

AN ESKIMO IN CHARGE OF A TRADING POST IS A phenomenon in the Far North. Clearly George Angulalik, the native trader at Perry River, was in every way an unusual man. In a single generation he had leaped from bow and arrow hunting to twentieth century commerce. Many natives, after years of trading fox pelts at H.B.C. posts, get deeper and deeper in debt. But Angulalik had built up a considerable credit. When, therefore, it was decided to close this costly and remote post, as not being a paying proposition, he made a bid for it and an arrangement was made that was satisfactory to all parties. I did not understand all the details. All I know is that a trader's license was issued to George Angulalik in 1937; it hangs on the wall of the Perry River post.

It was Angulalik's son, Oakoak, who welcomed us outside the post, where some gasoline barrels were aligned on a smooth stretch of ice—a landing strip for a plane that might, sometime, land there. Oakoak apologized, in fair English, for his father's absence. Angulalik had taken the dogteam on a trip to his new post at Sherman Inlet. After

Mingalik thaws out salmon at Perry River. Overhead hang fox skins to dry

Oakoak had made us comfortable, he told us with obvious pride about his father.

The Company had run the post at a loss—and no wonder. Only about 50 families came in to trade, and the cost of transportation of the trade goods was extremely high. When I was there, for instance, coal cost $240 a ton, sugar was thirty-five cents a pound, flour was $24 per hundredweight, rice was $1. a pound. These goods had to be shipped by rail from Edmonton to Fort McMurray; then by boat to Fort Smith; then portaged by truck to Fort Fitzgerald; then by boat down the Mackenzie River to Tuktoyaktuk. From there, an annual schooner carried goods to Coppermine and Cambridge Bay. Supplies destined for Perry River had to be transshipped from Cambridge Bay; or, if the ice closed in again too soon, sent across on the sea ice by dogteam in the winter. A long haul! To illustrate how long: imagine if New York had to be supplied from St. Louis *via* the Mississippi River to New Orleans and thence by sea. By comparison, simple!

Angulalik had prospered because he required little from the Outside for himself and family. They lived off the land. Caribou and seal were the chief items of their diet and furnished them, as well, with year-round clothing and tents for the summer. By 1949 he was ready to open a new trading post, still farther to the east, at Sherman Inlet, Adelaide Peninsula. He owned two schooners, the *Sea Otter* and the *Tudlik*, both equipped with engines. He used these for transportation of trading goods to Perry River, to take furs to Cambridge Bay, and also to supply his new post at Sherman Inlet. And, for a fee, he conveyed goods for the Hudson's Bay Company to their own post at Gjoa Haven, King William Island.

Oakoak, the son of the trader, was about twenty-four years old and had a young wife, Suzie Mingilgak, and a baby daughter, Flossie Ototakak.

Pulled to the shore on Wagstaff Island where the Perry River Post stands, this Diesel powered boat belongs to Eskimo trader Angulalik

I was interested to see how this family lived, what they had done by way of adapting a white man's house to their way of life. (Suzie Mingilgak was of partly white blood.) The family preferred to sleep on the floor—the bedstead had been taken apart and stored in one of the rooms. A slop bucket stood prominently in the kitchen. A mirror hung on the wall—but I never saw anyone look into it. There was an old gramophone, never used, and a few broken old rec-

ords on a shelf. There was a wind-charger to supply electricity, but it was out of order. The radio, thank God, did
not work. There was a table and three chairs. We used the
chairs the first night, but by the following day when we
were no longer outsiders, we all sat on the floor when eating.

A coal-burning cookstove provided what heat there was
—which was not much. What could you expect, with coal
costing $240. a ton? Large hunks of caribou and piles of
fish stood beside it, to thaw out gradually. The windows,
baseboards, and part of the ceiling were thickly frosted. I
never remember being colder than during those first hours
in that house, waiting for our supper.

Suzie had at once put on a caribou stew to cook. But her
movements were so languid that it looked as though supper would never be done. Her dream-like air added to my
impatience. She wore a calico Mother Hubbard over her
artiggi. She had been educated at the Aklavik mission
school, but had not let this bother her; she seemed to be a
typically calm and happy Eskimo woman.

At last we sat down to the caribou stew, feeling awkward
on those chairs. I dug out some unusual tidbits from my
supplies—a can of sardines, two chocolate bars—and supplied the tea. After the feast, we smoked and talked.

What I wanted to know was whether a dogteam could
be found to take me south to Garry Lake.

Oakoak looked thoughtful, meditated, shrugged, then
shook his head. Only one family lived near the post, and
they had no dogs. The hunters, inland, would not pay a
visit to the post until late spring. . . .

I would have to give up the trip to the south. Even if I
could find a dogteam to take me as far as Garry Lake, I
might be stranded there for months before I could get out
to Baker Lake. Instead I decided to go to Cambridge Bay,
across the sea ice, and from there take a plane out.

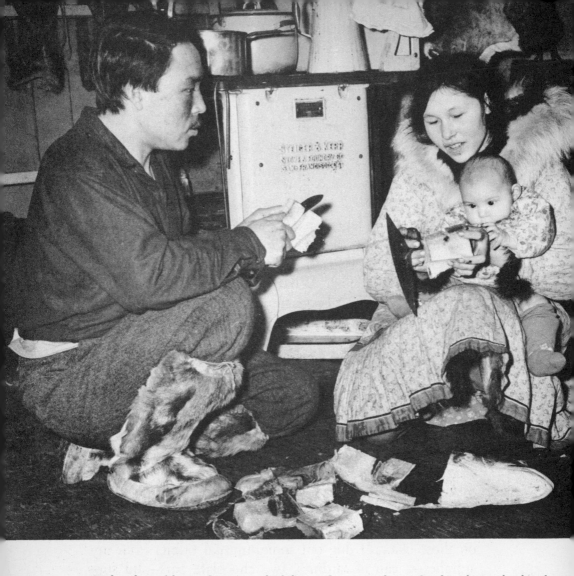

Oakoak and his wife Mingalgik have frozen salmon for lunch, in the kitchen of the Perry River Post

I did not want to go to Cambridge Bay. Having seen Fort Churchill, on Hudson Bay, I knew what army bases in the Far North were like, and I could do without seeing another.

Oakoak had been to Cambridge Bay recently and he talked with bewilderment of the waste. All the Eskimos could live on what was thrown out there. Things of great value—food, tools, clothing . . .

"The white man is wasteful!" he said.

I could not explain our ways to this Eskimo trader.

Useless continued to hang around, and our host fed him as a matter of course. Gradually I began to see him with Eskimo eyes . . . He was there—he was hungry—there was food. It was as simple as that.

We ate well at Oakoak's. There was always food for everyone.

Besides caribou, we ate quantities of red salmon and big tom-cod. I thoroughly liked raw frozen fish, much to the natives' astonishment. I passed a difficult test when I ate with enjoyment some dried meat dipped in seal oil. It had a slightly fishy taste, but was good. Seeing that everyone watched me swallow this, I asked Kamingoak the reason. Said he: "Usually it makes white men vomit!"

Angulalik's store at Perry River looked like any Hudson's Bay Company store, down to the last frosted nail head. I stamped around in there for some time, buying provisions for my trip to Cambridge Bay. Stupidly, at one point, I removed a mitt. My hand steamed like dry ice and when my fingertips touched my fur pants they were hard. I had frozen a couple of fingers inside a store, after coming through the inland patrol without serious mishap! It was a nuisance, for they were my most useful camera-fingers.

The store was well stocked with a variety of merchandise. There were bolts of stroud, of calico, stacks of heavy-duty woolen pants for summer wear. Caribou skins, frozen stiff as boards, were stacked to the ceiling. In the food line were pilot biscuits, canned meats, canned and dehydrated vegetables, and chocolate bars. The Eskimo is developing a

Oakoak behind the store counter at the Perry River trading post. The post belongs to his father Angulalik

sweet tooth—much to the detriment of said tooth. Prowling around, I discovered four gramophone records, three lanterns, two razors, and several cans of pipe tobacco. Hanging from the rafters were fish nets, snow anchors, buckets, and tea kettles. A few rifles were stacked against one wall.

Oakoak grinned happily, proud to have me see how much merchandise was in the store.

I ran across some things that surprised me. There was a great quantity of rope and twine. With caribou and seal so plentiful, I should have thought caribou sinew and seal-thongs would be used in preference to rope. Oakoak said that rope was "a new fashion" and that Eskimos now preferred it. Yet sealhide thongs are much stronger and easier to handle in cold weather.

Then I came upon a carton of baby bottles and nipples.

Kamingoak and Oakoak assured me that the white men were persuading Eskimo women to use these things, as being better. I would just like to see an Eskimo mother in a tupik or igloo sterilizing those bottles and nipples, heating the baby food to the right temperature! (I did see how this was attempted, on my next trip north.)

Most of the fur turned in by the trappers was white fox. Dozens of pelts hung from the rafters. They were exceptionally clean. I learned that Angulalik had a reputation for turning in clean, soft, and well-dried skins.

Neither Angulalik nor his son, Oakoak, had been to mission school and so knew little English. How, I asked, did these men manage to keep their accounts with the H.B.C. at Cambridge Bay? And how did they manage to write out their orders?

Oakoak smiled, and I did not have my question answered until a week later, at Cambridge Bay. There I was shown one of Angulalik's orders. Like all Eskimos, he had an artistic gift, could draw pictures. He simply copied the lettering on the boxes and cans. The result was quaint, and occasionally it was too cryptic to be understood. The Hudson's Bay Company men somehow managed to figure out orders such as this:

½ dozen cheap prices.
1 case Three Stars Flaming Light Matches, No. 50.
10 lbs. of women's underwear.
¾ the Okonite Company No. 8.
12 Icy Sesel. (ice chisels)
6 Ointment, capsicum Compound, Beware of the Eyes.
1 doz. Sale Price No. 288.

One night there was a real traffic jam in Suzie Mingilgak's kitchen. Two families had arrived. They were sightseers, according to Kamingoak; they were there to see me.

Eventually they stopped milling round and settled down for a quiet talk. The subject of conversation was the white man—not me, this time, but other samples of "kabloonas." Some of the men had driven dogteams for kabloonas at Bathurst Inlet, Cambridge Bay, and Gjoa Haven. They seemed to be talking with special eagerness, and I persuaded Kamingoak to interpret what they said. He did so intermittently. They thought kabloonas could hardly be rated as high as Eskimos. But one must be polite and kind to them.

When several of the men had their say—and Eskimos, unlike white men, do not all talk at once, but listen while another talks—Iksik began to speak. When he had finished, Kamingoak interpreted: "He says you are not too bad. He says you at least try to be like us."

I felt flattered. Iksik and I got along together famously. He had always been ready to do me small favors, helping me brush the snow off my clothes, picking tea leaves out of my mug—without servility, merely out of kindness. And I recalled very well that once he had offered me his wife. "You can sleep with her any time," said he. His old wife had not presented too great a temptation, but refusing had

Perry River native sets a fox trap. The snow block will conceal trap entirely

caused me an embarrassing moment. Well, apparently Iksik understood.

It was then Oakoak's turn to talk. He had once driven a dogteam for a carpenter going to Cambridge Bay. "He was always crabbing," said Oakoak. "He wanted to camp for the night at two o'clock in the afternoon. He never smiled."

The Eskimos all shook their heads and clicked their tongues at this. I gathered that the carpenter was being collectively damned.

There was time to sit around talking, for the wind had arisen during the night of our arrival at Perry River and continued to blow for the next two days. My arrangements were made for the trip to Cambridge Bay, so there was nothing to do but wait out the storm. I spent some of the time bringing on my journal. Always, I had a swarm of Eskimo children around me, their bright eyes following intently, their little faces getting in the way of my pen.

As usual, my maps interested everybody, although the names on them meant nothing. Try to imagine an Eskimo pointing to some islands and saying: "Those are the Royal Geographical Society Islands."

Oakoak told me the Eskimo names of a few of the lakes we had crossed. One of them was Kimaktun Lake. It was named for a native who had been killed "by lightning." Another lake was called Kaglilik, meaning "the large snow-house where the People used to dance." Krigalik, another lake, means "the place of the nose"—whether having to do with a real nose or the contour of the lake or perhaps a rock profile, I know not.

When I discussed distances with Oakoak, it was the usual thing. Miles meant nothing to him. He would look, listen, wrinkle his brow, then say: "That is two sleeps away." I judged that this represented roughly 70-80 miles of fair-weather travelling.

On the third day, the wind abated. We were wakened early by Niakok, Angulalik's brother, who came into the house, stepped over Kamingoak, Iksik, and myself in our sleeping bags on the kitchen floor, and went into the next room where Oakoak and his wife and baby slept. Then an older woman with a tattooed face came in. She was Niakok's wife, Haemok. Soon the baby was brought in and everyone sat round playing with it, while waiting for Mingilgak to get breakfast. She was going to make some bannock and fry it in seal-oil. Everyone liked that.

Niakok's wife, Haemok, was holding the child when it began to show signs of discomfort. At leisure, someone looked for the lard pail. Haemok transferred the baby to between her knees. The slow-motion search for the pot continued. It was not found soon enough. Calmly, Haemok cupped her hand to catch the trickle . . . Then the steaming little stream escaped her hand, splashing on the floor a couple of feet from some frozen salmon.

No one paid any attention. The child was not punished —nor was the frozen fish wiped off. Everybody smiled, including the baby.

Niakok was not the only man Haemok had. She had two husbands. All three lived together happily and had done so for many years. The men were very good friends indeed.

I liked Niakok, who seemed to have a good sense of the ridiculous. Kamingoak had told him about my medicine-man performance in the sleeping bag and about my weather predictions. The little gray-haired man looked across the room at me with a twinkle in his eyes and rattled off a string of gibberish. I replied with another string of gibberish. Niakok did not crack a smile, but his eyes twinkled merrily as again he replied, in still more jabberwocky. It left the rest of the crowd puzzled.

That day I jigged for fish through five feet of sea ice. Oakoak caught quite a haul of tom-cod. One minute those big fish were so alive and the next lined up on the ice, frozen stiff.

The temperature must have been thirty below. I froze my fingers again as I focussed my camera on Oakoak, absorbed in his fishing. I hoped for the best with my color film, for the colors that day were exciting: the bright blue sky, the white ice, Oakoak's brown furs, the opalescent fish, and the long, long purple shadows . . .

One Medalist camera was out of order. Three different things were wrong with it. As usual, near the end of my trips, I was beginning to worry, anxious to know what I had on my films.

And as usual I was dreading getting back to civilization. It's always a jolt. Eyes, ears, and mental reactions all need to be readjusted. That day, out on the ice with Oakoak, I realized that in less than two weeks I would be hearing the old banal questions—and would be giving the old, banal answers. The questions would range from "How did you ever stand the cold?" to "Did the Eskimos offer you their wives?" The voices would be shrill, my nerves a bit on edge. How senseless those clumsy looking beetles—automobiles— shuttling along in the streets! How idiotic some amplified voice announcing "In two seconds it will be exactly twelve-thirty!" It is hard to take this sort of thing when you are still, in imagination, hearing a komatik creaking beneath you and when your eyes are still looking out upon endless horizons. Again friends would say: "He's still bushed."

XIII

going...

Oakoak accompanied us part way to cambridge bay
the following morning. Our report of caribou on our way
in to Perry River had excited him, and gave him a welcome excuse to go hunting.

That last night at the post I was invited to join in a
poker game. I didn't, but sat by, looking on. The way Eskimos play poker, it resembled the white man's game in
only one respect—you win or you lose. I could not fathom
by what rules they played. In the end, the women were
summoned. They rose to get some caribou skins and other
articles that their man had lost. Oakoak lost heavily. Iksik
acquired Oakoak's alarm clock—it would be an ornament
for his distant igloo. Useless won a much needed pair of
pants and a calico artiggi. Kamingoak acquired a thermos
bottle, a new cigarette lighter, and a whip. It was a pleasure to play poker with a trader who kept on losing.

Next morning four sleds were loaded for various trips.
First to go was Oakoak. He travelled light, hoping to bring
back some caribou. Then Kamingoak and I set out, with

our eleven dogs jingling their bells. After us came Iksik, his dogs looking better fed for their stay at this hospitable post. Trailing at the end came Useless, who had attached himself to Iksik again.

Suzie Mingilgak did not even stand in the doorway to see us off. She was busy nursing the baby. So we just lit out, with yelping dogs, cracking of whips, and a groaning of loaded komatiks.

For a time we were retracing our tracks, still visible despite the blown snow. At noon we stopped for tea from the thermos bottles.

As we started on again, following a new trail, Iksik fell behind and turned off to the south. He went slowly, searching for a lost track. The last I saw of him was when he turned inland. He had gone without lengthy farewells. The immense land swallowed Iksik again, and in three sleeps he would find his home on the white snowy waste.

In his wake went Useless, with his scrawny dogs. A light wind fluttered his ragged artiggi. Then he, too, vanished from sight.

That night Oakoak built us a magnificent igloo. He was an expert, and I was becoming a judge of snow-craftsmanship. In the darkness his dark shadow moved, bent, with snow-knife probing the snow. Then he found a patch that was suitable. Expertly, rapidly, he cut and placed the blocks. Gradually the snowhouse grew up around him, in a rising spiral, block on block, neatly cut, neatly placed. It was masonry worthy of the old Incas, who worked in stone. The blocks scarcely needed chinking.

Sealed in at last, with the primus stove roaring, and with caribou skins spread over the sleeping bench, we cooked our evening meal. Outside, the dogs were curled up, dozing, waiting for their nightly feed.

Perry River man builds excellent igloo, now finishing the porch

We spent a good night in the silent igloo. Towards dawn —about 6—I woke up to see the snow blocks getting more and more translucent in the morning light. Small clouds of darkness flitted over the white dome from time to time. The wind had risen and was blowing drifts of snow over us.

It was a nasty morning, with low visibility. The sun was merely a luminous spot towards the south, its roundness was hidden by the ground drifts. But we set out.

After an hour, Oakoak turned abruptly inland. He went off, without even a wave of the hand. Within 200 yards, his komatik was lost to sight in the drifts of blowing snow.

We had a tail-wind as we set off over a wild jumble of pack-ice, skirting islands, striking more or less northwest.

For three days we travelled on the sea-ice, our trail being to the northeast of the Melbourne Islands. Smack in the middle of Campbell Bay we found a deserted igloo waiting for us, the first night.

Next day we were storm bound. Anyway, I was feeling sick—something I had eaten the day before had upset me. So we stayed in the igloo, which was old, had iced up, and dripped the minute the primus stove sent out any heat. Several times during the day Kamingoak went outside to dig the dogs out of the drifting snow, lest they suffocate.

The wind dropped a little on the second day, and again we set out towards the northwest. Towards night, on one little island, we came to an igloo where a man had recently died. His corpse was still there, and sitting beside it was his widow. Her face was impassive. Her kudele barely flickered. Immobile she sat, gazing into space, the flame dying.

We stopped at a seal camp in Anderson Bay next day. A mass of land we had noticed before the storm closed in once more turned out to be Melbourne Island. To ascertain such facts often takes hours of travelling.

Kamingoak's lead dog had his nose close to the ground, and we trusted him utterly. He would pull us out of this nothingness into a trail that led somewhere. I gave up trying to look into the wind. It simply made my eyes water and froze my eyelashes together.

190

A Victoria Island man wears the primitive wooden "sunglasses" still in use, and still the best

Dog fight

Circles of snow blocks had been erected around seal breathing holes. A few dead seals lay frozen stiff on the ice. An Eskimo, massive in furs, lumbered towards us.

I passed round cigarettes as Kaminkoak talked to him. He invited us to have some tea at his nearby igloo.

At the seal camp of two igloos, a woman was cutting up a seal. The blood was flowing onto the ice. Bending from the waist, in the immemorial attitude of the Eskimo, she wielded her ulu expertly. Our dogs trembled and whined with excitement. The harness got tangled as they tried to approach the kill.

The Eskimos said: "Let them eat!" And we decided for

Dog fight

once to break the rules. Peter Kamingoak unharnessed
them. In a tense circle, hackles raised, the dogs stood with
their noses pointing inwards towards the fresh meat. The
woman threw some pieces of bloody seal meat onto the
ice. The dogs made a rush, falling upon it like lightning.
Now and then two dogs reared at each other, snarling.
Then again they fell back to gulp down more. One dog
dripped blood from his nose and ears.

Timidly, then, the woman offered me a tidbit, with
blood-stained fingers. It was a piece of seal liver, a northern delicacy. I ate it gladly. How did it taste? Well . . .
like liver!

That night, in one of the seal-hunters' igloos, we all sat talking for a long time, quietly, after supper. We, did I say? *I* listened, drowsily. The kudele, burning seal-oil, flickered. Our shadows lay gigantic on the glittering white walls. The guttural voices were soft and low. It was like a chant, as it rose and fell. There were long silences. The men sat quietly, rarely turning their heads. When they talked, they did not address one another directly. From time to time the woman tended the lamp . . .

From Anderson Bay we struck out briskly across one of the southernmost tips of Victoria Island. In the dawn light the sky and the snowy landscapes were a pearly gray. In the distance loomed the great tower of the Loran (Long Range Navigation) Station at Cambridge Bay, more than 600 feet high.

Soon we beheld a dogteam coming towards us. Two oddly dressed individuals were sitting cross-legged on the sled. Jumping off a few yards from us, both excitedly pointed cameras in our direction. They shouted at us to stand still. Their voices were harsh, their gestures violent . . .

They were creatures from another world. Their eyes were invisible behind big black sun-glasses.

They were men from the army station, out for a ride. They were greatly surprised to find me a white man.

"I guess you don't know we're closed down officially," said one of the men when we had shaken hands. "This thing doesn't work up here. It's too costly to dismantle. We'll probably just leave the stuff behind. $26 million bucks it cost. Gone with the wind!"

The camp itself was a tiny cluster of huts, around which were little mountains of fuel oil drums, wires and insulators, boxes and ropes. About 60 men were stationed there, and most of them had come up for six months. They were all fed up, homesick and anxious to get Outside again.

"Anybody's nuts," said one of the boys, "that comes to the Arctic if he don't have to."

Countless barrels of fuel oil had been flown in to keep the boys warm. A wet canteen had been installed to keep the boys happy. Air Force planes came in weekly, or even oftener, so the boys could write home to Mom and Dad saying, "I now live 100 miles north of the Arctic Circle . . ."

At night the Loran Station tower looked like a gigantic Christmas tree, lit up. But even so, it was only a pinpoint of light in that vast land.

I was invited to stay at the H.B.C. post, until the plane took me out, via Fort Nelson to Edmonton. Kamingoak and I parted for good. After a day or two he would set off on the long trek back to Coppermine.

The first night at the post, no one went to bed much before dawn. I liked manager John Stanners, especially. He and his helper Jack Bourne and I could not get through talking. With John Stanners I could talk freely. A middle-aged bachelor and a Company man of long experience, he had travelled a great deal in the Arctic, was up on its history, and seemed to know everybody. He knew Learmonth well. That year he was being sent to Spence Bay. He looked forward to the new isolated post on Boothia Peninsula, near Ross' North Magnetic Pole. It was also near where Sir John Ross had spent several winters more than a hundred years ago. Like Learmonth, he was keenly interested in the lost Franklin expedition. Like Learmonth, he was loyal to the traditions of the Company. With me, he bemoaned the deteriorating influence on the people of such government enterprises as the Loran Station. He agreed that the Arctic was no place for white-collar boys who could not do without movies and modern conveniences. "Things were better," he said, "when the Company was here without outside influences. I believe the people were happier."

Stanners had a look at the maps I had used, and corrected some of them with their latest information. They had some of the results of the R.C.A.F. map information, and had seen some of the photographs taken from the air in 1946 and 1947.

The map-makers were going to have to change quite a few outlines of the islands in the Canadian archipelago, not to mention some of the lakes, rivers, and longitudes of the mainland. Take Perry River post, for instance: the latest observations moved it to the westward, out of Keewatin District. On the other hand, Pelly Lake would have to be moved over eastward. And say, did I know? The aviation boys had proved that Great Bear Lake was even greater than anyone had thought.

I wondered if it would make much difference to people like Iksik. He would continue to estimate his distances by so many sleeps; would continue to find his directions by the half-obliterated tracks leading from one camp to another; and would continue to call places by the names his forefathers had used, unaware of the names on the Admiralty charts. The thought gave me a feeling of stability.

Stanners, like other old timers, talked about the summer there as being something worth seeing. The break-up of the ice, the flowers appearing at the very edge of the receding snow, the flocks of geese and ducks that sometimes come north—I envied him his life in the Arctic.

"Well, any time you feel like coming up," said Stanners, as we parted, a couple of days later, "There'll be room for you."

"It's a deal," I said.

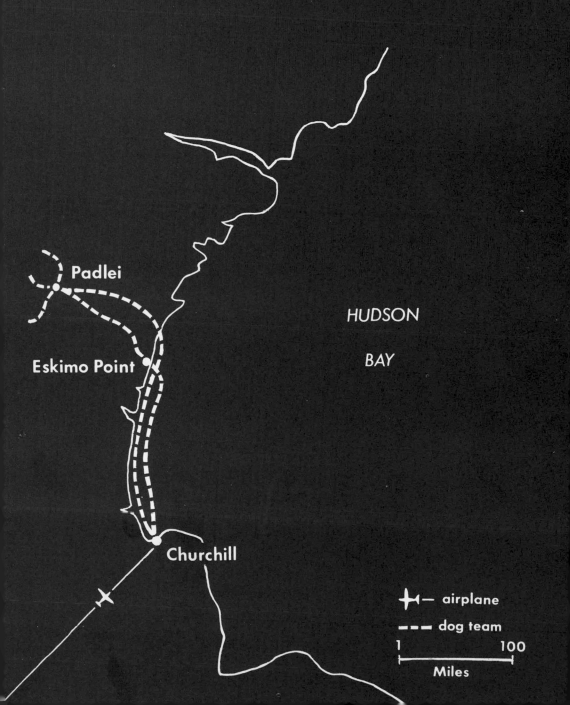

3. portrait of famine:

padlei, 1950

Padlei

Eskimo Point

HUDSON

BAY

Churchill

✈— airplane

- - - dog team

1 ⊢————————⊣ 100

Miles

XIV

cupid rides the komatik
to eskimo point

IN 1950 I VISITED THE LAND OF THE PADLEIMIUTS, WHO
are among the most primitive of the Eskimos. I had not intended going there. It was brought about by sheer accident,
for when I flew to Churchill from Winnipeg and The Pas
it was to accept a year-old invitation.

Delayed and misunderstood telegrams were the cause
of my being stranded in Churchill. I had planned to visit
John Stanners now at Spence Bay, Boothia Peninsula. I
had expected to catch a plane to Baker Lake and from there
go north by dogteam. But when I reached the military base,
Fort Churchill, on January 13, I was informed that the
plane to Baker Lake had left the previous day, and that
there would not be another flight for a month. In reply to
my distress, an officer bellowed that he had sent telegrams
to everyone, including Jesus Christ. This did not soothe
me, and for several days I wandered round in Churchill
like a lost soul, wondering what to do. To charter a plane
from "Arctic Wings," at that time a Catholic mission enterprise, would be ruinous—it would cost $800 at least.
There was nothing in Churchill I wanted to photograph,

and to stay on at the small hotel would be too depressing.

Then I met Bill Carey, R.C.M.P. corporal from Eskimo Point, about 200 miles to the north on Hudson Bay, and before I knew it I was buying provisions. Fortunately an extra Eskimo with dogteam had strung along with Bill and was willing to take me north. From Eskimo Point, Bill said, I could easily find another dogteam to take me inland for some close-ups of the Padleimiuts.

So that is how it happened that I obtained an eyewitness report of these people in a famine year and secured some help for them from a momentarily scandalized world.

Momentarily scandalized. That means, "relief" was rushed in. After that the Padleimiuts and all the other people of the Barren Lands were forgotten, except for the usual registration of births, deaths, marriages, and the issuing of an ever-growing number of Destitute Rations. In their annual autumn migrations, the caribou had by-passed the Padleimiuts. Weakened by hunger, the people had no resistance to disease, and there were epidemics of influenza, measles, and even poliomylitis.

But to get back to Churchill. I'm getting ahead of my story.

Bill Carey had come down from Eskimo Point on several errands, one of which had to do with the polio cases. Also, in connection with the disaster of an R.C. missionary, Father Dionne, the previous autumn. He had gone out in a boat with a native, been caught in a storm, and had vanished.

Bill had once been stationed in Coppermine. He knew Dick Connick and he knew Learmonth. In ten minutes we felt like old friends. Bill had many reasons to want to get back to Eskimo Point in double-quick time. His Eskimo Special Constable had been stricken with polio and had been flown out for treatment; Bill had found a man to

200

replace him, Joe Ulurksit, who accompanied him. Then, Bill was a newly-wed. Only six months previously he had married a childhood sweetheart, Alta, and he wanted to get back to her.

As we loaded our komatiks for the trip, on January 18, I learned that Cupid (in a caribou artiggi and with a musk-ox horn bow) also was with us. Joe Ulurksit, Bill's substitute Special Constable, was going to pick up a bride on the way north. His mother knew of a marriageable girl at Long Point and everything had been arranged. The girl, Mahpie, would be waiting for him. Only Tootoo, my dog-team driver, seemed to have materialistic aims: he wanted to take his dogs north for caribou hunting, and was glad to get pay for the trip. As for me, well, it was a case of renewing a long-standing love-affair with the Arctic.

With favorable weather, Eskimo Point should be reached in about five sleeps—it took longer, for it was a hard trip. We did not have favorable weather; in fact, the soldiers who did weather research stated: "Wind chill too great for dogteam travel." The temperature was near 50 below zero, with a strong ground drift. We set out, January 19, three dogteams crawling northward over rough sea ice along the western shores of Hudson Bay. It took two days to cross Button Bay.

Ulurksit's little bride-to-be was waiting for him at Long Point, where we spent the night in a native shack after a good supper of fried seal liver. Next morning she jumped onto his komatik, and we were off again.

Mahpie was a shy, small creature, who did not look a day over thirteen, although she had to be fifteen, said Bill, in order to be allowed to marry. "Oh well," he said, "Joe can take her along, we can find out how old she is from my records."

For total baggage, Mahpie had an antiquated and solidly

Typical pressure ice on Hudson Bay

frozen handbag. Dressed in fur-clothes, you could not see how developed or undeveloped she was. But when she ran beside the team with tall Ulurksit, she looked like a little girl. She was a valiant little girl, though, for when the sled got into difficulties, she lent an expert hand, lifting and pushing the komatik, untangling dog lines.

We teased Ulurksit about his bride, but he merely grinned. And that night, when we all slept together in a half-snow, half-canvas shelter on the sea ice, Mahpie crawled into her sleeping bag at one side, Ulurksit at the other, into his.

One night we struck an abandoned trapper's shack on the shore and slept there. The shack was a sieve, but it had a rickety stove which Bill put into order, for he had, luckily enough, brought some coal along. In the night, we woke up shivering. The coal had been used up and the wind had increased to a gale. So Bill tore up some shelves and boxes for fuel. "If worst comes to worst, we can tear the shack down and have a *real* fire," he grinned.

Next day we were storm-bound, but with odd bits of wood Bill managed to keep the shack warm enough for us to sit around playing rummy. Little Mahpie and her Joe, when not outside in the storm attending to the dogs, sat inside with us, eating, drinking tea, or dozing. I did not catch them exchanging a single remark. They only looked at one another from time to time with shy smiles.

Against an icy headwind we pushed on next day, travelling without even stopping for a cup of hot tea. Bill had some *quaag* in his grub box—raw frozen meat, cut up into cubes, like candy. It was good, but hard as a rock, dissolving slowly and sometimes freezing to the inside of the cheek.

Our goal that night was a white trapper's house. Long after sunset, a star appeared low on the horizon. As we advanced, it grew bigger. It was the light in the lone trapper's shack . . .

George Lush was the only white trapper in the region— he had been one of the first and now was the last of them. His license had been granted twenty years before, when he

Trapper Lush loaded with fox furs. His home in background

came to the North as surveyor for the Hudson Bay Railway. We were the first white men he had seen in seven months, and though he denied that he was ever lonely, he was eager to talk.

A gray stubbly beard, a partly bald head, and an almost toothless mouth when he smiled were all that betrayed his age, which was 55. He still had a slim, youthful figure. His eyes had that piercing look of sea-captains or men used to searching for something in vast distances.

George was not interested in what was going on Outside. He had a radio, but when the battery had worn out some years before, he had not bothered to replace it. His little world here, on the banks of the Tha-Anne River, interested and excited him. It was the subject of his talk. His dogs, the birds and animals of the region, his traps, the square-flippers (seals) in the bay represented his world. You couldn't be lonely, for there was always too much to do. And when you had finished work, said George, it was good to pass a pleasant hour in the silence, playing solitaire by candle-light.

He cooked us a good meal of caribou steaks and sliced a freshly baked loaf of raisin bread, which he said was not as good as usual.

"Lucky you found me here," he said, "I'm out on my trap-lines most of the winter. Got another shack 70 miles inland."

He said he caught anywhere from 17 to 100 foxes during the open season. It kept him busy setting and inspecting his 250 traps. He caught a few cross fox, many white fox, and sometimes wolves and whiskey-jacks (Canada jays).

George Lush went in to Churchill only once a year, for provisions. He lived on seal meat, caribou, fish, geese and ducks when he could get them. From the outside world, he got tea, coffee, flour, dried fruit, and butter—these in exchange for his fox pelts. He skinned and stretched the fox skins before taking them to the Hudson's Bay Company post to pay on his "debt" there, Eskimo fashion. His debt was evidently a mounting credit, since he was thinking of "pulling out."

"The North's gettin' too crowded for me," he said. "Planes roarin' overhead. Army boys, police boys, weather boys, bug boys—too many white men comin' up here now."

He had six well-fed dogs, and talked about them as if they were human. He was sure his lead-dog, Whitey, was the best in the world. "And don't let me hear you call huskies fierce," said he. "Mine eat out of my hands. I never beat up my dogs—don't have to. Treat 'em well, and they love you!"

They were his only love. In all the years he had been living in the North, George Lush had never spent a night in an igloo. He had little use for Eskimos, and avoided them. When he travelled, he carried a double tent and tent poles with him. He had never married.

The shack had two rooms and a kitchen, but one of the rooms was shut off for the winter. I peeped into it and saw a sewing machine. "Yep," said George, "I make my own clothes."

We all slept on the floor, and George kept right on talking until late. He said that next year he was going Outside for good. He could not, once he left the Northwest Territories, renew his trapping license, so going out meant for good. I wondered how he would fit into life Outside . . . Gradually I dozed off. George was still talking. At last he said, listening to our heavy breathing: "Aw, you bastards are asleep, while I'm jabbering away." Whereupon he crawled deeper into his sleeping bag.

The next day everything began to go wrong.

The wind continued to blow, the sun was only a faintly luminous patch. Sky, sea, and land were all one in a milky whiteness.

Pup tries teeth on frozen salmon

After five hours of travelling through this, we rested and had some tea out of our thermos bottles, and ate a few pilot biscuits. We had to make Eskimo Point that night, our grub boxes were nearly empty. There was no more dog food, and we were out of coal oil. That forced delay in the deserted hut had used up our supplies.

We were all suffering from frostbite. Bill was in agonies with a frozen nose—the second time it had frozen up that year, he said. So he hurried forward. Joe Ulurksit, with Mahpie on his komatik, followed after, and Tootoo, with me, brought up the rear. We stayed as close together as possible, as night fell.

Then Ulurksit's sled hit a sharp rock and lost chunks of mud from the runners. We stopped, and Tootoo lent Ulurksit his primus stove to thaw out frozen mud, for the runners had to be repaired there and then.

Little Mahpie climbed upon our komatik, and we pressed onward, slowly. Bill's team ahead was now completely hidden from sight.

Tootoo ran ahead, encouraging our tiring dogs. I had never, never felt such intense cold. Hours passed. Finally Tootoo admitted that we were lost. We would have to make camp—without fuel or food. All the food was on Bill's big sled.

We stood in the darkness with the sighing driftwind around us. Mahpie withdrew deeply into her artiggi hood and sat motionless. Tootoo got out his snow knife and began to probe the snow. Within a few feet of me he became invisible again.

Then methodically, Tootoo was cutting snow blocks.

Soon we were inside a very small igloo, but there was no welcome roar of a primus stove to cheer us. Exhausted,

208

George Lush and his lead dog

I crawled at once into my sleeping bag. Why Ulurksit had not caught up with us and where Bill had gone to were matters for conjecture, but I could think of nothing but my own misery. As I warmed up, though, I realized that Tootoo had not unharnessed the dogs or fed them before he had sealed us in. I thought with pity of the poor beasts out there with empty stomachs in the cold darkness.

Then Tootoo, as if by magic, produced a small piece of seal blubber and improvised a kudele with the top of an empty can and a rag for wick. The flicker of the lamp cast his shadow upon the glittering snow wall. He sat hunched over in front of the lamp, impassive, fumbling in a small box for some crumbs of tobacco. There were none, but his face showed no sign of disappointment.

Why was he sitting up? Vaguely I wondered about this. I wondered still when I woke up to find him still sitting there beside the light, which was at its last gasp. His head had sunk down over his knees. He was not frozen, he was merely asleep. I could hear the sound of his breathing. Then I realized what had happened: he had given little Mahpie his bed-roll. Hers was on Ulurksit's sled . . . The primitive man had been more chivalrous than the civilized.

The lamp went out. I was aching, now, in every limb, and felt cold. As I fell asleep once more, the thought went through my mind: "Remember to straighten out before freezing to death." Bill had described to me how difficult it was to handle curled-up frozen corpses—he had done so several times.

Faint light was filtering through the snow house walls when I woke up again. Tootoo and Mahpie were already stirring. We must start off at once—without breakfast, and with hungry dogs.

Slowly the komatik creaked onward through the icy mist. My hair became frosted, sticking to my forehead.

Evidence of frost bite

One eye closed up, the eyelashes freezing together. A swath of wrinkled white skin across Tootoo's cheek and nose showed that he, too, was freezing. Mahpie had frostbitten cheeks. The dogs were frosted to their shoulders, and were whimpering with pain.

On and on we went. Then, at the end of what seemed an eternity, Tootoo pointed joyfully ahead. I could see nothing. Yes, after a minute, I made out a speck in the distance. It looked like a rock. But it was a rock that grew bigger as we approached, and it changed its form, becoming a tiny house with a steeple. It was the R.C. mission, at Eskimo Point. The barracks could not be far off. Tootoo had brought us dead-on to our goal.

When we staggered in, it was 3 P.M., and Bill was about to send a radiogram to Churchill asking for a search plane to be flown out. Three native dogteams were already out looking for us, supplied with chocolate bars and hot tea. We had missed them.

Joe Ulurksit had arrived an hour before us. Bill had got home late the night before.

Within an hour, after warming up in that comfortable house, it all seemed like a dream.

Before going to bed that night, Bill and I stepped outside just to see what the weather was doing. The thermometer on the sheltered porch registered 52° below zero. Quickly we retreated indoors, wondering how anybody could stand travelling in such cold. And we rushed to the hot stove, luxuriously turning in front of it . . .

When Bill consulted his books it was found that Mahpie was only thirteen. She and Joe Ulurksit would have to wait two more years to be legally married, according to the white man's laws.

But Ulurksit serenely built an igloo and moved into it

212

with Mahpie. There seemed to be no law to prevent that. We knew what the sequel would be. Mahpie would soon be pregnant. Then Father Berube would perform the marriage ceremony, so that the child would be born in holy wedlock. And all would be well.

Inside the Roman Catholic mission chapel was a religious painting of Saint Theresa and the child Jesus. Young Father Berube, a French-Canadian, translated the inscription on the painting for me. It was in syllabics and read:

> "Here the native peoples got Him for their light and their end in Heaven. Pray for them."

Father Berube posed for me in his vestments. He also cooked an excellent dinner for me: caribou roast, canned asparagus, French-fried potatoes, and a cake with pink icing.

He lived all alone. Several times a year he made dog-team trips inland towards Nueltin Lake and the land of the Padleimiuts. He had a shack at Padlei, which he had visited in the autumn. It looked then, he said, as though it would be a "rather bad year" for caribou. Mysterious thing, the way the caribou migrations shift their course. "Even the naturalists can't explain it," said Father Berube. "One year the caribou flow over the land like a torrent. The next year, not a caribou!"

Everyone ate well at Eskimo Point. At the Careys' we had roast caribou twice that first week. Bill, as a government employee, had the right to shoot two caribou a year. Besides such delicacies there were imported foods of high quality, the R.C.M.P. larder being well, thought not extravagantly, supplied.

At the home of the Hudson's Bay post manager, Ches Russell, it was the same thing. But there, again, I heard a faint rumor of hunger among the inland people.

"They're improvident!" it was said. "They're turning into post-loungers! They all expect free hand-outs of flour!"

I wanted to go inland west to Padlei, and Ches Russell promised to find me a dogteam driver.

First of all I settled with Tootoo. His pay came to $23. Feeling a bit cheap, I gave him an extra $5. Some tip! For without him I would have been a corpse, no exaggeration.

Tootoo could not take me to Padlei because he had heard that people and dogs there had little to eat. He wanted to go north to hunt caribou. His dogs needed fresh meat. When he had got some caribou, he would come south again. By that time I might be ready to go back to Churchill. I asked if he would take me back, when that time came.

"Eee," said Tootoo, his version of "Yes."

"With many dogs?"

"Eee," said Tootoo, smiling.

And off he went into the vast white spaces.

For my inland trip, we found Kumok, meaning "Louse." Then I bought provisions and settled down to wait for good weather. The trip to Padlei was only about "three sleeps" distant—roughly, 125 miles—and Kumok's dogs looked ill fed.

Kumok was the usual quiet, smiling, and efficient Eskimo. The only thing unusual about him was that he shared his wife with his best friend, Attatsiark. Or, you might say that the woman in question, Pameok, had two husbands. She also had two children, and the question as to who was their father disturbed no one except the Mountie who had to register them.

Alta and Bill had been married in their home town in Nova Scotia, July, 1949. Alta had never been far from home until she went as a bride to Eskimo Point. All she

At Eskimo Point. Two men share one wife. Kumok became my guide (left)

knew of the Far North she had learned by reading *Mrs. Mike*, after her engagement. Most of what she knew about cooking and housekeeping she had learned from Bill, after their marriage.

portrait of famine: padlei, 1950

She took housekeeping seriously, and had no time to spend on the jigsaw puzzles, magazines, and embroidery her parents kept sending her to while away the presumably idle hours. Worst of all, she had little time to take any outdoor exercise. Yet she had resolved not to sink into the usual sedentary life of a white woman in the North, and had a complete fur outfit to face sub-zero temperatures. Whenever I went on a camera jaunt around Eskimo Point, she started out with me, bravely. But always she had to rush back home, to do some urgent work.

The house was kept bright and clean. Alta had managed even to raise some potted plants—tulips, narcissus, and shamrock—but they looked rather pale. She had become a good cook, and had invented several recipes of her own, some of them useful to Bill when on a dogteam trip. For instance, she ground up roast caribou with its fat and put it to freeze outside. In a crumbly condition this—a modern version of pemmican—was stored in bags. Alta gave me some of this and some freshly made doughnuts, frozen solid, for my trip to Padlei.

On February 4 the wind dropped and there was a promise of milder weather. Early next morning Kumok arrived with his team, and we set forth.

Kumok, as well as his dogs, had been on short rations for some time. I determined if possible to feed them well on this journey. It didn't turn out that way, for my supplies, which I had thought plentiful, were inadequate. They had to be shared with people who were much hungrier than we.

We met some of these people on the second day out . . .

Kumok on way to Padlei with a small load on sled and 8 scrawny dogs

We came to a small igloo on our way to Padlei

XV

on the track of hunger

IT WAS THE TINIEST IGLOO I HAD YET SEEN. OUTSIDE, A single mangy dog, the sole survivor of a full team, lay starving and motionless. A broken komatik was nearby. That dog and that sled told a story of suffering and defeat. Inside was a young woman with a baby. Her caribou clothes had lost most of the hair, and so could provide little warmth. She sat in darkness, without fuel or candles. Never had anything reminded me more of a primitive cave-dwelling than this dark lair.

A few caribou bones, sucked clean of marrow, lay on the frozen floor. Kumok questioned the woman gently, and learned that she had no food, no tea, no fuel. Her husband had gone on foot in search of caribou several days ago. She was simply waiting.

We gave Tetuk biscuits, tea, tobacco, candles from my stores, and left a small quantity of kerosene for the primus stove, along with some matches. Tetuk at once chewed up a biscuit, and fed it, a soft mass, from her mouth into the child's. We left them, heavy-hearted . . . We had not gone far when we met her man, Annowtalik, gaunt and stag-

Kumok beats his dogs when they slow down, with a 35-foot seal hide whip, folded

gering with weariness. He had made a long journey, hoping to bring back at least a ptarmigan or hare. He carried an empty game-bag.

A layer of soft snow made for hard pulling. As a result, we did not reach Padlei in the three sleeps we had expected, and our food was getting low. But Kumok smiled philosophically. No food? Well then, there was no food! **220**

As we neared the isolated Hudson's Bay Company post, we saw fox tracks, but none of caribou. Several ravens and one big white owl fluttered up ahead of us. In the distance were shimmering palisades, which sank lower as we climbed to higher ground. Tops of willow brush showed above the snow. We were in the land of the Padleimiuts, "the people of the willow thickets."

Ptarmigan tracks were visible, leading from one shrub to the next. Farther on, stunted spruce trees were plastered with snow, and whipped by the wind into fantastic forms. A serene sunset, cold gold, faded to gray as we drew up before the trading post, and Henry Voisey came out to meet us.

Henry Voisey was a trader of a bygone type, perfectly content at his lonely trading post. Both he and his wife Charlotte were part-Eskimo. They had a little fair-haired daughter, Mary. It was a calm household, almost like an igloo.

Hudson's Bay Company, Padlei

Mary Vosey, trader's daughter at Padlei, is much more at home in native ways. Eegie and Mary like each other, rub noses quickly

Kumok found that he could not stay here with his dogs, since there was no food. He must take them to caribou country, if he could find it. I would continue to pay him his $2. a day—in credit at the H.B.C. store—while he was away with his dogteam, hunting. At the end of a couple of weeks or so, he would return to take me back to Eskimo Point. I bought him some grub and he got some new harness, very happy at this arrangement.

Over supper, Henry Voisey and I discussed prices, trapping, dogs, missionaries, and famine. The Arctic white fox pelt brought only $3.75 that year. Almost no market for them Outside. The natives were feeding fox carcasses to their dogs, something they only do in times of famine. They were also jigging for fish in the lakes. This provided some food, but lake fish are not very fat and so are not very nourishing as a steady diet. And there were few caribou.

Kumok makes the mud covering smooth and rounded again with improvised plane

About thirty Eskimos lived in tupiks and shacks not far from the Padlei post. Most of these were on Destitute Rations. Others were camped more than twenty miles distant, in various directions. To the southwest, about forty miles away, was Pipkaknak's camp, which was still relatively well-fed, thanks to his expert hunting in the previous autumn. He had been able to lay up meat in his caches. But even there, famine would not be staved off much longer.

"Wherever you go around here," said Henry Voisey, "you'll see real hunger. Many of the dogs are dead. It'll take a few years to recover from this. You know how it goes: no dogs, no hunting . . ."

We talked about caribou hunting. Getting caribou is like getting deer of any kind. It takes skill and patience, especially patience, to stalk caribou. Sometimes you have to travel hundreds of miles from camp. Then you may catch a glimpse of a few stragglers. They will be travelling up wind. If you are in that wind, they will scent you at a great distance. You creep up on them. But just when you think you have them within gunshot, a wolf may pass to windward. They run off in another direction—and you have lost them. Their sense of hearing is keen. If there is a crust on the snow, they will hear you at a distance of five hundred yards. Yes, the biggest quality of a caribou hunter is patience—and that was why Eskimos were good hunters.

"But you know all about that," said Henry finally, "if you've hunted with the Chipewyans. And you also know how important caribou is to the people. No caribou means no dogs, they die of starvation. It means no food, no new clothing. It means hungry people that catch any germ that comes along. You have sick people, nailed to the spot . . . and that means no hunting next year."

After a while, speaking of the man I had met returning empty-handed to his starving wife, Henry went on:

"Weak as they are from hunger, some of them set out

We tried to save our dogs. (On way to Padleimiut starvation camps)

In the winter I was at Padlei (1950), a fox carcass could buy goods shown. Discs in center represent $3.75

on foot, going thirty miles and more on a long-hope search for caribou. The ones that have trapped foxes can get flour and tea at the post but caribou is their staff-of-life. Without dogs, they can't get to their trap-lines."

Henry had handed out destitute allowances of flour or rolled oats. But bannocks would not keep the people alive for long. Soon there would be no fat to fry them in, anyway. Some of the people already were eating dry uncooked flour, just by handfuls. And polio had struck down several people in Padlei.

I asked what the missionaries were doing about the situation.

"Praying, I guess," said Henry. "And wait till you see one of them that lives near here! You'll see him—he usually drops in at mealtimes."

Oolie , an Ihalmiut (Nueltin Lake) and my guide from Padlei south, wearing typical snow glasses with beaded strap. Pipe is made of soap-stone and a cartridge

Bernard Fredlund, of the Northern Evangelical Mission, lived in a nearby shack which he built with native labor. Ruddy, with fierce blue eyes, he looked like a Saskatchewan farmer—and was. He was a farmer who "got religion."

Eegie, at Padlei, Hudson's Bay Post

Snow sculpture, shaped by the wind, can be 6 feet long

I asked him why he had come to Padlei. He said: "To teach Christ." He had entered the Northwest Territories presumably for "language study" and often dropped in at the Voiseys' to ask them for help in this. He had been at Padlei a year and from his questions I gathered had made little progress in the difficult Eskimo language.

He stayed for supper. Henry and I did not give him an opportunity to say grace, but pitched into the soup at once. Bernard offered up a silent prayer for himself, then surveyed us disapprovingly.

He again frowned, after supper, when we smoked. He had a great aversion to Lady Nicotine and was trying to make the Eskimos abandon the evil weed. Bernard—or

Mary Voisey and her mother in their best artiggi

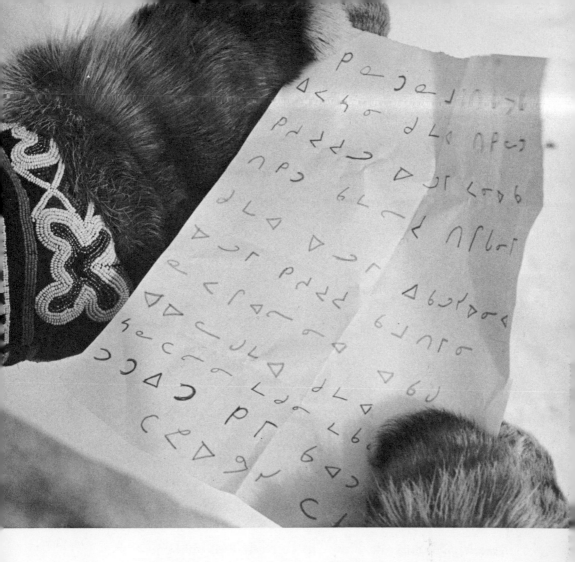

Mrs. Vosey wrote a letter in syllabics for me at Padlei

"Screwball," as we called him behind his back—was having a hard time with these pagan Eskimos. He began talking about their superstitions.

A medicine man (*angaruk*) in the country exercised great influence. He must be combatted. In obedience to the Angaruk, the people observed many senseless taboos. One man would not eat fish; a girl at Padlei would not eat bird-eggs; another would not eat caribou tongue.

portrait of famine: padlei, 1950

In the course of the evening, a native from Nueltin Lake came in, and was greeted warmly by the Voiseys. His name was Oolie, and his wife was pregnant. Until recently, he had let his hair grow, according to an immemorial tradition of expectant fathers. The Voiseys told me later that the missionary had cut Oolie's hair, unable to stand the sight of such a pagan demonstration.

Bernard had come to the Voiseys' ostensibly to get the syllabic lettering for a Biblical phrase, which Mrs. Voisey wrote out for him. She now tried to teach me to read syllabics, and for my benefit wrote a letter. Here is the letter in translation:

> Written to anyone: Yesterday Kumok arrived and also Kretsuyuyuk. Today Pangokak arrived to trade a fox. Today Kumok will go fishing, and Kretsuyuyuk is putting lazybacks onto his komatik. Kumok is leaving tomorrow, is going caribou-hunting for 2 Sundays. There are no caribou at Padlei. Dogs are hungry. Goodbye to everybody.

Mrs. Voisey was kindly to everyone. For my benefit, she dressed up in her beaded artiggi and posed for me. Her outfit came from Repulse Bay, and the ornate patterns were made with countless colored beads. The design of the garment, particularly the hood, was different from that of the Padleimiut women, whose hoods are inordinately long.

Out on the ice I got some pictures of the natives jigging for fish through several feet of ice. I photographed a nearby grave of a pagan woman. Her body was barely covered with rocks, a tiny mound as inconspicuous in death as in life. But Screwball was piously erecting a cross made from a shipping crate . . . much to the delight of the dogs. We send missionaries to assure the Eskimo a serene life after death—the Eskimo is too polite to send out one of his own people to tell us of his serene life before death.

Eegie with an adopted child called "Little Eegie"—who does not like dried milk mixed with water

The Voisey house was well kept, without any apparent effort. Mrs. Voisey always had time to sit down and rest, play with her little daughter, or talk to us. She was an excellent cook, but never forced food on her guests. The child, Mary, was happy and well-behaved. She played with her

Kinuk, at starvation camp takes last bit of meat, a caribou head, to eat inside her igloo

A piece of caribou skin is given to child to eat

Although skin is loose on her bones, her artiggi black and without warmth —she still goes on, uncomplaining, at starvation camp near Padlei

Near death. Note Government identification tag

Girl at starvation camp, just skin and bones, appears bulky in old fur clothes

Suspicious Padleimiut

Padleimiut woman scraping ice-window with "ulu"

A hungry Padleimiut who still has a good fur suit

Living quarters at Hudson's Bay Company, Padlei

Eskimo chum, Ootook, as long as she liked. When she was hungry, she came into the house for food. When she was tired, she went to bed. Mrs. Voisey had read no book on child psychology, but she got excellent results. She had no theories to foist upon the world, no plans for improving it.

My igloo on edge of tiny spruce grove during a storm, Padlei

I hated to leave this serene household, but I had taken all the photographs I wanted in the immediate locality. I wanted to visit the distant camps, and painful though it might be, get some close-ups of the face of hunger.

Henry Voisey found time to take me on his komatik to an Eskimo camp a long day's journey out. It was situated on the edge of a lake, in a grove of stunted spruce and tamarack, and there he built me a snow-and-canvas shelter similar to those we had used on the way up from Churchill. The walls were of snow blocks, the roof of canvas and a frozen blanket. I settled in. He left for Padlei, saying he would return for me in about a week.

I was alone with the people.

Henry Vosey, is well practiced in handling a seal hide whip 40 feet long

All this land was a network of lakes—endless stretches of muskeg in summer, a heaven for mosquitoes, a hell for any other living creature.

Two tiny windowless log cabins had been erected in this grove. My neighbor, Adjaruk, was a man with two wives; and several pot-bellied children played around the place.

I managed to make myself understood a little with an Eskimo vocabulary of barely fifty words. With the aid of pantomime, and proper distribution of tobacco, we set up friendly communication.

244

Padleimiut grave on rise of hill with Kumok standing in ground drift

This family lives in a filthy shack near Padlei. The man has shaped a fiddle from a bacon tin, a branch and caribou sinew

The young woman, Tetuk, whom I had first met on the way inland from Eskimo Point was there with her husband Annowtalik, Adjaruk's eldest son. It was almost like meeting old friends, and gradually I heard their story.

246

portrait of famine: padlei, 1950

Annowtalik was a good hunter and had owned a fine
team of dogs. The dogs had died this winter, one after
another, of hunger. As long as he had a team, Annowtalik
had managed to go hunting. He shot a few caribou and
cached some of the meat. Then, when all the dogs had
died, he made two trips on foot going as far as fifty miles
to bring back the buried caribou meat on his back. Finally
there was no meat. He was now too weak to hunt except
close by for ptarmigan or hare. He had scarcely enough
strength to walk in to Padlei, to get the hunter's rations of
flour, baking powder and tea, and other food with the family allowance for the baby.

On the way in, he had come upon a caribou and shot it.
With understandable zest, he and Tetuk had attacked the
carcass, gorged, then suffered terrible pains in their dis-
tended abdomens. They had walked the rest of the way,
and looked haggard, although the baby looked well.

In both cabins, the caribou skins that had served as
ground-sheets had been fed to the dogs. There was no floor-
ing and the ground underfoot was half-thawed, filthy and
damp. The people's fur artiggis were worn thin and almost
hairless. What extra skin clothing they had had was long
since used as food not only for the dogs but themselves.

They were hungry and cold. But no one complained.
They kept busy. They ate dry flour or made bannocks when
they had fuel. The men went out each day on the lake, jigging for fish through the ice, but not always with success.
The women gathered firewood. And in the gloomy huts all
played with the babies or amused themselves with string
games, stories, and music.

Annowtalik had contrived a fiddle out of an empty bacon can, long and narrow, some wood, and different thick-
nesses of braided caribou sinew. He sawed away at it, with
the primitive bow of wood and sinew, actually managing
to play a recognizable tune.

portrait of famine: padlei, 1950

In the shack, a child was still unweaned. The mother had gone for days without food and her breasts were dry. She looked gaunt and hollow-cheeked. I gave the women a can of powdered milk and, lo and behold, they found among their rags a nursing bottle and nipple! One woman mixed the milk with water. To warm it, she filled her mouth with the mixture, then spat it into the bottle. The old man in the hut wiped off the nipple on his greasy artiggi, fitted it on the bottle, and urged it upon the howling child. The baby drank a little, struggled, and howled again. A woman came over, picked up the infant, and twisted a heavy breast over her artiggi. The baby gurgled with contentment.

I handed out a few chocolate bars, some tea and biscuits, feeling helpless and ashamed. They had no candles, and I had barely enough for my own needs. In a few days, these little handouts drained my supplies.

In the midst of this misery, I took photographs. Time and again, when I used my camera in a dark, grimy hut, or when out of doors and the lens clouded up, I could hear in imagination picture-editors saying: "This don't do for reproduction. Poor focus, poor exposure . . ."

I photographed a woman delousing her child. She ate the lice as she worked. Horrible? It represented a tiny amount of nourishment, would quiet the pangs of hunger.

These pictures would, I hoped, show the outside world what real suffering was. They would also show the strength, endurance, courage and ingenuity of an almost exhausted people. Maybe after seeing them, white men would stop referring to Eskimos as "children" and "incompetents."

They did not whimper and whine. They did not yell for social security. They held no demonstrations. They did not even think of criticizing the white man. They were totally unaware that a mass of government officials in Ottawa looked after the welfare of the Eskimo. During this time of hunger, the missionaries did not help; the R.C.M.P. had

248

Padleimuit using bow-drill to make hole repairing komatik

no instructions to help; officials were bent over triplicates of vague statistics.

Only a few individual men of the H.B.C. knew what it meant, and gave out rations to the hunters until their shelves became bare. Henry Voisey gave away many items out of his own mess supplies. I had seen it before, in case of actual need, the Eskimo always came to these quiet and unpublicized men for help.

I hoped these pictures of wooden shacks would show white men how absurd wooden houses are for Eskimos.

One night, above the seething wind, I heard a comforting sound outside. It was Adjaruk. He had come over to my hut in the dead of night and was reinforcing the snow walls. I recognized his heavy tread and the sound of his voice, for he grunted laboriously as he struggled against the wind. Slowly, his badly-shod feet crunched around in the snow. Gradually my walls were made weather-tight, all the holes were well chinked and the canvas roof lashed down.

When he had finished, I took my snow knife and cut an opening in the wall, inviting him in for some hot tea. He slid in, we drank tea and smoked. All this, practically without a word, but with understanding smiles.

At the end of a week, Henry Voisey sent Keegootituk ("The Toothless One") for me with a team of four dogs, and we started back to the Padlei post in the worst weather yet. Drifting snow plastered us, and layers of soft snow made the going hard, even had the dogs been strong. To help out, Keegootituk and I pushed the komatik. For a time I thought we were lost, that we would never find the isolated little trading post. But when the dogs realized they were going home, they picked up speed and I knew we were on the right track.

250

Padleimiut woman, in child labor, at starvation camp

It was good to be back at the Voiseys'.

Bernard Fredlund, the missionary, dropped in to hear my news When I described the suffering I had seen, he said the people were doubtless being punished for their sins. When I told of a childbirth in a famine camp and described the difficult labor of the exhausted woman, he blushed, lowered his eyes, and edged away . . .

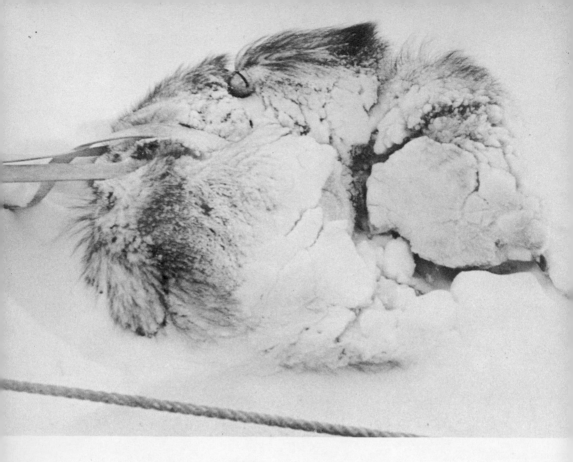

A dog in harness during storm, caked with flying snow

Two days later I was off again, this time on a journey to the southwest, to Pipkaknak's camp, about forty miles distant. Oolie, the Nueltin Lake native, was my new guide.

As we jolted off into the sunny morning, Henry tried to take a picture of us with his camera. But it froze on him.

Oolie spoke no English, but Mrs. Voisey had given him a letter written in syllabics which would explain to Pipkaknak why I was visiting his camp. I took along with me, this time, some surplus food. Luckily. For, just outside the post, we were joined by Ayook, with a team of four dogs.

Ayook worked as "native helper" for Bernard Fredlund, and at first I thought the misisonary had sent his dogteam out for some wood. But no, Ayook stuck with us all the

Dog, dead from starvation, at Pip's camp

way. He followed us like a scavenger, and he was just that. He was helping himself not only to our tea and tobacco and biscuits, but ate our flour—dry, by handfuls. The missionary's helper was half-starved, as were the dogs.

Next morning one of his dogs began to stagger in a drunken manner. Ayook released him from the harness. The thin, mangy creature stood for a moment staring ahead, with glassy eyes. Then he flopped down in his tracks. He would be dead with the cold in another few hours . . . We left him. Eskimos have a prejudice against shooting their dogs.

Now, with only three dogs, Ayook trailed behind us.

By noon, another of his dogs wobbled and stumbled. He

picked up that one and put it on his komatik. It did not whine, but lay there, listlessly.

Shortly afterwards we stopped for a rest, the boys erecting a small snow block wall against the wind, which had risen. After our lunch of tea and pilot biscuits, Oolie squatted near the shelter. Then he picked up the half-dead dog and carried it over to the fresh excrement. The dog lapped it up eagerly, and seemed to revive.

Late that afternoon one of Oolie's dogs began wobbling. Oolie slipped the harness off, and the dog flopped down on the trail. We went on. Soon the dog was only a dark spot in the drifting snows.

Starvation is a frightening thing. Suddenly the great frozen land itself terrified me. I tried in vain to recapture some of the ecstasy I had felt in the past when looking out over these vast white horizons. I had felt at times that the Arctic was like a great symphony, not yet written, but waiting for the right composer to come along. The symphony would be something like Bach's *Toccata and Fugue*—vibrant, resonant, relentless.

Relentless. Yes, the Far North could be that.

XVI

at home with the padleimiuts

PIPKAKNAK REMINDED ME, SOMEHOW, OF KOIKHOK, WHOM I had met on the Coppermine inland patrol. Both men had great dignity, both were pagans, both were extraordinarily good hunters.

Pip—as the Voiseys called him—had a spacious home. In shape, it was roughly oval, in size about sixteen by twenty feet and about seven feet high. The walls were of snow blocks, and the roof was of caribou skins sewn together and held in place by cross-pieces of thin peeled tamarack sticks. You entered it through a long tunnel of snow, and down four steps. Within, it was amazingly light—four ice windows were set into the snow walls. A small stove, contrived out of scrap-iron, glowed redly and threw out heat intermittently, when fed with the fuel of these regions, the stunted willows that have to be dug out of the snow. Order and cleanliness prevailed. Also, there was food here. Pieces of caribou meat stood by the stove to thaw out gently, and there was a pile of marrow-bones that had not yet been cracked and sucked dry.

Padluk, Pip's wife, soon gave us some hot tea. Pip and

Starving does not cut off affection at Pip's camp

I sat down on the sleeping bench, with an upturned box in front of us for a table. Maybe civilized people depend too much upon words, I don't know. But almost without words Pip and I felt at ease with each other, right from the beginning. I accepted his hospitality without question. He accepted my biscuits and tobacco with more restraint. He knew no English. I knew very little of his dialect. We communicated with smiles and signs. Sitting beside him, I indicated my box of pilot biscuits and he took one. After which, he looked first at his wife, then at me. I motioned to her to take one. She did so, shyly. We sat there drinking tea and munching the biscuits without feeling any need to talk. When Pip's four children appeared they had to be invited to have their share of biscuits. After which, I offered some tobacco to Pip and Padluk. They filled their soapstone pipes. We sat there for some time smoking in almost total silence, enveloped in the fragrant cloud of tobacco.

Then Pipkaknak read Mrs. Voisey's letter, discreetly. He smiled. We were friends.

I stayed a week at Pipkaknak's camp, sleeping in his tupik, eating his meat, sharing with him my coal-oil, candles, biscuits and tobacco. My vocabulary increased, and I learned that he had a trapline of about sixty miles, round-trip. He had about fifty traps set out. That winter he had caught some foxes to trade for tea and ammunition at the Padlei post. He made fewer visits this year, in order to save his dogs' strength.

Pip was a patient hunter, full of ruse. He had made many caches of caribou meat in the previous year—but not enough. When Padluk cooked a tuktu stew, she cut the meat into small morsels to make it go further.

Nearly every morning Pip and his sons went out on the lake to jig for fish through more than four feet of ice. He

Pipkaknak enters his igloo with a dead fox in his hand, at starvation camp

Oolie has good luck fishing through 4 to 5 feet of thick ice behind wind break near Padlei

took along his snow knife, to build a shelter against the wind, his ice chisel, a scoop, and a sinew-line. Some days he brought back excellent trout, big fellows. I liked them raw and frozen, but still better when cooked.

Pip's dogs were not fat. But even so, they were better fed than any for miles around. A litter of pups, recently weaned, played inside the igloo, standing hungrily waiting for small bits of meat or fish.

portrait of famine: padlei, 1950

Pipkaknak was not baptized, nor were his children, Henry Voisey told me. He was a pagan "not yet ready for religion," according to the missionaries. He had learned to read and write syllabics from other Eskimos. Those cuneiform symbols which resemble shorthand, are said to be easily mastered, but they baffled me. In turn, Pip admired me when I wrote my journal at night. He and Padluk and the children crowded around, watching in silent wonder the movement of my pencil.

Because of the scarcity of new caribou skins, Pip and his sons were often occupied in repairing dog harness, while Padluk and her daughter spent much time mending boots and artiggis. Every scrap of skin was precious.

Sometimes the children played roughly. But never was there any howling or fit of temper. Padluk went about her work, letting them play, stopping occasionally to pet the youngest with a gentle nose-rubbing.

I was a centre of interest. A kabloona living in this camp —it was unheard-of. Sometimes the tent was invaded by a dozen visitors, my smiling spectators. A covey of children usually trailed me from one habitation to another.

On this windswept lakeside—the lake called South Henik on my map, but according to Pip the name was Shaneujuak, "Crosswise-to-the-wind-lake"—stood three tupiks and one igloo. In the igloo lived an ancient hag, resigned and ready to die. She and her man were on destitute allowance. Their dogs had died. The old woman sat in that dark igloo, sucking an empty stone pipe, and spitting everlastingly. When I gave her some biscuits and tobacco I was surprised at her *Namakto*—"Thank you."

Polio had struck this camp, too. One of the strongest of the young hunters had been the first victim. He had been hauled by dogteam to Padlei and flown out to Churchill. From there, with other polio patients, he had taken off

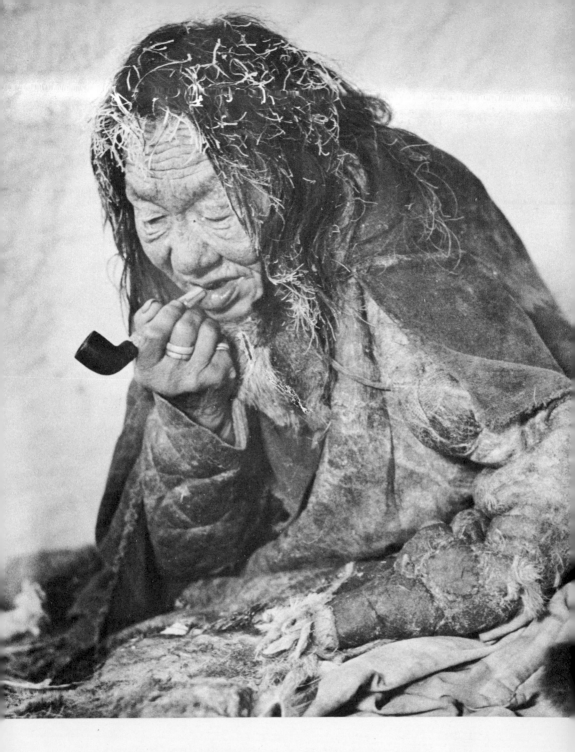

Starving Padleimiut sits resignedly in igloo. Frosted over, she no longer moves about, will quietly die in a day or so. I had filled her pipe

for Winnipeg. They did not reach their destination, for the plane crashed and all the passengers perished. His young wife, unknowing, was still awaiting his return.

Oolie's igloo was small, low, dark, and dirty. It must have had a bad smell—but I did not notice it. And I realized, not unhappily, that I must now smell like these people—a mixture of old caribou skins, smoky fires, grease, and stale perspiration.

In the tent was a swarm of kids, runny nosed and ill fed. Two of the children were part white. Who their father was did not seem to bother Oolie. His wife was big with child, she moved about heavily, with a patient look on her face. Oolie was letting his hair grow again. He, too, had a patient look. Another mouth to feed? Well, they would somehow manage.

One night Pip and I discussed his income. He told me he had caught 24 foxes. From this I was able to work out his budget for that year:

24 foxes	$ 90
Family Allowance (3 children under 16)	$200
Total	**$290**

Under normal conditions, his family and 8 or 10 dogs required nearly one caribou per day throughout the year —let's say, 300 caribou—in addition to a few fish. During this year he had succeeded in killing only 90 caribou. Somehow, they would have to manage.

In Pip's tupik everyone slept naked under furs, two and three together. My sleeping-bag caused much comment at first, as did my habit of sleeping partly clothed. It wasn't white man's modesty. I was cold!

One day his place became very cold. There was no more fuel.

I discovered how cold it was in the tupik when I tried to use my camera and found that it had frozen. I juggled it under my artiggi, thawing it out with my body-warmth. But the lens persisted in fogging up. Trying to use a filter, it fogged too when I touched it.

I always enjoyed watching Pip's family get the sled and dogteam ready—they had gone out one day several miles to a cache of caribou, the last one. Now, a trip must be made for wood. Pip said something in a soft voice, one brief sentence. Immediately his eldest son, Nanow, and his eldest daughter, Ajartook, bestirred themselves. The girl put a pail of ice on my primus stove. When the ice melted and the water warmed, she took it out to Nanow. Nanow filled his mouth with warm water, sprayed it on the sled's mud runners, and smoothed it down with his mittened hand. He had to work quickly, running up and down, for the water froze instantly making a stone-hard icing over the mud. All the while Pipkaknak was busily harnessing the dogs.

Two dogteams went out with Pip. Karyook and Oolie also needed firewood. The old man Serko dragged his sled himself, since all his dogs had died of hunger. The four men returned that night with their loads of wood. Oolie brought back a few skinny sticks, some willow branches, wrapped up in my sled canvas. Karyook, his brother, brought back a slightly larger load of smaller stuff. Old Serko brought in a very small load of willow branches. Pip brought back two logs 12 feet long and almost 10 inches in diameter, besides a big bundle of willow twigs. Even when it came to hunting firewood, Pip was the best man of the lot.

At Padlei I had heard Voisey discuss the "timber" situation in this region, "The Land of the Little Sticks." According to him, the wood—small stands of spruce and tamarack, besides the ground-willow—will last only another 15 years. After that—what? There has been no "re-forestation" program. It has taken those stunted trees hundreds of years to grow. I know, for I have counted the rings of some of the trees. It will, therefore, take hundreds of years to replace them . . .

Kumok had returned from his caribou hunting, looking as plump as the proverbial partridge. His dogs also had a well-fed look. Kumok had killed ten caribou and had travelled several hundred miles in the two weeks he had been away. But he brought back only three nights' feed for the dogs and a small amount of meat for ourselves. Eight hungry dogs and an active man on a long sled trip make short work of ten caribou, and probably he shared his hunt with friends he had met.

We had to leave at once, for the shortage of meat was very serious. In fact, we were finally feeding the dogs on expensive canned meat from the store shelves, at 95 cents a tin and two tins per dog per day. But that supply was limited. Mrs. Voisey suggested that our dogs should wear can-openers around their necks. Henry, in the same vein, swore that one of the dogs had come to the store and demanded a can of Klik, saying "Charge it to Harrington!" In spite of our jesting, the situation was serious.

Kumok and I returned to Eskimo Point by a roundabout route. After several days hard travelling, we came upon an Eskimo encampment. Perhaps it was spontaneous, perhaps in Kumok's honour, but that evening there was a drum dance. One of the men in camp, Ahkpa, found the frame of a drum, stretched a caribou skin over it, tightened it with sinew around the willow frame, and then apparently lost interest in the whole thing.

But later on in the evening, all the women came and sat side by side on the snowbench. At length Ahkpa struck the

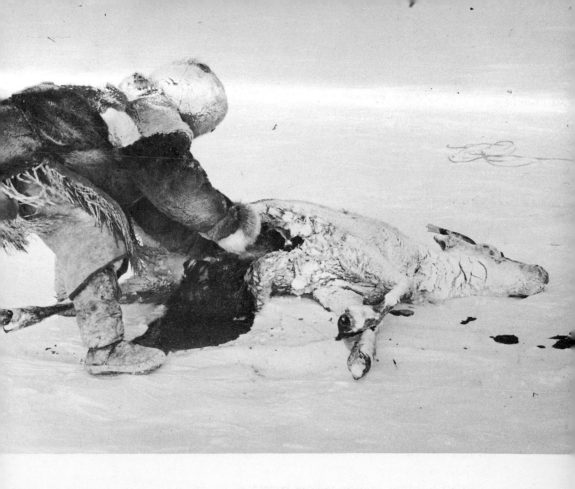

Kumok at last shoots a caribou as we near coast again, east from Padlei

frame of the drum slowly, twisting it back and forth. The women took up a monotonous chant which eventually gathered volume, though the tempo never became faster. The drummer stamped in a small circle, swaying his body, shouting from time to time. He perspired, but was urged on, though his breath was coming in gasps. Then someone else took the drum and the chant continued.

Ahkpa tightens skin on willow frame of drum

My two candles gave a fitting light. In the midst of that great wasteland, in the absolutely silent night, only here, in a pin-point (relatively) twelve feet in diameter, were a dozen people crowded together, chanting knew not what. I thought of this violent land and of these brief moments in which I was permitted to sit in the shadows amongst its inhabitants as a privileged onlooker. As we walked back to the igloo Kumok had built for us, that night the sky was filled with great bolts of Northern Lights.

Ahkpa strikes frame of drum only

The next day on the trail we sighted caribou and the dogs went wild. The men fired at two hundred yards, and missed. Then farther on four more caribou were sighted. Six shots brought them down. Two were quite small. We stopped, while the Eskimos cut up the carcasses. Fresh quivering meat at last!

The dogs were ravenous. When the entrails and some pieces of meat were thrown to them, they dived into it wildly, tearing and ripping, snarling and rearing. A storm came up, driving snow into everything, as the meat was at last loaded onto the komatiks.

That night we built a large igloo, and had a feed. It is good to eat when you know what hunger is. It is good to kill when it is to satisfy hunger. The contentment of my companions was infectious, and I shared it. But I recalled, while famine was in this land, the well-fed soldiers farther south who thought it great fun to turn their guns on the migrating caribou and on the schools of white whales in Hudson Bay.

We were back at Eskimo Point by March 14. The day was calm, the land was dazzling white in the sunshine, which gave some warmth.

"I'll bet," said Alta, "that Mrs. Voisey didn't even offer you a bath . . ." And she went off to heat water for me, murmuring something about some people *never* taking a bath.

Things had changed at the Careys'. Bill told me the news. Alta was going to have a baby. He already made plans for her to be flown out next summer for proper medical care.

Somehow, the gaiety had gone. Or was it that I had changed?

Bill also told me of a new ruling made at Ottawa: henceforth adoptions were illegal. From now on, a child had to *belong* to its parents, be of their blood. This would greatly simplify keeping the records, both on the part of the R.C.M.P. and the government clerks.

"And thank God," said Bill, "I'll soon be able to get out of this country. Only two more years to go and I'll be free to settle down somewhere. This is no place for a white woman . . ."

Kumok, paid off, went out of my life without any good-bye, in the Eskimo fashion. He had built me many snug igloos. We had shared food, when we had it, and had gone almost without when supplies were low. He had taught me patience and calm obstinacy—by example. Undemonstratively, he had been kind. How many times had he looked at me, when the wind blew and he knew I was tired, asking me sympathetically, "Ik-kee?"—Are you cold?

I stood in the doorway watching until he was out of sight. On the way to his friend and their wife . . .

On March 17, Tootoo turned up, ready for the trip southward to Churchill. He had gone on his caribou hunt back of Rankin Inlet, and all told, had travelled 300 miles. He looked well-fed, as did his dogs. But the few caribou he had killed had all been eaten on the return trip.

On March 20, Bill and Alta Carey waved goodbye from the barracks. Alta had stuffed some doughnuts into my grub box and filled my thermos bottle with tea. Bill and I had thrived under her excellent cooking, topped off with freezers of rich ice cream mixed with strawberries from Nova Scotia. Such hospitality is beyond price.

In clear sunshine and with a tailwind, the dogs felt happy, and Tootoo and I ran along in sheer exuberance.

Tootoo swerved later toward the floe edge to hunt seals. The gurgling and splashing open water a few miles from shore startled me. There were many birds and gray vapor rising. An unreal scene, after all the solidly frozen country.

Then we had to cross a wild jumble of pack-ice, pressure areas that stretched for miles. We shoved and heaved over the rough ice and fissures of open water, breaking our gear. Then one afternoon, on smooth ice, the grain elevator of Churchill, that wonderful landmark for all travellers returning southward, loomed on the horizon.

portrait of famine: padlei, 1950

Again reluctantly, I saw it slowly grow larger. A few miles from it, I asked Tootoo if we could camp for the night. Once more we went through the pleasant routine of building an igloo, unharnessing and tying up the dogs for the night.

Inside, Tootoo and I turned our grub box inside out, and stuffed ourselves until the last crumb had vanished.

It was a calm and peaceful night. A night to encourage plans for new trips . . .

4. the smiling face of the north arctic spring

spence bay, 1951

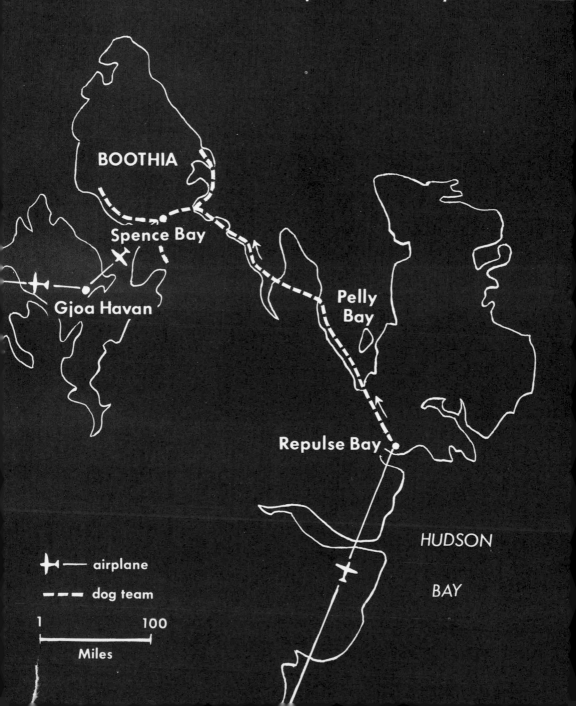

BOOTHIA

Spence Bay

Gjoa Havan

Pelly Bay

Repulse Bay

HUDSON

BAY

✈—— airplane

--- dog team

1   100

Miles

XVII

to pelly bay and the end of night

I HAD ALWAYS LEFT THE ARCTIC JUST WHEN THE SNOW was beginning to get soft and the sea-ice showing signs of breaking up. Yet for years, the very phrase "Arctic spring" had a kind of magic for me.

At last, in April 1951, I hoped to reach Spence Bay, on Boothia Peninsula near the North Magnetic Pole, and 200 miles north of the Arctic Circle. This trip would take me to one of the least accessible of the Hudson's Bay Company posts during break-up season. Again the journey would be by plane and dogteam.

The plane that took me north to Repulse Bay belonged to Arctic Wings, Ltd. of Churchill, and I was the only passenger other than Bishop Lacroix. The Bishop was on one of his periodic rounds of the Hudson Bay diocese, and so ours was a zigzag course via Eskimo Point, Baker Lake and Chesterfield Inlet to Repulse Bay.

We took off early in the morning of April 19, and in less than two hours came down at Eskimo Point for three minutes—just long enough to throw off two mailbags and give Father Berube an opportunity of kissing the bishop's ring.

At Baker Lake an H.B.C. clerk from Scotland entertains with his bagpipe

He called out a surprised "Hello, Dick!" . . . and we were off again.

For what seemed an endless amount of time, we zoomed over a glaring white emptiness, where coastal lines merged with the frozen snow-covered bay, lakes with the snow-covered land. Charlie Webber, the pilot, could be trusted to find his way. But how these northern pilots do it is nearly as much a mystery to me as how an Eskimo guide finds the next igloo.

That night I slept at the H.B.C. post at Baker Lake, "You can sleep on the chesterfield," said Sandy Lunan, the manager. "Make yourself at home." He told me that the best sewing in the region was done around Baker Lake, and on his advice, I bought a new caribou skin outfit for $25, quite different in design from those I had before. His young clerk, fresh from Scotland, had remembered to bring his bagpipes and was already serenading the ladies. But he declined to pose for me in his kilt!

At Chesterfield Inlet, Dr. Corbett ran out to meet the plane, and invited me to stay at his quarters. Conversation surged until after midnight, mostly about cameras. Chesterfield Inlet with its 32 white inhabitants, was practically a town, and recently the first Eskimo nun had taken her vows there. I gladly left behind white man's progress next day, and the plane deposited me at Repulse.

In Churchill, the temperature had been 30 above zero. At Repulse, smack on the Arctic Circle, the thermometer still stood at 10 below. But the sun was already shining brightly at six in the morning. It would shine at that season for eighteen hours each day, and later on, for the entire twenty-four. Spring had already touched the Arctic.

The total white population of Repulse was four men: two Oblate missionaries, the H.B.C. manager and his clerk. Two hundred and ten years had passed since Captain Middleton reached this landlocked bay in his search for the Northwest Passage. Yet this was the extent of its growth. Still, things had changed even in the thirteen years since Henry Voisey had clerked here. Windchargers now supplied electricity. The trading post was equipped for sending and receiving radiograms. And the missionaries had a projection machine and instructive film-strips supplied by the government.

Father Philippe at Churchill had told me of this as we puttered around in the mission's newly-installed darkroom. The Eskimos were now to have the benefits of pictorial education.

At Repulse, the missionaries showed me a typical selection. One sequence pictured the "Beauties of Ottawa" —architectural beauties. Another was a "Tour of Canada," showing the provinces something like differently-shaped-and-colored cookies. "Feminine Hygiene" showed colorful anatomical cross-sections of the female body. Father Didier thought this one unsuitable.

There were no dogteams available at Repulse, so I radioed Spence Bay. While waiting for a reply, Alex Spalding, the manager, let me play over his collection of Chopin records. I hung around the store, watching him take in furs (fox pelts were up to $13 this year) and hand out trade goods in exchange . . . tea, tobacco, ammunition, flour, calico for Mother Hubbards, and so forth.

I noticed that some of the young women wore the tails of their artiggis slightly rolled up. "Oh," said Alex, "that's a sign that they are still not married." Nowhere else had I noticed such differentiation.

Then by luck, five days later, an Eskimo arrived who was willing to take me north as far as his spring camping grounds near Pelly Bay. From there, he said, I would easily find someone to take me on to Spence Bay. The overall distance would be about 350 miles.

This bell calls the Eskimo to early mass at Repulse Bay

Kanayok, my new friend, said we should reach Pelly Bay in "eight sleeps, maybe not so many." He would take me as passenger on his komatik for a flat rate of $35 plus food for his family and his dogs.

Kanayok's nine small dogs were hitched fanwise to the sled. I bought a seal from the missionaries to supplement the dog-food Kanayok had cached on his way down to Repulse. His sixteen-year-old son, Angotialu, would be very useful on the trip, except that he could not build snow-houses very well yet. But, Kanayok said, we would not have to build igloos going north. We would use the ones he had built on the route south from Pelly. His tattooed wife, Arnaktasak, rode on the komatik constantly, as if lashed to the load.

Another young Pelly Bay Eskimo went with us. Erkuak-tok's twelve dogs hauled a heavy load of stove-pipes, window-sashes, tent and mail to Father Henry, the well-known Oblate pioneer missionary. The material was intended for a new mission on King William Island. And of course Erkuaktok had his family: his wife, a three-year-old daughter, and a three-months-old baby.

We were quite a crowd.

By force of habit, I had stocked up with candles. Candles at this time of year, when we had at least fourteen hours of sunlight, and could easily travel at night!

My friends regarded this trip as a holiday. Why should they hurry? There was plenty of frozen salmon and walrus, biscuits and other foods for both man and beast. Trapping had been profitable this year, and now was the time to take things easy.

Kanayok enjoyed life. His rubbery face, under a thatch of graying hair, could twist into any number of comical grimaces, all of them cheerful. He would turn somersaults at tea-time, and after a hard day's travel, he would stand on his head just for fun. He had us all doing it, and I was surprised how relaxing it proved to be.

278

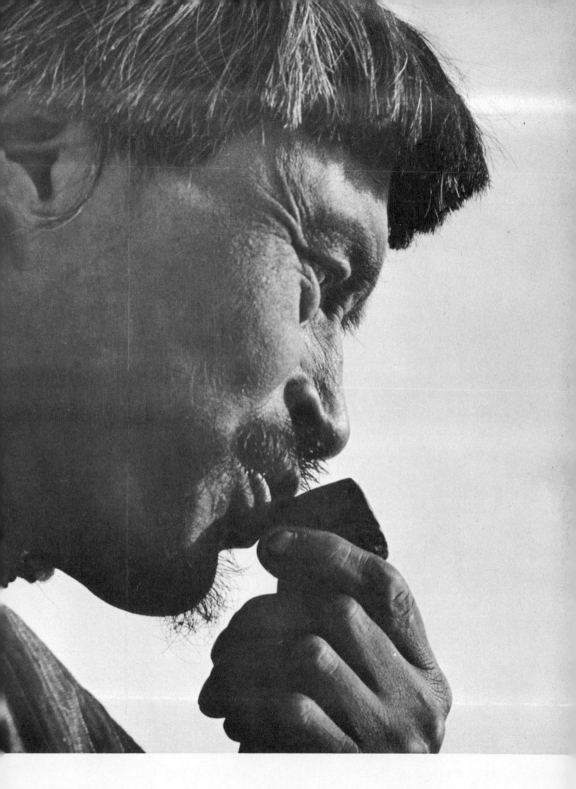

Kanayok, guide from Repulse Bay to Pelly Bay. His stone pipe has lost stem

The old lady—I guess Arnaktasak would be about 45—liked to take her time, too. And almost anything served as an excuse to stay over in an igloo. One day, watertight sealskin boots had to be made. Another time, new clothes must be sewn, for summer was just around the corner. She carried with her all kinds of gear, such as her stone kudele in which the lighted seal-oil made a rosy light, and her hand-operated sewing machine the clatter of which seemed oddly out of place in a snowhouse.

By the third igloo out, we were all wearing sun-glasses, and all had cracked lips, and cheeks burning from sun and wind. My friends had wooden goggles, whittled from driftwood, with a slit for vision. They were better than my store glasses made of wire mesh that scratched my forehead, plastic which clouded up, and felt which faded quickly in the strong sunlight.

At first it was hard to fall asleep when the sun was still shining. But I got used to it, and could crawl into my eiderdown and sleep no matter how bright.

Following a chain of lakes, we reached the fourth igloo at the foot of Committee Bay, and from then on travelled on sea-ice northward along the coast. The snow was getting soft on top of the caribou moss.

To warm up, I often ran alongside the sled or ahead to encourage the dogs. They would strain at their load, trying to catch up. Once, yelping loudly, they nipped my white caribouskin boots. "*Nanook*," explained Kanayok. I didn't care to have the dogs mistake my legs for a polar bear's. It wouldn't take much for a determined set of dogs to chew up a man.

After a rest and tea, I would ask Kanayok, "Which way now?" He would point out our general direction. Then I would walk sedately ahead, self-consciously pleased with my ability to keep a direction on an overcast day in a fea-

Building in his own image, snowman carved from single block of snow

tureless land, by fixing my eyes on some almost invisible speck in the distance. I always had the feeling that I should be commended . . . But Kanayok never recognized it as any achievement. Any Eskimo did it as a matter of course.

We did not carry a compass. No Eskimo ever·does. Near the North Magnetic Pole, a compass is almost useless. Kanayok did have a clock, however, an alarm clock which he had just acquired. It had never been set, but ticked merrily away.

With almost continuous daylight, and later a curtain of mist, we lost count of the days. Was it the fourth or fifth day we stopped over at an igloo for a whole day and night?

We unloaded our komatiks and ate and slept whenever we came to one of the igloos. "Tamoa-shuk-tunga," I would announce. Someone else would echo it. We were all hungry! Therefore it was mealtime. And how we ate! My grub box was soon half empty. This, despite the fact that Kanayok had dug up several caches of frozen fish, buried under the snow on the route south. Arnaktasak was a good cook. Her bannocks fried in seal-oil! Her salmon fried in its own belly fat! We gulped it down, licked our fingers, belched happily, then turned to my biscuits, jam and tea. My knife was always licked clean by someone before being put away.

After which, we slept. Sometimes the woman would sit up for hours by her flickering kudele, crimping bootsoles with her teeth. She was making summer footgear for her men.

About the fifth day out, Kanayok said we must stay over, for he had to find an *umiak* he had cached somewhere the past summer. Soon he would be needing that 18-foot boat again. After this explanation, he and his son took off on the komatik, and vanished over a small hill.

I wandered over to chat with Erkuaktok. Scratching crude diagrams on the snow, we reached an understanding.

Erkuaktok showing string games. Eskimo "cat's cradels"

He would take me on from Pelly Bay to Spence Bay, a distance of three igloos.

Erkuaktok was in a merry mood. We turned somersaults, stood on our heads, wiggled our ears. Then he mounted his largest dog and rode around as long as the dog would allow. He decided to build a snowman. With his snowknife, he cut out an eight-foot-long block of snow. We stood it on end, and he carved Eskimo features and mode of dress. (An Eskimo—naturally, he would create in his own image. I wondered how the Christian saints appeared to him?)

Moving boat through soft snow. Committee Bay

I added eyes and a mustache. This was such a huge success that Erkuaktok promptly made a second smaller figure for his little daughter.

Then his eyes lit on a fox track. "We will follow it," he decided. So we trailed it for what seemed miles through the soft snow. I was sweating and said so. "In a little while, we will find *treganja*," Erkuaktok promised. We kept on going. After more than an hour, the fox tracks brought us back exactly to our starting point. Erkuaktok doubled up with laughter—what a joke!

When Kanayok and his son appeared with the heavy umiak on their sled, I wondered how in the world they expected to transport it to Pelly Bay. We had already quite a load. And the big boat must weigh at least 500 pounds, and was the length of the sled. How could the dogs pull the additional weight in the softening snow?

284

Well, they managed. Four of us hoisted the boat onto the sled, upright, and Kanayok skillfully lashed it in place. All our gear went into the boat, including the old lady and a nursing pup. Both slept most of the way.

Off we went, at snail pace. Wind and sun had cleared away patches of snow, exposing gravelly sand. It didn't make things any easier, and as the mud got knocked off the runners, the dogs couldn't pull the load. With serene good nature, the Eskimos stopped, and even with crumbly snow, managed to put up an igloo. But instead of a dome, they used a piece of canvas over the snow walls for a roof.

Kanayok again went over a hill, and re-appeared with a couple of lengthy steel bands. Our accident had occurred not far from a cache where he had stored the steel runners the previous fall.

We unloaded the boat with its gear, and overturned the komatik. Then Kanayok screwed the steel bands onto the wooden runners. The komatik was harder to pull than with mud, but the wood had to be protected from wear. Steel or whalebone shoeing is necessary for travel in that period. With the calendar, Erkuaktok had indicated that he used the komatik all but two months of the year.

The load was back-breaking. Father and son and I walked and pushed, panted and wheezed, sweated and broke through the crust at every step for hours. Whenever the komatik stopped for a time, it was extremely hard to get it started again. Load limit and dog-power have a rather loose association for Eskimos, and I felt sorry for the poor brutes. But when I saw how these beasts, which should have been worn right out, fought at night—I hardened my heart.

We simply could not travel the following day, for the temperature had risen to just under the freezing point. The sky was overcast, and any gear piled on the snow was slowly sinking out of sight. "It is too warm to travel today," said Kanayok. "We will wait until after the sun goes down."

It was time for "spring changeover."

First, Kanayok had a haircut of the soupbowl type, and it suited his straight hair. He climbed into a new suit of underwear over his old ones—quite a tricky business, much like getting dressed in an upper berth. For the igloo roof was not very high to begin with, and it had sunk with the thaw to the point where he could not stand upright. He pulled on overalls, and a new plaid shirt.

For outdoor wear, he would add a parka of blanket cloth, and over that a canvas parka, both made by his wife. She sat barelegged on the snowbench, running up a new coverall for herself on the portable sewing machine.

Bannock was cooking over the primus stove. The young lad and I were working the wire puzzles I had brought with me—when the roof caved in!

Without any warning, big blocks of snow, not really wet but breaking on contact with our heads, fell down upon us. Kettles were knocked over. The primus stove hissed unburned gas. Only for a moment were we astonished and speechless. Then the most uproarious laughter broke out. How screamingly funny—our house fell down! We shook with laughter as the wet snow melted down our necks.

Kanayok and his wife hopped around bare-footed, pitching out snow, like sailors bailing a boat. The sewing-machine had to be dug out. Angotialu was so weak with laughter that he was useless. Erkuaktok and his wife came running, and peering over the walls at us, laughed themselves into stitches.

Once the mess was cleaned up, we sat down comfortably, without a roof, while Arnaktasak made tea. And I marvelled at their attitude toward disaster. Had the weather suddenly turned cold again, their sodden clothing would have become a frozen suit of armor. Eskimos have died thus.

Kanayok replaced the roof before nightfall with the canvas. Fortunately, for of all things, it rained during the night. Rain pelted down with that hollow dropping sound, and soon found ways of dripping through onto our sleeping robes. Kanayok went outside to pull the canvas taut, while the old lady scooped up the puddles into a can. Angotialu reinforced the igloo with wet snow, and pounded it hard to keep it from leaking. They all smiled cheerfully, and soggily we went back to sleep.

By morning, the rain had loosened most of the mud on Erkuaktok's runners. And he had no steel shoeing. Patiently as ever, the Eskimos unloaded the sleds. The building supplies were cached—Father Henry's mission would have to wait another year. Kanayok left his big boat on the beach, thank goodness. They overturned Erkuaktok's sled on Kanayok's, and piled the travelling equipment, the women and children on that.

Erkuaktok's twelve dogs were added to the string, and now we had twenty-one dogs pulling. But they hauled with their bellies close to the ground, while we pushed, strained and heaved. We averaged perhaps a mile an hour.

The going was so slow that I had plenty of time to take in the vegetation. Here and there grew tiny pussy-willows, white sprouts one or two inches long showing amid the brownish moss. I saw a clump of what looked like cedar, also only a few inches long, already with red buds at the tips. More and more ptarmigan were seen, starting up ahead of us, making a frightened querk-querking sound.

Our previous progress seemed excellent by comparison with our speed in a jumble of sea-ice. Ice stood piled on end as high as houses. We moved an inch at a time, with great effort, covering perhaps a hundred yards in two hours. A new crust had formed on the shore ice, but it was not heavy enough to support our unusually heavy load. It seemed to me that Arctic travel consisted mainly of hard trips, and harder ones.

the smiling face of the north

We were chilled, making camp after midnight. That night the colors of the cold golden sunset became also those of the sunrise. The sun just dipped below the horizon, so to speak. A single bright star shone to the north, and a slender sickle of moon. But of course it was not dark. In fact, the nights had ended.

I had brought plenty of food for all, for the estimated eight days of travel. But now, on about the twelfth day, Kanayok lifted the lid of my grub box, thoughtfully studied its contents. Soon afterwards he left the tupik (the skin tent he unearthed from still another cache) and shortly returned with three frozen salmon and some seal meat. I let go and brought out dehydrated soup, two biscuits apiece and two gumdrops each. We licked our knives, our fingers, and ate the tea leaves happily.

We were held up again next day by wet snow which made it impossible to travel. At a word from his father, Angotialu went hunting, and returned with half a dozen ptarmigan, which his mother boiled over the primus stove. They were delicious in a greasy gravy, and surprisingly warming. The Eskimos spit out feathers which had not been cleaned away and ate the intestines, cracked the small bones and sucked out the marrow.

All morning Kanayok amused himself humming an old melody softly. Erkuaktok's family drifted in. We made fun for ourselves by placing gumdrops on our noses, and guiding them into our mouths. My wire puzzles, never any problem to the natives, could be done with their hands behind their backs, or with their teeth while one of them still baffled me.

Kanayok began a story in a gentle sing-song voice. I could get words here and there, such as fox, bear or man, and had some faint idea of the hunting story. The others sat absorbed, listening quietly, to a long-familiar tale.

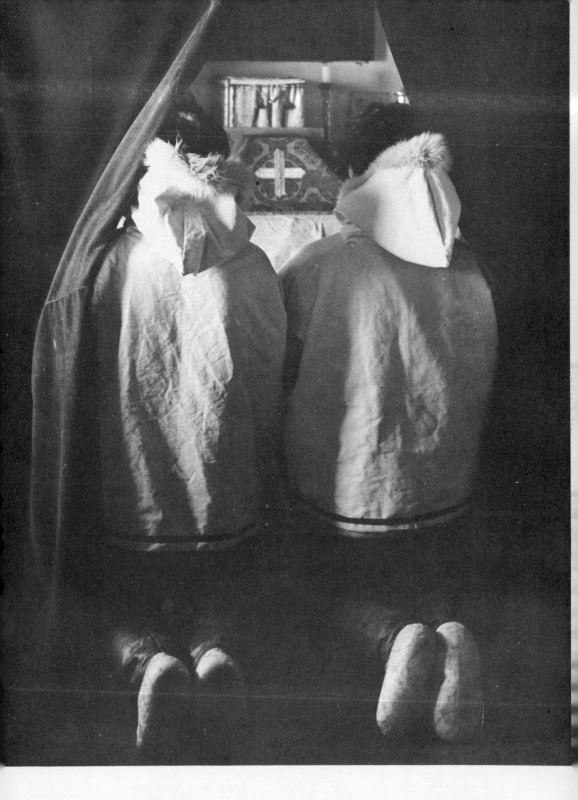

At Pelley Bay mission two Eskimos pray for a safe journey

Father Vandevelde holding mass at Pelly Bay mission

Netchilingmiut mother delousing child. Pelly Bay mission

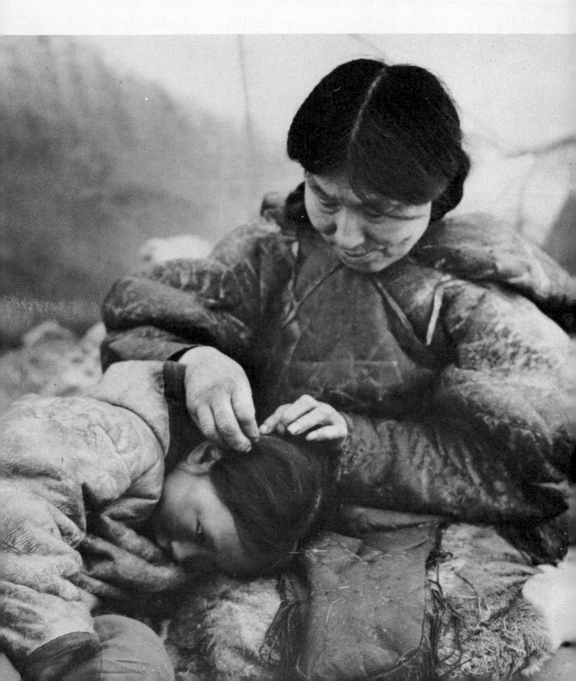

the smiling face of the north

Kanayok packed the komatik with the same care he had used thousands of times. Through snow flurries, we followed a wide shallow river valley, between sheer rugged rocks, boldly standing through countless centuries. More and more sled tracks, old and new, joined in the valley until it seemed like a highway.

I scanned the barren hills, and all seemed to have buildings on them, which dissolved into angular rocks. On among islands and between them and over them, we sped, now on the sea-ice of Pelly Bay.

At last one of the rocks did become a building. It was St. Peter's Mission. Father Vandevelde, who knew of our coming, appeared at the door briefly in his vestments, waved and vanished inside again.

Leaving my friends to unharness the dogs, I went inside, and stepped right into High Mass. It was just ending, to the lusty accompaniment of Eskimo girls singing in Latin. A moment later, Erkuaktok came in. With no self-consciousness, he at once went to the altar, kneeled there a minute. Then the curtains screening the sanctuary were closed, and the chapel at once became a hall. Erkuaktok sat on the floor, made the sign of the cross, and attacked his frozen fish, nearly slicing off his nose with his knife in his haste.

Father Vandevelde, his dark beard mixed with gray framing a weather-beaten face, extended a rough hand to me in greeting.

XVIII

the world's most remote mission

FATHER VANDEVELDE WAS A NATIVE OF BELGIUM. HE SPOKE French and Flemish, as well as English, fluently. He also spoke Eskimo with ease, he told me that he even dreamed in Eskimo!

Yet this scholar and priest in his ordinary indoor clothes —heavy gray flannel shirt, dark woolen breeches, fancy seal-skin boots—looked with his long beard like an old-time trader.

He was a chain-smoker—with his bishop's understanding permission. Now he at once rolled a cigarette and lit it. He explained that his superior, Father Henry, was away having taken the dog team north to Thom Bay, a mission established only in 1949. As he smoked, he put hunks of seal blubber into the kitchen stove, and fried slices of frozen caribou in a heavy pan.

"What an extraordinary year for visitors!" he exclaimed, his face beaming. At Christmas a Mountie from Spence Bay had dropped in. Then a doctor had passed through on a plane bound for Spence Bay. After that, Father Papion from Thom Bay had come south for his annual visit. "And now you!" He could hardly believe it.

Father Henry on way to establish a new mission on King William Island

The only other visitors here since 1935, when the mission was founded, had been Gontran de Poncins, author of *Kabloona*; Miss Oldenburg, who had been flown in by Ernie Boffa; and a geodetic survey party some years back. Father Vandevelde had been at Pelly Bay since 1938, arriving three years after Father Henry established the mission. He had helped build the present mission house of rocks found nearby, chinked with local clay and sand.

294

We had brought mail for him and Father Henry. I had thought he would seize on it avidly. But he merely smiled, "I have a whole year to read it in," he said, "and another year after that to wait for the reply to my letters."

The pleasant aroma of smoked caribou steaks now filled the little kitchen. Father Vandevelde had prepared it himself. It took about three weeks of intermittent smoking, he said. The meat was sliced, seasoned and bound together. He hung this bundle over a smudge fire of dried seaweed, inside a canopy made of old coal sacks. It was left to smoke three days at a time, removed for about the same length of time, then smoked again. Prepared like this, the meat would keep for years in that latitude.

"You shall have some of the smoked tongue for breakfast—it's two years old," said Father Vandevelde. "It tastes like very good salami." Then his brown eyes lit with pleasure, as he recalled something else. "And you shall have eggs. I was given a dozen hen's eggs two years ago, and I still have some."

They were frozen hard as hand-grenades, but edible. Several round rocks turned out to be potatoes. He insisted upon sharing things that in the Arctic are rare and precious.

Pelly Bay is cut off from the world. No boat can reach it, for the ice never entirely leaves the bay. The natives use small boats brought overland from Repulse Bay, and the mission owns a tiny and antiquated outboard motorboat. All cargo must be brought in by dogteam from Repulse Bay, and the Eskimos were paid $7.50 in trade, for hauling each 100 pounds. Small teams could haul only 200 pounds, say, which hardly justified the trip. The biggest loads each year are the Family Allowance rations, which Father Vandevelde distributes to his 130 parishioners scattered along the coast.

To haul coal or fuel oil would be out of the question. Father Vandevelde and Father Henry devised a stove that

Father Vandevelde making a batch of bread

would burn seal blubber; it made a crackling hot and rather smelly fire, which was short-lived. But it sufficed for their fortnightly bread-baking, and gave some heat.

Father Vandevelde made bread while I was there. He stayed close to the stove while mixing and kneading it, for even a few feet away would chill the dough. Then he placed the loaves in oblong pans which had once held tinned bacon.

Nothing was thrown away. Sardine cans were turned into ash trays. When I opened my last can of peanuts and carelessly tossed the can away, Father Vendevelde immediately picked it up, put it on a shelf for some future use. Similarly he unrolled the strip of tin with its key, and put them aside.

He had learned to practice an economy similar to the Eskimos, and to do without most of the amenities of civilization. The mission furnishings were of the sketchiest. The tableware consisted of two plates, two cups, one saucer. As guest, I was given the saucer. The furniture boasted one home-made chair and stool, and a wooden bench about two feet wide on which the missionary slept. Packing cases served for other seats. Indeed, all the wood used in the mission was old—it had previously done service in Repulse Bay, and before that in Churchill.

Aided by a few Eskimos, Father Henry and Father Vandevelde had constructed the mission buildings, six small edifices of stone. One of the smallest was for use in the coldest weather. One February the temperature had sunk to 62 degrees below zero.

To compensate for the long darkness of winter, Pelly Bay has long summer sunshine. And to make use of that continuous sunlight, the fathers had built a tiny hothouse, six by ten feet, where on May 10, the temperature was up to 77 degrees. They intended to plant radishes and beans, and already the lettuce seed was in. Earth had been gathered by the spadeful from here and there, and the rake was a section of caribou antler.

They had many plans for the future. Father Vandevelde said, with an exalted look, "We hope next year to build a bell-tower. How wonderful it would be to hear the sound of a church bell in this place."

The thought of a church bell breaking the cold Arctic silence did not warm my heart. And the mission cross, which I had taken for bits of driftwood had actually been blessed by the Pope, on one of Father Vandevelde's two trips Outside in thirteen years. In 1947, he made a visit to his home in Belgium, and then a pilgrimage to Rome. He carried with him the mission cross, which had been presented by Captain Larsen, when the *St. Roch* wintered in the ice at Pasley Bay.

Father Vandevelde's other trip Outside was in 1942. He had fallen ill, and with an Eskimo driver sledded south to Repulse. From there he was flown to Churchill and then to The Pas, where he was operated on for appendicitis. The doctor's orders were to rest, but he returned soon after, making a thousand-mile dogteam trip back to his mission.

The most poignant feature of the whole journey was in Churchill.

"I wept," he said simply, "when I saw the things that were being thrown away in the army dumps at Fort Churchill. Food and lumber and bedding destroyed in great piles! I was not ashamed to scrounge around at night, picking up useful things to bring back here to Pelly Bay. What waste!"

I mentioned the famine conditions I had seen among the Padleimiuts. He nodded his head. "Yes, I know what it is to be close to starvation."

In 1939, the year of the dog epidemic, the mission had lost eleven dogs. Unable to fetch supplies or go hunting, the fathers had been reduced to a diet of fish—and fish only —for four months. Finally they were able to make up a team which they sent to Gjoa Haven, King William Island, for food supplies.

The native driver went and returned in 21 days, a record time, bringing not only flour, matches, and other necessities, but a Christmas cake made by the H.B.C. post manager. Some old newspapers were also sent, and thus the missionaries had their first news about World War II —six months after it had begun.

"And the Thom Bay mission is lonelier still," said Father Vandevelde. "If you should get the opportunity to visit, Father Papion will be so glad."

We spoke of our respective dogteam trips. Father Vandevelde estimated that he had travelled 10,000 miles by dogteam, all told. One trip had been marred by a series of accidents, and he and his driver had run out of all food. Then Father Vandevelde remembered the sugar. Eaten by handfuls, it would keep up their strength for a while. All day he nursed the thought of the pleasant surprise for the evening. But the sugar was gone. It had broken open and scattered when the komatik overturned on the sea-ice.

"I was afraid my driver was killed, for he fell beneath the sled," said Father Vandevelde. "I had a terrible time lifting it, expecting to find him dead or badly injured. He got off with a few bruises. I will never forget how he laughed when he saw my woe-begone face! Like so many near-tragedies here, the whole thing became a joke. The Eskimos are an admirable people . . ."

He went on to speak of the Eskimos' generosity, of the communal sharing of goods. During the food shortage of 1939, when everyone was barely surviving on fish, a man would return with a load. He would put it down in the midst of the encampment, and each woman would go forward and help herself to a fish until all had been distributed.

"On so many occasions," said Father Vandevelde, "I have to recognize that the Eskimo is a better person than I am. They are Catholic by conviction," he ended.

I think he meant that they are innately Christian, and certainly they are patient, unselfish, gentle and humble. I could never claim to "know" the Eskimos, to penetrate deep into their character. I could speak only of what I had seen. And I knew that they held in warm affection this kindly Belgian whom they called "*Attata Vi-ni-vi*" (Father Vandevelde).

He was proud of the mission. But in preparing for mass next morning, he said whimsically, that it was too bad he was out of candles for over a year now, but that the Lord would understand. Candles? I had a dozen of them in my grub box. He was rapturous over this trifling gift, and merely smiled when I described their purchase as a blunder.

"This must be almost the most remote mission in the world," I suggested one day.

"It is perhaps the most inaccessible, but Father Papion's is lonelier," he insisted. "And on the way there you would see many other things, such as the remains of pre-Eskimo cultures. You must photograph these things," he said eagerly, "then we will see the pictures in the papers that people sometimes send us."

He had barely said this, when he clapped his forehead, and exclaimed, "Now I remember! I have seen your name and some of your pictures. Come into the library."

The library was a small chilly room which boasted two rows of books and a stack of much-thumbed magazines. He rummaged through them, and came up with a Belgian paper which had a four-page spread on my Coppermine trip of 1949.

"There is only one error in it," he said hesitantly. "See, the caption of this igloo picture. It says the blocks are of ice—*glace*. But it should read snow, *neige*."

I knew, of course. The caption had been re-written, wrongly, in the editorial office.

300

The little library also held relics of northern expeditions. Like most well-read people stationed in the Arctic, Father Vandevelde was keenly interested in the history of Arctic exploration. He was well-informed on the lost Franklin expedition, and the many search parties that had been sent out later. He had some iron hooks salvaged from the wrecks of Sir John Ross's ships. Like others in that region, Father Vandevelde on his dogteam trips always kept an alert lookout for some trace of the past.

The mission's single chair was in the library, and it had once belonged to Amundsen. Rasmussen's sled runners had been used as supports in the main building.

All sorts of absolute necessities were lacking in that mission. I wondered what would be the most acceptable gift?

"Send us the *Beaver* magazine," he said without a moment's hesitation. I was staggered. The Hudson's Bay Company quarterly is an excellent magazine, devoted to the north, but in the face of so many shortages . . .

At the last minute, Father Vandevelde further added to my debt of hospitality, by putting into my grub box, despite my protests, a supply of frozen salmon and a whole pound of butter from the mission's lean stores. Erkuaktok carried my repayment back from Spence Bay. But doubtless Father Vandevelde would stash it away until the next visitor chanced by.

Crossing the "waist" (isthmus) of Boothia on way to Spence Bay

XIX

"taku-vunga"

IN ERKUAKTOK I HAD HIRED A LANGUAGE TEACHER AS WELL
as a dogteam driver. Seeing my efforts to learn the language
—or rather bits of the Netchilingmiut dialect—he earnestly
tried to help me. He eagerly gave names to everything,
words which I would repeat, and then promptly forget
many of them.

But I thoroughly learned one phrase on our journey from
Pelly Bay to Spence Bay. *Taku-vunga*—I see! And since in
the latter part of May there is much to see in the Arctic,
and since he made no effort to teach me the conjugations,
I couldn't forget it. *Taku-vunga!* By merely pronouncing
it I can evoke the feelings of the trip, probably the most
light-hearted I ever made in the north.

"Akkedia-taku-vunga!" Erkuaktok calls, as we trot beside the komatik. Our shadows stretch long ahead of us,
for we are travelling northward on the blue sea ice with
the sun behind us.

"Akkedia-taku-vunga!" I echo. The ptarmigan vanishes
in a frightened flutter of wings as we speak.

Inukshuks on Boothia Peninsula

"Kog-taku-vunga!" shouts Erkuaktok, as we pass the frozen mouth of a river. And I repeat the phrase, "Kog-taku-vunga!" I see a river!

But now, ahead of us is a seal out on the ice. Erkuaktok brakes the sled, and this time barely whispers "Netchik-taku-vunga." He does not wait for an answer. In white ar-tiggi, he is creeping noiselessly toward his prey. He kneels, aims his rifle . . . too late. With a plop, the seal has slipped down into its breathing hole out of sight.

"taku-vunga"

Erkuaktok grins, cracks his 40 foot sealhide whip, and
the twelve dogs lunge ahead at the ends of their traces.

Sometimes my friend sings a haunting melody, and he
has a good voice. I can sing it with him, but when I try it
alone, the tune eludes me. In the song I can identify some
words such as *nanook*, polar bear, *ukala*, rabbit, *treganja*,
fox. And the phrase *sinik-tu*, sleep thou, occurs more than
once. He also likes to chant the Latin masses. I am not
critical of his Latin, nor is he of my Italian when I burst
forth into *"Un bel di vedremo."* We are good companions.

Travelling without any sense of time, we camped when
tired, ate when hungry, wakened when we had enough
sleep. There was no night and day, for the sun never set
now. It was always there, low on the horizon. We didn't
hurry, for we had plenty of food, though we were seven
sleeps on the way, instead of the estimated three.

This was a comparatively new route to the Eskimos, since
there was nothing at Spence Bay until the Hudson's Bay
Company established its post there in the summer of 1949.

Northward as far as Ross Peninsula we travelled on the
sea-ice. Then we cut westward, crawling up a long deep
bay, across the chain of lakes to Lord Mayor Bay. Erkuaktok named all the islands and prominent hills, and I wished
I knew the translation, for the names on the maps meant
nothing to him. From Lord Mayor Bay, we went westward
again, crossing the narrow neck of Boothia Peninsula towards Spence Bay. Sheer bluffs, laced with snow-filled
crevasses, towered hundreds of feet above us. Flat-topped,
carved by the winds, these solemn survivors of the ice-age
seemed to be eternity itself. And again I heard in my mind
the surge of the *Toccata and Fugue.*

Snow flurries caught us here. The sun was obscured, and
we moved through a pearly gray haze, in which sky and
snow-covered land were one. The dogs broke through a

Sealskin shoes for dogs

thin crust of ice at every step. One dog left tiny spots of blood on the snow. Sympathy? He was the most vicious fighter of the lot at the end of day.

During the last two days we passed *inukshus*, groups of rocks in four-foot piles, which looked at a distance like little men. When caribou swept over this land in great numbers, these *inukshus* were erected to herd the caribou through narrow valleys and to their death. Erkuaktok said that some were also used in drying fish. Few caribou were left in these parts.

We were making camp the last night out when three Eskimos drove up. One of them stuttered. His companions laughed every time he spoke, and so did Erkuaktok, and I. We all imitated him—and then he laughed. But somehow he got everything said.

Later we sat quietly in the tent, drinking tea. The dogs had been fed—one was even snoring. I was thinking ahead of Learmonth, that man of Arctic legend, who was substituting for John Stanners at Spence Bay. Tomorrow he would stand in the doorway of the post, quite unruffled and say in soft Scottish accents, "Hello there, Mr. Harrington. Come in, and take off your fur clothes." And we would drink the rum that I had brought over 350 miles by dogteam, and 2,500 by plane.

Reality was different.

Coming around the last bend, we saw the half-dozen red and white buildings of the H.B.C. post on the bare rocks rising out of Spence Bay. The clerk, who introduced himself as Ernie Lyall, welcomed me. Born on the Labrador, he had an Eskimo wife and a swarm of youngsters.

"I'm sorry Mr. Learmonth's away just now at King William Island," said Ernie Lyall. "Come on it, though, and make yourself at home."

At 3 a.m. I woke up suddenly. I was unused to sleeping in a well-heated house and soft bed. But it was not discom-

H.B.C. post, Spence Bay, taken at midnight in June

fort that awakened me. It was the sound of voices. Learmonth and his dogteam driver had returned.

Nose peeling from sunburn and eyes bloodshot from the wind, the sixty-year-old Learmonth looked as though he had been through one more ordeal. Disaster seemed to dog his steps, and calamity was no stranger to him.

"taku-vunga"

Nowadays, the H.B.C. rarely owns dogteams, it being much more economical to hire team and driver on the few occasions they are needed. This time, the driver had a couple of heart attacks on the way. Learmonth doctored him with the only medicine he had with him—bicarbonate of soda which he carried as tooth powder. Then he bundled the Eskimo up on the komatik and undertook to drive the dogs. At first the dogs refused to obey the unfamiliar voice. But somehow he got them going, and brought them in, travelling without any rest.

Considering this, and that he had just completed a 200-mile round trip, he looked well. We had met briefly years before in Toronto. He then wore city clothes, and had seemed extremely shy. Now in his fur clothing, he looked more at ease. His chronic reserve momentarily vanished as he moved about, laying aside his travelling gear, and making tea for himself and the Eskimo.

His gait was hurried, his gestures few. He spoke softly, with a marked Scottish accent. "Anyhow" became "anyhoo" on his tongue. Dressed for Arctic travel, he seemed short and bulky. In indoor clothing, you could see that he was slight, almost boyish in build.

I had heard, and before we finished our tea I knew, that here was a man no one could know intimately. He eluded questions, merely agreeing with what you said. His "hmm" of agreement reminded me of the Eskimos. He had little to say about his many hair-raising "adventures" in the north. He was vague on facts he had gleaned regarding the Franklin expedition. Only when he talked of the Eskimos did his face light up.

As he got up from the kitchen table to catch a few hours' sleep, he said, "I'm afraid you've come at a very busy season. Foxes are coming in at a great rate, and I'll be busy with the book work. But anything I can do for you . . ."

"White Gold" of the Arctic

"taku-vunga"

A "servant of the Hudson's Bay Company," as the old record books phrased it, L. A. Learmonth has been with the fur trade for forty years, and his life is still bound up with it. Every phase of the work interests him; no task is too small, none too large for him. When replacing someone in a post—for technically Learmonth is retired—he works late into the nights at the bookkeeping.

Finding locations for a "farthest north" post has fascinated Learmonth for years. He had a hand in founding Fort Ross on Bellot Strait, and in inducing the Dorset Eskimos to move to Somerset Island, north of Boothia Peninsula. The *Nascopie* which supplied the eastern Arctic posts could usually reach Fort Ross from Hudson Bay. But for two or three years in succession, shifting sea-ice had prevented the ship from calling at the post. So the post had to be moved. Learmonth selected Spence Bay.

Spence is more accessible than Fort Ross, but it is still remote and is the costliest trading post to supply with goods. Freighting costs are $250 a ton, as all supplies must come via the Mackenzie River. Deposited on the Arctic coast more than a thousand miles to the west, the cargo is picked up by a small coastal schooner which, with luck, reaches Spence Bay some time in September. Freighting by dog-team would be still more costly, and by plane is quite prohibitive.

It may be years, if ever, before Spence Bay post justifies its outlay. For trading in the Arctic, while very profitable in some years, has far more years which show red.

Soon after the company established its trading post, the R.C.M.P. followed, to set up its barracks about three-quarters of a mile distant. Two young constables were in charge. Just before I reached Spence, two student entomologists had been flown in via Yellowknife. "The bug boys" were staying at the barracks, though all four were frequent guests at the post.

the smiling face of the north

The people kept coming in with their fox pelts. It had been a good year for trapping, and all the country north of Spence Bay was drained of natives. They were all gathered around the post, or on their way.

At the post, a special room was set apart for the natives. They sat on benches and floor, chuckling, smoking, chatting or smiling thoughtfully. Learmonth trotted back and forth, making tea and serving it to them, along with biscuits and jam. It went on for hours. A dogteam might come in at 2 a.m. L. A. would put on a fresh kettle of water for tea. With no sign of reproach, he would jump to close doors the Eskimos had left open. He would enter into conversation with a venerable man. The people obviously regarded him with more than respect. There was affection in the exchange of glances and words.

Learmonth had a special care for the Eskimos, true. But throughout the north, more than any other group of white men, the traders are concerned for their welfare. Apart from sentiment or altruism, it is only sensible, for the Eskimos are their customers, their sole reason for being in the country. Yet they must operate economically, if they hope for any profits.

With sunshine at midnight, I drifted into the Eskimo routine of falling asleep at odd hours, whenever I felt like it. I would go to bed say at 4 a.m. and be wide awake at 8 o'clock. Going to the door I would see the people—men, women and children, wandering over the sea-ice. There was never any regular period of activity—life went on at all hours. It was the one time of the year when they might relax and enjoy life with their friends for a short while.

In the store, Ernie and Learmonth were kept busy. The shelves were fast being emptied, as the people stocked up for the summer to go to their fishing camps. In a few days, all the candy and tobacco had gone. And some essential trade goods would be low until boat-time.

Polar bear skin stretched to dry

the smiling face of the north

Daily new canvas tents were set up near the post on a windswept hill. Dogteams were everywhere. Towards the end of May, some of the dogteams went out to meet the last stragglers—Dorset Eskimos coming down from their hunting grounds near Fort Ross. It was said they were pulling their komatiks themselves, having lost nearly all their dogs. There was a great stir when they arrived, weary but smiling, their few dogs listless with fatigue.

As for Learmonth, his usually closed face showed emotion as he greeted them. No wonder. For it was Kavavouk's group, and with them last autumn L.A. had shared a perilous situation.

The previous September, a party of thirty or so Eskimos with a dozen dogs set out from the new Spence Bay post to go to their hunting grounds near the recently-closed Fort Ross post, more than 200 miles to the north. The trip was made by sea, following the west coast of Boothia Peninsula. Learmonth went with them, hoping to find relics of the lost Franklin expedition.

Kavavouk owned the schooner *Seal*, Takolik the whaleboat with its small marine engine. Six days out they struck a gale, and the temperature fell suddenly. Within a few days they were caught in treacherous rubber-ice, which threatened to encase them. With saws and chisels, the Eskimos tried to cut a lane out to open water, but daily the ice increased. The fuel for Takolik's engine grew scarce. Dogfood ran out, and there were no seals.

The vessels could not have stood the beating they received, had they not been sheathed with metal salvaged from an R.C.A.F. plane wreck near Bellot Strait. Patiently, in slow relays, they moved forward, unloading the cargo onto the ice, bringing it up by dogteam, the women and children working along with the men.

Towards the end of the month, fortunately, some seals

3 1 4

were procured, and a polar bear was shot. This food, plus an occasional ptarmigan kept them in meat.

Then ice floes came in toward shore, pushing up big pressure ridges. The strain on the anchors was terrific, and it looked as if all were lost. They unloaded the ships, and camped on a big iceberg, just in time. The ice floes shifted, beating against the shore, pushing the *Seal* on top of one of them, crushing its sides, tearing off the keel.

And then the iceberg itself split. Most of the supplies were lost, but the whaleboat was pulled up on one section. By the eighth of October, they were altogether stranded.

There was nothing to do but walk. The party split up, some going north to Bellot Strait, where ammunition, traps and sleds had been cached. Two or three of the people returned to Spence Bay with Learmonth, a walk of 120 miles against an icy wind.

No wonder L. A. greeted Kavavouk with special warmth.

And now he heard the sequel of the story. The people in their northward walk over the sea-ice had suffered great hunger. They scraped old polar bear skins for any fat that might be on them, and finally boiled the skins. Many of their dogs had starved.

Although Learmonth and the Mounted Police had some dogfood caches in the country, Kavavouk's party touched only a small part of it. Even that much made them feel apologetic, and wounded their pride, Learmonth said. They would have felt no embarrassment at sharing the cache of another Eskimo.

Fortunately their trapping had been good that winter. They brought down many white fox, apologizing for their condition. Because of lack of fuel, they had not been able to thaw out the carcasses and skin them. Learmonth assured them the foxes would be accepted as they were.

Now they could buy the things they needed, clothes,

315

dogmeal, ammunition, tea. Soon Kavavouk's people were well-clad. He himself had brought down sixty pelts. With a good summer of sealing, their worst days would be over.

Learmonth found time to talk only over our meals, many of which I prepared at this busy time, and after which I washed the dishes.

On the subject of the people we were in almost complete agreement: we both admired their ingenuity, their native intelligence and their character. But we sometimes reached a deadlock, as on the subject of the young man who would return soon from two years' "hard labor" at Cambridge Bay barracks.

On a visit to Creswell Bay, Learmonth found the people suffering from malnutrition and gangrene in their feet. He used up the remaining foodstuffs at the Fort Ross post—carefully entered in a notebook—then under greatest difficulties he made a trip across shifting ice to Arctic Bay. There he was able to get out a message which eventually brought rescue. He was equally reliable in reporting a case of murder he encountered on his return trip. A young hunter had throttled his mother-in-law.

"Judging from the motive—she jabbered and nagged at him all the time—and the fact that she had already attempted suicide, he simply restored peace in his igloo by silencing her. No one objected, except white men," I protested.

"The people must be taught that they cannot kill one another," said Learmonth quietly.

One day we reached a similar stalemate on clocks. Who cared what time it was? In a land where part of the year you had continuous daylight, and then for a great part of the year continuous twilight, clocks seemed ridiculous to me. There were no trains to be caught on the hour.

"I like the ticking of a clock," Learmonth maintained.

"It's companionable without being demanding. In fact, when I was at Fort Ross all alone, the clock was good company."

He pointed out, too, that syllabics were a deterrent to the Eskimos learning English. "The syllabic system does not give them access to our knowledge, our books. It's useless in intercourse with white men, since few of them can read it. It's now used mainly in the prayer books and hymnbooks and in notes the Eskimos write to one another."

I was not so sure of the value of the Eskimos having access to our knowledge. It seemed something they had done very well without.

Learmonth smiled, said "Hmm," and closed up.

Another day, discussing missionaries, we found ourselves on common ground. We shared an admiration for the courage of some of them, though we felt it misplaced; but agreed that most of them were fanatic, intolerant, and destructive.

"There are still many shadows lurking in the people's minds," he said, "and they are replaced by new fears, instilled by the missionaries."

There is not the least doubt that Learmonth is happier and more at ease with the Eskimos than with white men. He has become almost Eskimo in many ways. He is a lonely figure, with a philosophy and knowledge he cannot readily share with others. The Arctic is his "frigid mistress." He can combine frankness and reticence. No writing could do him justice, nor even describe him fairly. Somehow the vast barren land enthralled him. In turn, the Arctic shaped him so that ordinary life Outside is repulsive to him. He is never direct in his approach, rarely asks questions outright.

He has made countless long walks, dragging his own camping gear, a double tent, very light toboggan, some grub, notebooks. He has collected birds and minerals; knows the history of Arctic exploration as few others and made numerous contributions to the lore of the Franklin expedition.

In single walks he has covered hundreds of miles, a lone figure in a lonely land, and profoundly enjoyed that loneliness. No wonder his philosophy despises all hypocrisy and make-believe. But he is never a crusader. He has found the life that suits him.

At the song of a bird, L.A. would look up quickly from his plate, and say with assurance, "A horned lark." Or the faintest glimpse of fluttering wings and he could pronounce, "A snow bunting."

At any time, now, those bird sounds could be heard mingled with the voices of the children.

XX

fun under the midnight sun

ABOUT 150 ESKIMOS WERE NOW ASSEMBLED AT SPENCE Bay. Dogfood had run out and several men had gone sealhunting. They would not go far, for "Sports Day" had been set for May 28, and they all wanted to be present.

On the eve, the two Mounties came over to discuss with Learmonth the last-minute arrangements for this spring festival. The "bug boys" accompanied them, and as usual the four men made great inroads on the mess supplies, especially the tins of fruit juice and preserves. "Ah, the company's lousy with money!" said the government employees. As we cleaned up the debris in their wake, I seethed over their unthinking arrogance and thanklessness.

Learmonth was unperturbed. He'd seen plenty of it in his forty years' service. "Hospitality is a tradition with the Company," he said calmly.

The Mounties were going to run Sports Day—all prizes contributed by the H.B.C. of course. The contestants were to be rigidly divided according to sex and age.

"Is that unusual?" I asked Learmonth.

Competition, he explained, is foreign to the Eskimos.

Kids at Spence Bay

They have no fierce determination to excel or win. In these athletic contests, the only division they made was between young and old; and often that too is forgotten. Left to themselves, in a dog-race, a man with only two dogs, for instance, would happily race against a man who had ten dogs.

That night, before turning in, I glanced into the room where the people were as usual assembled. All had recently acquired new riches in exchange for their fox pelts.

The women were decked out in bright cotton Mother Hubbards (which remain bright for only a few days). The men had new wool pants, cloth artiggis, and maybe a new pipe. And they showed the effects of a few days' rest and good eating. They were excited and happy. This was the peak of the year. After Sports Day, they would disperse quickly all along the coast for fishing and seal-hunting.

May 28 was a brilliant and cloudless day. The voices on the ice sounded just like those of people on any sunny holiday beach. The children, who had intermittently played and slept throughout the night, were alert and lively, ready for more games.

Among the assembled people, the Mounties moved briskly, regimenting them into groups, according to age and sex. The people smiled and did as they were told. Soon 18 dogteams were lined up on the bay ice. Each team had seven dogs hitched fanwise, for the Mounties believed in fair play.

The Mountie raised his arm: a gun barked, and the teams were off on a 10-mile route which took them around an island in the bay. The winning team returned in less than an hour and a half. Prizes of ammunition, tobacco and tea went to the first three winners.

Then came an igloo-building competition, for men only. (What a lark if the women had been permitted to help their husbands!) The Eskimos worked with shouts and laughter, as the snow blocks, too soft at this time of year, crumbled in their hands. But finally the first igloo was completed in exactly half an hour.

After this came tug-of-war: one for the men, one for the women, one for the children. The rope was stretched out on the ice. Captains selected by a Mountie, stood at both ends of the rope and chose their teams. The Mounties marked the snow with limiting lines and tied a white ribbon in the exact middle of the rope. Then one shouted, "Go!" and the contestants pulled and sweated and tumbled. Shrill laughter rang out in the women's contest.

Winners. Losers. It was all quite decorous, and well-organized.

The next event was a footrace. Again the men raced against men, women against women, children against children.

I could not help but think that the Eskimo way would have been far more fun for them, and much more amusing to watch, when all of them raced at once. The slowest and smallest would be greeted with cheers as loud as those for the biggest and fastest. Probably an older person would have darted out, picked up a toddler, and run like hell with him. Cheers! The child had won the race!

Now came the "scramble," a favorite game. For this, a haphazard lot of trade items was thrown into the air, several at a time: women's wool bloomers, bright pink; a package of tea; some plug tobacco; candies; a box of .22 shells. All pitched in, roughly snatched and grabbed, shrieking with laughter. I noticed that each person made a pile of his winnings, and that the pile on the ice was respected by the others.

This went on for some time. The white men got bored, strayed into the house, helped themselves to tea, sardines and cookies.

Now the rope lay where it had fallen on the ice. A youngster grabbed one end of it, shouting. Someone grabbed the other end. A second, a third, a fourth jumped to one end or other and heaved. There was a mass attack on the rope, of both sexes and all ages. Whenever one side gave way, new ones jumped in to help out. Eventually one group, exhausted, was pulled down into a pile. The game broke up in laughter. But a few minutes later, quite unrehearsed and uncoached, the same thing would happen again. It was much more fun than before.

Ancient game of skill

Then someone started a favorite Eskimo game, the ball-and-peg game, with a pointed stick and a section of musk-ox horn. You had to catch the horn, which had a few tiny holes at the base, on the point of the peg. At this, the women were just as skillful as the men.

Ancient game of skill

Another group had found a softball. In this game two played together, tossing the ball between them, and others tried to intercept it. Pregnant women were mixed up in this, mothers with babies on their backs, a very old man, and all the children. I joined them. We slid, we stumbled, we took many spills. The game shifted here and there over the ice, the ball bouncing in all directions. Sometimes a tiny kid would grab the ball, then patter across the ice, hell-bent for the hills, with all of us in pursuit yelling.

My parka was ripped in a dozen places.

The sun had completed its circuit, not far above the horizon. Long shadows crawled across the bay. The air was still, except for the incessant birdsong. The people had collected in their tents and were drinking tea, smoking their pipes, resting up for the dance that was to follow.

Mangy dogs slept on the ash heap outside the tent. One, gaunt and starved, raised his head and howled, a lonesome eerie sound. He had come through the ordeal by hunger, and had not yet gathered enough energy even to fight.

All the people assembled in the company warehouse that night for a dance. A scratchy gramophone record played square-dance music. The Dorset people had been familiar with these dances ever since the whaling days, and Learmonth said they were going back to the old dances again. Last night, the white men had stood on the sidelines, watching the dancers and making critical comments. The people could not understand their words, but knew they were being ridiculed, and felt embarrassed, as they moved, toes turned in, with a heavy grace like the figures in a Gauguin painting.

Tonight we all shuffled together, sweated and whirled. We wove in groups over-and-under, in the intricate pattern of the "Ocean Wave" square-dance figure. We shouted and stamped our feet. My partners ranged from tattooed old crones who performed lithely to shy teen-agers, who shrieked when we twirled them around. Babies were nursed on the sidelines, or slept peacefully on the gyrating backs of their mothers.

Then a sudden hush fell on the frolic. The white men arrived en masse, this time to take part. They joined in clumsily, self-conscious in this new role, hopping stiffly and wildly. But they soon drifted away again with remarks that the people stank . . . were damn fools . . .

The moment they were gone, the atmosphere changed

once more. Ernie Lyall and I stayed and danced until four in the morning. By then, some of the children were piled up in corners, sound asleep, and my sealskin bootsoles had worn thin. The next day, my back felt nearly broken.

Learmonth had not attended the dance. He was hard at work over accounts, and had spent most of the night at his desk. I recounted to him the women I had danced with.

He listened, then smiled quietly. "I know," he said politely. I wondered just how much he knew.

On May 31, a radiogram came for me. It was a message from Arctic Wings. "Sorry we cannot pick you up. Beyond us."

I was upset at first, for this might mean I would be here until August. So I radioed Ernie Boffa at Yellowknife, asking whether he had any calls to make nearby, or what chance of chartering a plane. The reply came next day: Ernie could not pick me up. The disappearance of a plane during a flight had left him short.

Somehow it didn't bother me as much as I had expected. The enforced delay would give me time to make several shorter journeys on Boothia Peninsula.

Each day, now, some of the people packed their komatiks and gaily set off in various directions. One by one, they were swallowed up again by the land. Some were headed for Thom Bay, up on the other side of the Peninsula, where sealing was good. Perhaps I could go too and call on Father Papion at the mission there.

Arrangements were quickly made. Anijah was going seal-hunting near there, with his wife and adopted child. He would take me along, and we would go on by ourselves to the mission, thus combining business with pleasure. Hastily I packed my cameras and bought provisions at the store.

Anijah at fish hole—fish spearing implement in foreground

"Wish I were going too," said L. A. sadly, when he heard my plans. "You're lucky to be foot-free." He had been sticking so hard at the paper work and the radio schedule and the heavy trading, that he was looking weary and harassed.

I expected to be gone ten days or two weeks. Learmonth quietly filled corners of my grub box with small luxuries—peanut butter, pancake flour, beans. Once again I realized how priceless to the traveller in the Canadian north are the hospitable traditions of the Company. Their constant help, their generous accommodation to a passing traveller can never be rated too highly. Indeed, their very presence in the country makes northern journeys possible.

Ochoopau

XXI

break-up around boothia

Anijah had fourteen mangy, ill-fed dogs that would soon be fat and in good coat again. The load on the komatik was small, and we travelled easily. Light-heartedly, we struck eastward on June 5, travelling in dazzling sunshine, so warm that I fell asleep on the komatik. I wakened when the sky became overcast and a chill wind sprang up, filling the air with ice particles. I was glad that Learmonth had persuaded me to take my fur kulitak.

We made camp at the head of a long narrow fiord, which the natives called Shaguak. It was a favorite sealing place. Seals were always to be found there sunning themselves on the ice at this season.

Some hunters preferred to advance upon the dozing seal behind a screen made of white cotton. Anijah wore a special white cotton artiggi which covered him to below the knees. He ventured out on the ice with his rifle.

Shining and sleek, the animals lay drowsing beside their breathing-holes. At the least fright, with the mere flicker of a muscle, they could slide out of sight, dropping back into the water. It takes infinite patience and skill to get within rifle range.

Playing store in summer

We sat on the komatik, watching from a distance. Cautiously Anijah advanced upon his prey, knees bent in a half-crawling position. Whenever the seal raised its head, Anijah ducked and hoped to be mistaken for a hummock of snow. As soon as the seal's head went down, Anijah moved forward again.

330

The first seal, alarmed, slipped out of sight. The second seal also vanished. Then from a distance of a hundred yards or more, Anijah's rifle cracked.

The moment the dogs heard the faint "ping," they dashed forward with the sled, and reached the hunter before the seal stopped twitching. The round helpless-looking animal was silver-gray, mottled with darker patches. Anijah quickly slashed it open, removed the warm tender liver. We all ate it, blood running down our chins. The rest of the carcass he lashed to his komatik.

At Lord Mayor Bay just beyond, we met Eskimos with half a dozen seal loaded on their sleds, each weighing perhaps 80 pounds. That night we camped on a beautiful rock-surrounded raised beach. In many places, the snow had melted in patches, and where the snow had lately been, were clusters of tiny purple saxifrage.

Spring campsites are usually on a bare patch of beach strewn with small boulders which give good drainage, even though snow and ice and running water are all around. We spent warm nights on such beaches—though "night" still seemed a strange word to me in that period of continuous daylight.

In the tent, it was a happy family scene. Anijah and Shaunak laughed over the little girl's baby-talk, like parents everywhere. Then Shaunak would draw the little girl close in her arms, and flip a breast over her artiggi. The child suckled happily, though it was a dry breast. No one paid any attention. But it was a simple marvel of social security. Shaunak's own children had died in infancy, and this was an adopted daughter. Now Shaunak's pangs were over, Anijah was content, and the child had a good home.

As we travelled north, we saw as many as a hundred seals dotting the ice in all directions. Anijah shot one without even leaving the komatik. Hunting was really good! The

Anijah with dead seal at breathing hole

time of scarcity was past, and already the dogs were looking fatter and pulling more lustily.

Four canvas tupiks perched on the dry pebble beach at
Thom Bay, which the Eskimos called Ik-chok-to-ro-vik, evidently from the special type of seal-hunting done there. An
igloo is built on the ice over a seal-hole. The top is reinforced so that no light comes through, and the hunter shuts
himself up inside. He watches in silence and in darkness
until a sleek head appears. Then swiftly, the hunter's harpoon flashes . . .

Barren lands not so barren

Seal hunting is done through igloos at Thom Bay

We shared the tent that night with two visitors who drifted in singly.

The first arrival was a tattooed woman, her artiggi soiled with grease and blood. Her stringy gray hair was matted and she was nearly toothless. But she moved with a sinewy grace. Her eyes flashed as she spoke, and she smiled with vivacity. When she caught my eye, she smiled alluringly, and with great self-assurance. I was a little alarmed when I saw her spread out her caribou sleeping skins and begin to remove her upper garments.

Shortly after a young man entered. He was barely twenty, hardly half the woman's age, and full of talk and laughter. He spoke to the woman gaily. Then he crawled under her caribou sleeping skins, pressing himself close to her . . .

Anijah left his wife and child at the camp, and with lightened sled we went on along the shore in the direction of the Thom Bay mission. On the way we came to a tiny snug harbor set amid stark hills. Up on the beach, partly covered with snow, lay remnants of the *Victory*. This was the side-wheeler steam yacht specially designed for Sir John Ross's second Arctic voyage of 1829. The ship spent the winter of 1831 in Victory Harbour, then was abandoned. It was later carried out to sea by ice action and sank, but not until the crew had partly dismantled it. Much of the gear (ironwork, levers, hooks) still lies on the shore, in surprisingly good condition. Some of the metal has been put to use by the Eskimos and in northern missions.

We were now coming to the loneliest mission of them all.

Father Papion could not do enough for me, so delighted was he to have a visitor. The young bearded missionary lived all alone. He had come over from France in 1949, and in two years had had exactly two visitors—Learmonth and myself, not counting Father Henry, his superior.

Father Henry had just recently paid a short visit to this mission which he had built, and was now on his way to Gjoa Haven on King William Island. Otherwise Father Papion saw no one except his few parishioners—three Eskimo families, and even them only for a day or so every four or five months.

In one of the two rooms, Father Papion cooked, ate, read, and slept. The other room, about ten by fourteen feet, was the "chapel." It was plenty large enough to accommodate his congregation. For the people did not come to the mission with any regularity. Father Papion said mass in the altar alcove daily, all by himself.

Victory Harbor, Thom Bay, remains of Ross' polar expedition of 100 years ago. Ship "Victory"

Father Papion and his mission at Thom Bay in July

Thom Bay mission was well over 400 miles from Repulse Bay, yet that was the source of all supplies. Father Papion had learned to get along without most things considered essential by white men. He and his three dogs lived mostly upon seal (he had killed 168 in the previous year), fish, ptarmigan and Arctic hare. He used seal blubber in the stove only in the coldest weather, and cooked most of his food over the primus stove. He never ate dessert, and baked no bread.

One of Father Papion's followers

He showed me over his little domain. The house had double windows which could not be opened. His supply of frozen meat and other foods was kept in the attic. But he was building an ice-house, a hole about seven feet by two in the gravel bank near the house. He had braced this cellar with pieces of steel from Victory Harbour.

That night I slept on a hard wooden plank bed, two feet wide. It was Father Papion's sleeping bench, but he insisted that I use it, while he slept on the floor. The gravel beaches were softer than that cot, let me say.

Next day we carried on our conversation again with the aid of a much-thumbed English-French dictionary. Birds? Ah, yes, *oiseaux*—and away we went. Fortunately we were both good at pantomime, which filled the gaps when words failed.

I learned that ice remains in Thom Bay until August, drifting around with the tides; that September and October were the loveliest months, when waterfowl abounded; that Ross's North Magnetic Pole cairn was situated a little more than a hundred miles due west of the mission.

The young missionary talked of the Eskimos with affectionate admiration, praising their politeness, gentleness and honesty. The only thing wrong with them, apparently, was that they were not Roman Catholics. He was studying their language with great earnestness and intelligence.

With hard work, study and prayer, Father Papion passed his time. "And then, too, I play my two records." He played one of his old scratched records for me. It was Caruso singing "Miserere." Like Father Vandevelde, he studied the history of Arctic exploration, and especially a thick volume on the travels of Sir John Ross.

Father Papion seemed content. But as we left, he stood a lonely figure on Ikpik, that high bank of gravel, beside his little shack. He could hardly expect visitors within a year. In a low light, the sheer jagged hills looked stark and hostile. The uncompromising hills were unaware of him, and would outlast him. The tiny figure waved as long as we could see it.

Anijah and child at beginning of walk

Travelling on the sea-ice was so warm that we shed our fur clothing, and in spite of the melted surface, the dogs panted with the heat. When we paused they lay down on snowbanks to cool off. Two flocks of eider ducks passed overhead.

Anijah and child near end of walk

Once off sea-ice, however, travel was more difficult. At the first small lake the dogs sank shoulder-deep in slush. Shaunak walked ahead to encourage them, while Anijah and I pushed and tugged and jerked at the sled. It was still bright sunlight at two o'clock in the morning, and we were

Anijah and a dog ready for cross country hike

sweating, though icy water ran over the tops of our seal-skin boots. Two or three times the dogs had to swim.

When we paused for tea, Anijah and I were wet from head to foot. Still, he found time to play with his little

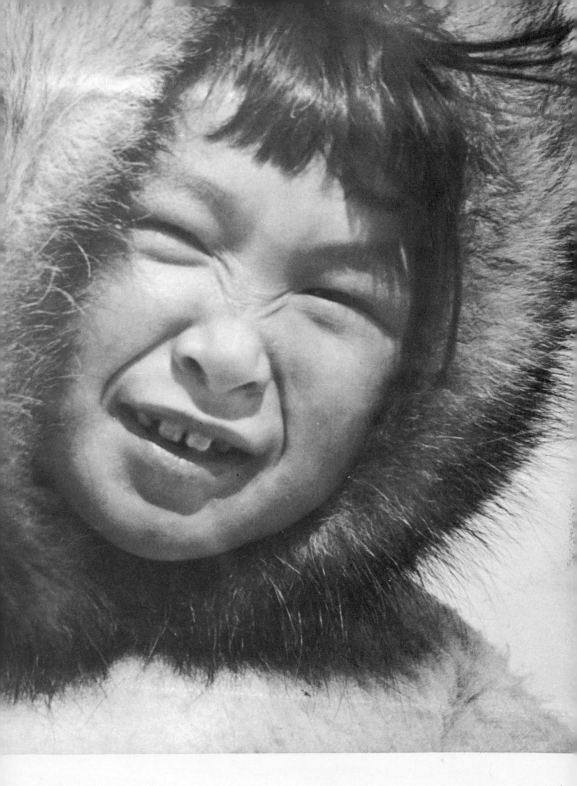

Spence Bay child registering "I do not like"

Anijah's adopted daughter carrying a pup inside her artiggi

daughter, and to teach me a few words of Eskimo. I followed the family's example of eating handfuls of red and purple flowers. Some tasted sweet, some bitter.

Travelling on shore was not as wet, but it was very hard going. As I trudged ahead of the team, plowing alternately over slippery moss and through slush, I was quite content. Birds in myriads twittered and chirped and sang. Three more flights of ducks honked over us.

A country clean-cut. On way to fishing camps

On June 13, I was back in Spence Bay, where Learmonth greeted us warmly. He listened intently to my account of the journey, saying "Hmm, hmm" by way of understanding and agreement. But it was never convenient for him to give me further explanations of the people, nor help me plan my time, nor further my trips around the country. In a way, he was jealously guarding the secrets of his own stamping-grounds.

At Spence Bay the scene had changed considerably in that short space of time. Bleak, black rocks were now exposed, and melting snow rushed seaward in a thousand tiny rivulets. The ground had emerged, giving new contours to everything, exposing the debris that had accumulated beneath the snow. When I left for Thom Bay, the post at Spence had been sunk in snowbanks. Now I was surprised to find that two steps led up to the door.

On the sea-ice, the water drained away through cracks, and here the people gathered to jig for Arctic char. Much like salmon, this fish has a delicious flavor. A strip of open water now stretched between shore and ice-pan which still filled most of the bay. When the wind and temperature dropped, the strip was covered with a thin film of ice.

Numerous flies had already sprung up, and I noticed a couple of fat bumblebees humming through the air. The people found eggs of gulls, geese and ducks, and sucked them.

Learmonth was very occupied again with the monthly account. I was eager to go north along the western shore of Boothia, to see the ancient tent rings and cairns which Rasmussen had described. I hoped that L. A. would accompany me.

He never said a definite "No," but kept postponing the day. The entire year lay ahead of him, but my time was running out. When Kavavouk's party, heavily laden, went north to Josephine Bay, I hoped Learmonth would suggest we follow them.

But my hopes were dashed, when instead, he announced that he had to make a trip to Gjoa Haven on company business. He would be gone about a week. I was alone with Ernie Lyall and his Eskimo family.

Immediately the post acquired a different atmosphere, and I realized how much of the neatness and order were due to Learmonth's presence. "Oh, he's too fussy," Ernie said, "always driving himself and everybody else." By contrast, Ernie himself was much too casual, good-natured and lackadaisacal.

346

Tools of prehistoric Eskimo. Cape Isabella

L. A. has a vast fund of knowledge but only tells of the things he wishes to reveal. A bit of a mystic, he cannot be drawn out. He has plans for the future, which concern pre-Eskimo sites, Ross's expedition, Franklin's fate—far more plans than can be included in his life-span.

I have an idea for a photograph but . . . "The sun isn't shining, perhaps later". . . Later, L. A. finds it impossible to take time off, and the opportunity is gone. "Oh, well, you'll get lots more pictures." Or I want to go in a certain direction, "Nothing there to take pictures of," or "Nobody here right now to take you there". . .

It is quite true that the natives must procure food in certain places, at certain times, and with certain equipment. To take them from their seasonal occupations means that they will suffer later from missing a brief but important hunt. Credit at the trading post does not make up for such loss. So my trips had to fit into the natives' annual routine.

It was just a short trip to Josephine Bay, only thirty-five miles from Spence. I thought of walking it. But Kunok, a lad of perhaps 14, was eager to take me with his five dogs, so we set out.

We slid quickly over the blue ice. But soon the surface puddles became larger and deeper. Rounding Cape Isabella, we ran into a shower of rain, while the sky beyond showed a beautiful mauve over the brown hills. We waded along, the dogs getting cold and stiff in the icy water, and the sewing in my sealskin boots gave way. Long cracks became wider, and the dogs had to be beaten into crossing. Rain drove through our clothes, and shorelines became obscured.

As we cut across between mainland and an island, with open water at both shores, the komatik came to a halt. The cake of ice we were on broke loose, and we sank on it to our hips. The dogs became frantic, and clambered on top of the load. I thought of my cameras in a box on the sled, and helped Kunok beat them off. We finally heaved the sled onto more solid ice.

It rained even harder, and I wondered why I had ever left the comfortable monotony of the post. Kunok was so exhausted that he fell asleep on the sled, and I had to nudge him awake so that we wouldn't approach a crack broadside and plunge in.

We at last rounded a hill, and saw before us Kavavouk's camp on the shingle. The white canvas tents looked very inviting, and the four families were hospitable and friendly.

3 4 8

Spring change-over at Spence Bay

Netchilingmiut

Kayak with extra passenger

They offered us seal meat and fish, and I contributed biscuits, tea and jam and tobacco. My few words of Eskimo proved quite useful.

The maps called this spot "Artist's Bay," though it didn't look very picturesque at that moment. But next day provided the balmiest weather yet. The sun brought out the delicate tints and tones of a huge sheet of white sea-ice, fringed with a narrow band of open green water along the shore, bare brown rocks partly snow-covered, and stained with ochre lichen.

Sitting in the lee of boat making tea

In the four or five days that followed, I often tramped for miles. There was a curious stimulation in treading where few had been before. Ross's North Magnetic Pole cairn was about forty miles to the north; and in this region, Sir John Franklin's expedition came to grief just over a hundred years ago. Old tent rings—stones placed in a circle about seven feet in diameter—were numerous, indicating that this had long been a favorite tenting spot for Eskimos.

On way to fishing ground on lake Netchilik

I knew these Dorset Eskimos were hardy. But their predecessors must have been still more rugged. Kavavouk brought me a lichen-covered scoop made of muskox horn, probably over a hundred years old, which he had found. He thought "Adeeliorli" (the Eskimos had long since dubbed me "picture man") would be interested, as I was. It was clear that here had lived a people who knew nothing of steel, nothing of white men and their ways. The earlier

Dorset beauty—Petecutie by name

Fishing with "Kokivok" on Spence Bay in July

culture must have been far more resourceful and hardier than this present race.

On our return trip to Spence Bay, we found that the rift between shore and sea-ice had grown wider. The "leads" in the ice-pan were wider, too, and the surface was as sharp and jagged as coral. My young driver put little sealhide boots on his dogs' feet to protect their pads from the knife-sharp edges, and we started off on a calm bright night.

Slithering along, we were seldom stopped by a crack, and never by one so wide that we couldn't throw the dogs across it one by one. Then the long komatik bridged it as

Tidal cracks and unwilling dogs near Josephine Bay

if no crack existed. We saw hundreds of birds, but the amount of birdsong had dwindled sharply. They were now nesting. We also saw two mosquitoes, which for the moment, seemed a novelty.

The snow was now all gone from Spence Bay, and a different type of fishing was in operation. The men carried *kokiwoks*, long harpoons with trident heads of muskox horn. Equala, for instance, would crouch over a hole in a cake of ice perhaps three or four feet thick, watching for signs of fish below. Then he would plunge in the harpoon. The flexible horn would slide down around the fish's body,

Josephine Bay camp

and the two iron prongs would keep it from escaping. He got about twenty Arctic char that morning.

After a few days at Spence I was off again, with Anijah and his family to Lake Netchilik, about 18 miles from the post, toward the south. By now, the middle of July, the ice had melted or drifted so that the lanes between it and the shore were fifty feet wide in places. Pelang, Anijah's brother, rowed the boat which contained two men besides himself, sundry children, two women and two dogs, in addition to

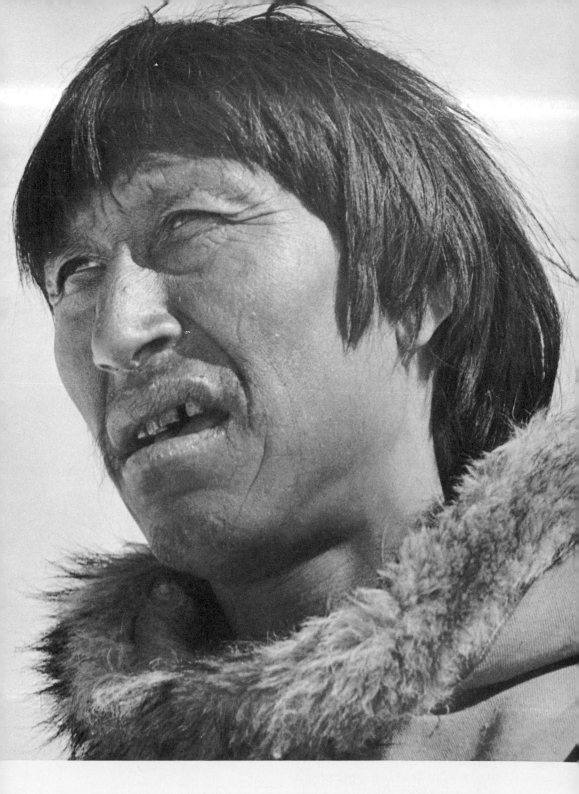

Pelan from the Back River area

fishing and camping equipment. He worked the boat between the rocky shore and the ice-pan which still covered most of the bay.

As we reached land, the load was removed from the boat, packed on men's shoulders and on the dogs, which did not seem to resent the burden.

We started across long sloping meadows, towards the camp on Lake Netchilik where the people were catching and drying fish for the coming winter. The air was chilly, though the warm weather should have been at its peak. A long range of hills lay to our left, with some patches of snow still lurking in sheltered spots. Many birds, some of them sandpipers, flew up as we plodded along amongst many varieties of low brilliant wildflowers. It was like an alpine meadow.

The walk must have been eight or ten miles. Anijah's little girl grew tired, and he perched her up on top of his load so that her legs came under the tumpline. Finally she fell asleep, secure on her perch. Obeluk, a tattooed old lady, never slackened her pace, although she must have been more than fifty Arctic winters old.

From a distant ridge, we looked down and saw the wide ice-covered expanse of Netchilik Lake. On a spit of land, four or five tents were pitched, and there we found Eskimos gutting fish, splitting them into strips, which they hung on sealskin lines stretched between *inukshus*, or even on the upturned komatiks. Anijah and his family put up the tents, and started in to fish.

Where the lake drains into the river, the water races to the sea. The Eskimos here had turned to yet another type of fishing, that of throwing long barbed spears at fish sighted in the water. Each spear had several barbs on it, and a light line for retrieving it.

Not far from the lake stands a remarkable pile of stones, shaped like an igloo, called "The House of the Thunder

Obeluk's tattoos. Spence Bay

Even in June snowstorms occur. Pup seeking warmth near bitch

Sisters," according to Rasmussen. He had been told about it on his Fifth Thule Expedition of 1921–24, when he collected legends and songs of the Netchilingmiuts. But Learmonth was apparently the only person who had seen it so far.

Obeluk, her handsome adopted boy and I, started off across the barrens, after Pelang had rowed us across the

Fur baling at Spence Bay

river. My Eskimo was much too limited to understand
what Obeluk said, but she knew as much as anyone about
the weird place, for she was one of the few remaining sha-
mans, who still communed with spirits.

She led the way past remains of a Tunik campsite, and
on to the ridge where stood the mysterious Thunder House.
Of unknown origin and obscure meaning, it was a tiny hut
built of flat stones. Ochre lichens covered the rock, and

363

Thunder House

the old lady seemed in awe of the place. Only reluctantly did she stand close to the hut, so that I could photograph both together.

Obeluk was glad to get away from the haunted site. Our legs felt tired as we left there, but she led the way at a brisk clip through the multitudinous Arctic flowers. We couldn't help but step on them, and in so doing, we stirred up hordes of mosquitoes. Their high-pitched sound was intense in every direction, threatening a mass attack if ever

Fish spearing on Lake Netchilik

the wind died down. But the blood-thirsty song came only to our knees. As we neared the lake, the cold wind over the icefield discouraged the insects.

Another day I walked alone far inland, climbed the wind-swept palisades and looked down over the lake. From that vantage point, it looked still larger. As I came down by a different route, I walked through a valley red with what I took to be oxidized iron ore. I saw bird nests, tent rings of another spring, *inukshus* and fragments of caribou bones. It was infinitely soothing, and somehow spoke of the unchanging centuries that have passed over this land.

At night, the sun dipped behind the hills, though there was no darkness, and the wind dropped. The icy air be-

Pipshi dried fish on Lake Netchilik

came perfectly still. Even the lapping of the waves ceased. Other worlds, other lives still called me, but for the time being, I knew complete peace and harmony.

During my last few days at Spence Bay, Ernie and Learmonth were even busier than before, for fur-baling was in progress. The bundles of white Arctic fox pelts were packed into the fur press, and wrapped in burlap for shipment Outside. Komatiks around the post were upturned. They would be useless for another month or two, until fresh snows fell.

Fish spearing near Lake Netchilik

The "Norseman" arrived July 27 at Spence Bay to take me outside

On July 27, the Hudson's Bay Company plane arrived, carrying John Stanners back to Spence Bay, Peter Nichols, District Manager of the western Arctic, six-foot-four Joe Coombes, the pilot, and a mechanic. They brought with them a radio beacon which they set up.

Spence Bay would have more gadgets, more noises, more cares and less peace.

And it seemed to me that our planes did not bring us closer to the natives: rather they widened the chasm. Men come in with the birds, and leave with them, carrying out incredible versions of Arctic life . . .

break-up around boothia

Fortunately, there was just room for me aboard the *Norseman*. I climbed in, carrying messages and letters for friends Outside. My long plane journey would take me on a now-familiar route—Cambridge Bay, Coppermine, Yellowknife and Edmonton.

Eskimos and whites stood around as the plane made ready to take off. The white people were gesticulating, shouting out admonitions and instructions. I looked wistfully at the Eskimos, standing there quietly, smiling. The plane roared, raced down the water, and Spence Bay fell away . . .

7877